The
UNKINDEST
CUT

The UNKINDEST CUT

HOW A HATCHET-MAN CRITIC MADE

HIS OWN $7,000 MOVIE

AND PUT IT ALL ON HIS CREDIT CARD

Joe Queenan

 HYPERION

New York

To my mother, Agnes
And my father, Joe

Copyright © 1995, Joe Queenan

Designed by Nicola Ferguson

Library of Congress Cataloging-in-Publication Data
Queenan, Joe.
The unkindest cut : how a hatchet-man critic
made his own $7,000 movie and put it all
on his credit card / by Joe Queenan.—1st ed.
p. cm.   ISBN 0-7868-6090-1
1. 12 steps to death.   2. Motion pictures—Production and
direction.   3. Motion picture authorship.   4. Low budget
motion pictures.   I. Title.
PN1997.A2123Q44 1996
791.43'72—dc20   95-23402
CIP

First Edition

1 2 3 4 5 6 7 8 9 10

If a movie costs less than five million dollars, and has a beginning, a middle and end, there is no way it won't make money.

—MENACHEM GOLEN

Contents

The
UNKINDEST
CUT

one

A Tree
Grows
in Manayunk

When I was a small, doomed child growing up in a deadly housing project in the mean streets of North Philadelphia, my life was a cesspool of anguish and despair. The only respite from the hideous quagmire of poverty, theft, disease, and homicide that we called home, the only beacon of glamor in a hopelessly wretched universe, was provided by the local movie house, the Alden Theater. Every Saturday afternoon—that is, every Saturday afternoon that I was not forced by my neo-Dickensian parents to work at some backbreaking, ill-paying job—I would beg, borrow, or steal 35 cents so that I could steal away from my rat-infested, litter-strewn, gun-crazy neighborhood and slip into the Alden. There I would spend hour upon hour in a state of nearly catatonic rapture gazing up at the idols of the silver screen: Stephen Boyd, Fess Parker, Gig Young.

Usually, the Alden presented a double feature, and quite frequently one of the films was a horror movie like *13 Ghosts* or *The Head* or *The Tomb of Ligeia*. In low-budget affairs of this ilk, men with huge fangs would invariably sink their teeth into the alabaster necks of winsome virgins and suck out every last ounce of their blood. As their dainty corpuscles spewed forth in a cataract of pure crimson—or what passed for pure crimson in low-budget, black-and-white horror movies—I would suddenly find myself transported leagues beyond the frontiers of my dreary existence, borne on a magic carpet to a Never Never Land where passion, terror, and redemption merged in the magic crucible of the ineffable. Gazing up at those grisly motion pictures every Saturday afternoon, I would forget for a few precious moments that I was marooned in a gloomy housing project riddled with crime, rodents, fallen women, and the ugly specter of racial enmity. As those flickering images danced across the screen I would find myself swept away from my abject misery to a fairyland where all the men were lionine stalwarts and all the women were winsome virgins.

It was in these moments that I made a fateful decision that would change the course of my life. One day, I swore to myself, I would sojourn to the Shangri-La I merely glimpsed every Saturday afternoon at the Alden. One day, I swore to myself, I, too, would live a glamorous, thrilling life; I, too, would be a radiant supernova like the creatures I worshipped on the screen every weekend. Right then and there, buried in the shadows of the Alden Theater, I promised myself that when I grew up I would grow really, really sharp teeth so that I could sink my fangs into the alabaster necks of winsome virgins and suck out every last ounce of their blood.

But never once did I dream about growing up to direct, produce, script, or star in my own motion picture.

WHATEVER DREAMS I may have had as a child, the idea of growing up to be a director or a producer or an actor or even a lowly screenwriter was not one of them. I would have dreamed about being a quality-control person in a factory that made alligator-skin wedgies for Peruvian cross-dressers sooner than I ever would have dreamed about *that*. I don't know whether it was lack of ambition, a hopelessly pedestrian worldview, a complete inability to see beyond the gray horizons of North Philadelphia, or what; but at no time in my youth or my adolescence did I ever dream about making my own movie, writing my own movie, producing my own movie, or starring in my own movie. I just never had dreams of that ilk. Nobody else I knew did, either.

Things were no different when I grew up. I always *liked* movies—I thought they were Milk Duds for the Soul—but I never had any interest whatsoever in finding out how they were made. I never read interviews with directors. I never read interviews with producers. I never took film classes in college, at a time when everyone and his brother was trying to corral an easy A by writing interminable term papers about the virginity imagery in *The Virgin Spring*.

Even when I lived in Paris for a year after graduating from college, I went out of my way to avoid reading anything that had the word "Cahiers" in the title. And when I'd go to see famous directors present their films at the Cinémathèque on Friday night, I'd make a point of leaving the room *before* Alain Resnais or Jean-Luc Godard got up to discuss the lighting in *Hiroshima, Mon Amour* or the influence of postwar American gangster movies on *Breathless.* I enjoyed films, but I had no more interest in finding out how they got here than in finding out how bananas got here. It just wasn't something that tickled my fancy.

Even when I grew up and became a movie critic, it never occurred to me that I might one day make my own film. I'd drifted into film criticism in the late 1980s purely by accident when a friend who worked at *Rolling Stone* called me up one night and asked if I could interview Sean Young the next day. "Sean *who*?" I asked. "Sorry, but the name doesn't ring a bell." My friend said that Young was the leggy, rake-thin actress who'd starred in *No Way Out* with Kevin Costner and in *Blade Runner* with Harrison Ford. Oh, boy, now I remembered her. Hot damn. Still, I had reservations about the assignment. One problem was that I'd never interviewed a movie star before. My friend said that didn't matter—anyone could do this kind of work—and besides, Sean wasn't *that big* a movie star.

I was still sort of hemming and hawing about the proposal when my friend mentioned that the assignment was kind of an emergency. Ms. Young, it appeared, had been accused of leaving a mutilated doll on the doorstep of actor James Woods, with whom she had co-starred in *The Boost,* a very bad movie during the course of which they had seemingly had a tiff. Dismayed by this news, two different journalists who had originally agreed to conduct the interview had backed off at the last minute, fearing the ire of the unpredictable starlet. I said that leggy, rake-thin unpredictable starlets didn't scare me one bit, since I'd grown up in a rat-infested, litter-strewn, gun-crazy neighborhood, but again I emphasized that celebrity profiles lay a bit outside my area of expertise, in part because I thought all celebrities were idiots and couldn't guarantee that I would be civil and attentive once they started talking about the war in El Salvador or the plight of the whales. My friend said she didn't care what I thought or said or did: She really needed this story. She was sure I could handle it; my credentials didn't matter; the assignment would be a piece of cake. So I agreed to do it.

The *Rolling Stone* article completely changed the course of my career. Up until then, I'd been making a living in two ways: by writing sarcastic op-ed pieces and book reviews for *The Wall Street Journal, The New York Times, The New Republic,* and other publications, and by writing sarcastic financial journalism for *Barron's* and *Forbes.* But after I wrote the article about *ma nuit chez Sean,* I became a movie critic for life. When I got to the leggy, rake-thin actress's apartment that night, she made me sit in her living room for an hour while she had her weekly algebra lesson with a local high school teacher whose name she'd found on a Laundromat bulletin board. There was a part of me that wanted to believe that this was your typical rehearsed celebrity iconoclasm, the kind of carefully choreographed idiosyncrasy (Buddhism, polo) that *Premiere* and *Vanity Fair* always fall for. But the longer I sat there listening to Young trying to make heads or tails out of the Pythagorean theorem, the more I became convinced that the actress already realized that she'd blown her shot at screen stardom by alienating so many people on the set of *Wall Street* and was now desperately attempting to prepare herself for a second career as the world's most beautiful high school algebra teacher. And that's what I wrote.

When *Rolling Stone* published "Are Sean Young's Days Numbered?" it drew the attention of *Movieline* magazine, a peculiar, irreverent Los Angeles publication whose editors called and asked me to begin writing celebrity profiles for them. I was more than happy to accommodate them. First I did Jessica Lange, then I did Keanu Reeves. And that was the end of that. After those two articles appeared, it was impossible for me to get any more interviews with anyone, because PMK, the Borgia-like agency that handles P.R. for virtually everyone in the film industry, hated my guts.

Ordinarily, not being able to get interviews with anyone in the film industry would have sounded the death knell of an entertainment writer's career. But not at *Movieline*. *Movieline* simply didn't care. So, over the course of the next six years, I wrote dozens and dozens of articles for the magazine, none of which required actually talking to anybody in the motion picture industry. These ranged from a piece in which I impersonated Mickey Rourke for a day, to a study of auricular trauma (ear mutilation) in contemporary films, to a scientific investigation of directorial name recognition in New York City. For that assignment, I stood outside Manhattan movie theaters to see how many people standing right next to a marquee reading "A Mario Van Peebles Film: *Posse*" could tell me who had directed *Posse*. The answer? One person in ten.

Some of these stories appeared in my book *If You're Talking to Me, Your Career Must Be in Trouble*. Some didn't. Anyway, by the time January 1993 rolled around, I was making a pretty good living trashing movie stars without ever having to meet them. Which suited me just fine, because I really do hate talking to movie stars about the whales. I was perfectly happy doing what I was doing: getting paid good money to make fun of people I despised without actually having to move to Los Angeles and meet any of them. This made me different from every other entertainment industry writer I knew. Everyone else I know who writes about the movies for a living secretly dreams of moving to Hollywood and getting rich by writing screenplays that never get produced. Not me. From what I could see, Hollywood was the closest thing to Hell on the face of the earth: this from a person who'd grown up in a rat-infested, litter-strewn, gun-crazy housing project in North Philadelphia.

So there I was, just drifting along, doing a bit of this and a bit of that, when one day I happened upon an article by Bernie Weinraub in *The New York Times* about a twenty-four-year-old Tex-Mex filmmaker named Robert Rodriguez (Bernie got the guy's name wrong—he said it was

Richard). Rodriguez, the article explained, was a *maverick* filmmaker who had become rich and famous overnight by winning an award at the 1993 Sundance Film Festival. He did this with a movie that he claimed to have made for $7,000 with a bunch of friends down in Mexico. *El Mariachi*, so it would appear, was a mistaken-identity black comedy whose central character was a destitute mariachi musician, carrying a guitar case, who turns up in a small Mexican town the very same day that a hit man with an arsenal in his guitar case arrives on the scene. Many amusing incidents thereupon ensued.

The film, originally produced for the Spanish direct-to-video market, went down well at Sundance, winning the coveted Audience Award, which is given to the film that the five thousand festivalgoers pick as their favorite, even though the judges and critics usually hate it and give their award to somebody influenced by Satyajit Ray or Billy Wilder or Fidel Castro. Emboldened by this success, and flush with the $5 million Columbia Pictures had thereupon handed him to make a sequel to *El Mariachi*, the *maverick* filmmaker gave a bunch of other interviews to major magazines and newspapers in which he encouraged other people to emulate his success and make their own films. *Ordinary* people. After all, you could make three of these things for the price of one Toyota Previa van, options not included.

I really enjoyed reading Rodriguez's heart-warming story, in part because it put a great new spin on a tired cliché. For once, here was a maverick indy who hadn't said anything about putting his low-budget film on his credit card. In the world of maverick-indy-low-budget hype, such an admission was virtually unheard of. For years, everytime an independent filmmaker, a *maverick* director, or some pathetic hack trying to make one final comeback was asked by a gullible reporter how he'd managed to pay for his movie, the obligatory response was: "I ran so low on funds that I put the whole thing on my credit card." It was standard material. It was generic schtick. If you were a bona-fide-maverick-indy-low-budget filmmaker, you had to use this cliché when speaking with the press. It was a federal law.

But Rodriguez never once resorted to this hopeless banality. Instead, he threw in all this colorful south-of-the-border stuff, telling people that he'd paid for the movie by working as a laboratory rat, and having his best friend sell some real estate, and getting the leading man's mother to do all the catering for the movie. I liked that. I admired that. I even envied that. In the world of mav/indy/low-budget filmmaker poorhouse chic, this was a novel approach to moviemaking hype.

A couple of months later, I went to see *El Mariachi* at a New York art house. I was impressed. The director really knew how to get a lot of bang for his buck. But did I believe that Rodriguez had actually made the movie I saw up on the screen for a measly $7,000? *Really* believe? To be perfectly honest, no. There was still a part of me that suspected that Rodriguez had made his movie for about $30,000 and then lied about making it for $7,000, because nobody would be impressed if you said that you'd made a mildly amusing black comedy about a mariachi musician for $30,000, whereas if you told them that you'd made it for $7,000 with your pals down in Mexico, they'd act like you were the second coming of Orson Welles, or at the very least the fourth coming of Roger Corman. But then I reminded myself that the $7,000 figure had appeared in *The New York Times,* the paper of record. So it had to be true.

This got me to thinking. Since Rodriguez had *ostensibly* proven that it was possible to make a movie for $7,000, and since he was going around telling everybody within earshot that they, too, could make a movie for $7,000, wouldn't it be neat to try duplicating the young Tex-Mex's achievement? To my way of thinking, all Rodriguez had proven was that *someone* could make a movie for $7,000. What would be really cool was proving that *anyone* could make a movie for $7,000.

And that anyone was going to be me.

I DO NOT want to create the impression that I jumped into this low-budget filmmaking thing headfirst. No siree, bob—not this crack journalist. There was no way I was going to embroil myself in a project as complex as writing, producing, and directing my own movie without making sure that all the t's were crossed and all the i's were dotted before I got the cameras rolling. First, there were a lot of important questions that needed answering. How much time would I have to devote to this project? How much effort? How much income was I going to lose by making my own low-budget movie? Or could I just do it at night and on the weekends? How many other people would I need to help me do it? Were there any hidden costs that I didn't know about? Was it possible, for example, that Rodriguez's $7,000 figure was a complete load of horseshit and this undertaking was going to clean me out?

In the weeks and months to come, I spent a lot of time investigating the *El Mariachi* hype to find out what was gospel truth and what wasn't. In doing so, I unearthed several clear advantages that the ostensibly penniless Mr. Rodriguez enjoyed over me. One, he'd been making films since he was a little kid, whereas I could barely operate an Instamatic. Two, he had access to somebody else's camera, which I did not. Three, he was a film school student who could borrow equipment and thus edit his film for almost nothing. Here our paths neatly diverged. I had no experience as a filmmaker. I had no friends willing to lend me a camera. I had no access to free editing equipment. So, without trying to take any luster off his rising star, I recognized that Rodriguez had started out with a number of advantages that neither I nor any other maverick/indy/low-budget filmmaker would enjoy.

On the other hand, I had the $7,000. As a ruthless hatchet man who was generating about one-third of his income by writing mean-spirited articles about the film industry, I could pull down $7,000 in a couple of weeks. This was important, because it would spare me the humiliation of having to work as a laboratory rat, or steal waitresses' tips, or collect recyclable soda cans, or indulge in any of that other low-budget/mav/indy cinephile mythology crap. So that put me and the mariachi man on a more even keel.

At this point, the reader may be asking himself: But even if you already had the $7,000 you need to make a film, why would you want to make your own movie? Simple. The old those-who-can-do, those-who-can't-criticize thing. Yes, much as it pained me to admit it, I'd always hated it when people threw that old put-down in my face. Especially people named Merv. But they had a point. Here I was making all my money by ridiculing other people's efforts to be creative. Here I was pretending to be a know-it-all. Well, if I knew so goddamn much about movies, why hadn't

I made one of my own? Wasn't it high time for me to put my money where my mouth wasn't and get down in the trenches?

For too long, cynical wiseasses like me had been poking fun at serious filmmakers without ever admitting how difficult it is to make a high-quality motion picture, or even a low-quality motion picture. For too long, malingerers like me had been content to tear down without ever building up, never once sticking out our own necks and exposing ourselves to the same withering abuse that we so gleefully visited upon others. For too long, people like me had been going around saying, "I could make a better movie than *Kickboxer III* any day of the week," or, "You write me a blank check and I guarantee you I'll make a picture that will blow *Red Sonja VI: The Viper's Birthright* right out of the water." Well, now I would have the chance to find out whether any of these haughty suppositions was true.

The next question that presents itself is this: What made me think that I could make a good movie? Well, for starters, I wasn't a moron. Most people in the film industry are. Movies often *look* great but their plots are cretinous. Their plots, in fact, are subcretinous. Not even a scintilla of intelligence is present in a film such as *Swing Kids*, the 1993 offering that dealt with the plight of twenty-something Benny Goodman fans starved for thrills in Nazi Germany. Films such as *Indian Summer* (a *Big Chill* with more moose) radiated an incandescent stupidity that had an almost otherworldly quality to it. Movies such as *A Stranger Among Us*, which is best thought of as a Lubbavitcher *I Saw What You Did and I Know Who You Are*, seriously expected intelligent audiences to believe that the cerebrally inoperative Melanie Griffith could just sort of blend in with the Brooklyn Hassidim and nobody would notice—the way Shaquille O'Neill could just kind of disappear into the crowd at a Shriners Convention. The people who made these movies were almost criminally stupid.

I, on the other hand, was not. I was mean, underhanded, cynical, and calculating, but I was not stupid. So I approached this undertaking with a certain swagger. What interested me in embarking on this epic adventure was to find out whether it was possible for an ordinary person, who was not criminally stupid but who had no previous experience in the motion picture business other than to have seen thousands of movies, to just walk in off the street and make a film that people could watch without gagging. No, I did not expect the film to be as good as *Howard's End*. But I did expect it to be better than *Howard the Duck*. Much better.

This being the case, I started to spend all my free time dreaming up possible plot lines for a film. At the very beginning, I have to confess, my ideas were disconcertingly sophomoric. One thought that crossed my mind was to make a sequel to the famous Ingmar Bergman film *The Seventh Seal*. Because I would not have enough money to film the further adventures of the Grim Reaper in rural Scandinavia, the entire film would be shot in black-and-white in an even more depressing locale: South Philadelphia, a place so daunting that not even people from North Philadelphia go there.

It did not take me very long to realize that *The Seventh Seal II: First Blood* was not going to work. For starters, there was no way Ingmar Bergman was going to sell me the rights to his title. Second, even if I concocted an absolutely brilliant parody of a ponderous Ingmar Bergman movie, film buffs would accuse me of stealing a page out of Woody Allen's book. Grrr. Third, Keanu Reeves had already done something exactly like this in the second *Bill & Ted* movie, where the two Valley Boys fight for their lives by playing Battleships with the Grim Reaper. So nix *that* idea.

The next brainstorm I got was to make *Jaws V*, a summer thriller with a deft ecological twist. A few months earlier, I'd read a strange article about sharks in *Sports Afield*. I use the word "strange" because it was the first article I'd ever read that actually defended the tigers of the deep. The author of the article, whose name presently escapes me, contended that of the 370 species of sharks dwelling in the planet's vast oceans, only 50 were actually dangerous to humans, meaning that if you got washed overboard in the middle of the Pacific Ocean with blood gushing from your stomach, there was only a one-in-seven chance that the fins encircling you in ever narrowing concentric circles would belong to sharks that were likely to kill you. Eighty-seven percent of the time, the sharks closing in on you would be merely curious.

But that wasn't the most important point in the article. The thing that really grabbed my attention was the author's contention that because of overfishing and mankind's irrational hatred of the tigers of the deep, many species of shark were now starting to turn up on those endangered-species lists compiled by responsible, high-profile, wildlife organizations. In other words: Sharks were in danger. Therefore, sharks needed our love.

Tapping into the burgeoning sense of ecological sensitivity that was apparently spreading like wildfire throughout our environmentally conscious republic, I dreamed up a riveting idea for a film: the world's first pro-shark motion picture. *Jaws V* would deal with a peace-loving, non-man-eating species of sharks living a few miles off the coast of Massachusetts whose safety was menaced by the arrival of a bloodthirsty shark-eating man in the area. The movie would include terrific scenes in which the newly appointed police chief in the tiny Massachusetts resort town of West Calamity would keep warning the local citizenry that if they didn't get rid of the shark-eating man, Greenpeace would come and wreck the resort's reputation and ruin the summer-rental business by telling the rest of the world that West Calamitites were ecologically insensitive pigs. As an additional spin, I decided that all the props and clothing in this eminently middle-American film would be purchased at Sears, as I attempted to become the first director anywhere to put an entire motion picture on his Discover Card.

This idea stayed with me for a while, but ultimately it had to go the way of *The Seventh Seal II: First Blood*. My paltry $7,000 budget simply wasn't large enough to cover the purchase of the *Jaws* trademark. And on a $7,000 budget, what was I going to do about the denizens of the deep? Use real sharks? Too risky. Plastic sharks? Too cheesy. Scary-looking trout shot through a magnifying glass?

No, thank you.

My third idea was *Cold Reception*, and this one really got me worked up into a lather. Here's the basic story line: A useless, talentless, horrible, washed-up stand-up comic who has never made any money in the comedy business finds out that he has only six months to live. For years, Leo Mertz has dreamed of honoring a promise he made to his mother on her deathbed. The promise? That one day he would make his whole family proud by being the *funniest man on an entire continent*. His family, the screenplay would explain, was still pissed off at him for quitting medical school.

Determined to bring his dream to fruition, Leo rehearses his best material and flies off to Australia, the smallest continent on the face of the earth, and a region not known for its glistening stand-up comedy tradition. Imagine his disillusionment when he gets off the plane and finds out that Australia is in fact packed to the gills with hilarious, fabulously talented stand-up comics, including Bruce "The Human Whoopie Cushion" Bartlett (to be played by a Patrick Swayze type) who literally blows Leo right off the stage when the two compete on Open Mike Night at a comedy club called Mirth in Perth.

Heartbroken, Mertz returns to the United States, where he begins to contemplate suicide. But then his girlfriend Esmerelda tells him that even though Australia is the smallest continent on the planet in terms of physical size, it is by no means the most sparsely populated continent. Antarctica is. And Antarctica has only 587 people, mostly Russian and Finnish scientists, and not a single comedy club. So how tough could the competition be? Mertz checks with his agent and discovers that every Wednesday night, to help folks get through the long winter, the scientists at the South Pole mount an amateur talent show featuring a smattering of musicians, jugglers, impressionists, and yes, stand-up comics drawn from their own ranks. It sounds like a gig Leo can dominate, so he gets on the next plane to the South Pole.

Tragically, when our forlorn hero arrives at the South Pole, he learns to his dismay that *several* of those Russian and Finnish scientists and oceanographers who spend the entire summer in Antarctica are amazingly funny guys. (The film, as I envisioned it, would even include a wonderful scene where a translator has to render Russkie Henny Youngmanisms into English. This would not add to the film's budget, as I had a friend who speaks Russian, and she owed me a favor.) Well, to make a long story short, Mertz does his routine and gets a few laughs, but then gets blindsided by a wacky Russian physicist who does an unbelievable impression of Billy Crystal, and by a Norwegian acid rain researcher who is even funnier than Alan King.

Devastated, Mertz returns to the United States and is next seen on the Golden Gate Bridge preparing to leap to his death. But just as he is ready to jump, he is dragged down off the trestle by a mysterious Japanese-American florist named Banzai Willikers. The florist, who would be played by a Pat Morita type, had once been the funniest stand-up comic in the history of Japan, but he has not told a joke in thirty years, since the night his routine at Ha-Ha's in Hiroshima was so side-splitting that three audience members died laughing.

Learning of Mertz's plight, Banzai agrees to teach him the secrets of Zen Stand-up Comedy. We now see Mertz and Banzai walking on the beach, rehearsing one-liners, as Mertz rigorously prepares for his return engagement in Antarctica.

"The joke is not in the punch line," Banzai will intone to his student at various junctures, preaching that all true stand-up comedy derives from a cosmic sense of inner peace. "The joke is in the stamen of the lotus petal."

The high point of the movie would be the scene where Mertz, who has now gotten a whole lot funnier, returns to that comedy club in Australia. At first, he does quite well, but then loses his nerve and gets humiliated once again by Bruce "The Human Whoopie Cushion" Bartlett, who is not a very nice man. At this point, Banzai tears off his jacket, leaps onto the stage, and rips into the funniest five-minute routine in the history of stand-up comedy. The crowd rolls on the floor as Bartlett, an unlicensed abortionist by day, skulks off in disgrace.

"The joke is not in the punch line," Banzai will intone to his student for the very last time. "The joke is in the stamen of the lotus petal."

Now, at long last, Mertz is ready to return to the South Pole and blow those Scandinavian and Russkie cocksuckers right off the stage. Which he does. The movie closes with a shot of the dying but happy stand-up comic drifting out to sea on an ice floe, clutching a cordless mike and whispering over and over again, "The joke is not in the punch line. The joke is in the stamen of the lotus petal."

I really liked this idea for a movie. I liked it a whole lot. But *Cold Reception* posed a number of serious structural problems. First, I didn't have the money to go all the way to the South Pole to film it. Second, *Cold Reception* was basically a parody—a send-up of the *Karate Kid* movies. And parody, as all students of the classics can appreciate, is the very lowest of the comic arts. But there was another, more fundamental problem with this idea, as with all of my other ideas. Basically, all of the movie ideas I'd come up with so far were big goofs. They were funny, yes, but they didn't resonate beyond that initial level of cleverness. They did not engage the moviegoer.

They did not speak to the heart.

I don't want to get all maudlin about this, but let's face facts: To succeed, a movie has to reach out and touch somebody. A movie can't just be a series of gags. It has to be about something important. Otherwise, who gives a shit? I'd seen enough movies, and written about enough movies, to realize that the most memorable films in motion picture history were the ones that addressed a universal human concern. Whether it was friendship (*Midnight Cowboy*) or honor (*Grand Illusion*) or deathless love (*Wuthering Heights*) or why you can't trust the government (*The Conversation*), the great movies always spoke directly to the human heart. They concerned themselves with something of value. They addressed the great issues of the day. They weren't just big yuckfests.

So, after carefully mulling over these extravagantly foolish movie themes for several months, I finally sat myself down and started to think about the Vision Thing. What was the single issue that spoke most directly to the viewers I was trying to reach. Love? Too corny. Racism? Too downbeat. Poverty? Been done. Greed? Cut too close to the bone. And then it hit me. One day, while paging through my local newspaper, I read a story about a support group for people who had trouble dealing with their emotions. The group was called Emotions Anonymous, and it claimed to be a twelve-step program for the emotionally undernourished.

The concept came to me in a flash. Deep down inside, wasn't everybody in this country sick to death of people who claimed to be suffering from pop dysfunctions? I'm not talking about cokeheads or boozers or heroin addicts; I'm talking about porkers who blamed their obesity on genetics, about goldbrickers and layabouts who claimed to be suffering from Chronic Lateness Syndrome, about greedy, acquisitive fuck-knuckles who claimed to have credit card addictions, or addictions to sex, or fatal predispositions toward slamming away bacon double cheeseburgers when in fact they were really nothing but standard-issue assholes.

"Assholes!" I thought. Now there was a subject with universal appeal. Everybody hates assholes. But nobody ever does anything about them. Well, here was my chance to strike a blow for all of us. Somewhere along the way, the plot line for a movie about twelve-step programs started to take shape. Somewhere along the way, I decided that a black comedy called *Twelve Steps to Death* was what I was looking for. Over the next few days, a vague plot began to take shape. My basic idea was a murder mystery in which a psychiatrist is found brutally murdered and all of the suspects are his dysfunctional patients, every one of them in some sort of twelve-step program. The viewer would thus be kept glued to his seat wondering whether the murderer was the sexaholic, the gambler, the porker, the Valium addict, the wife-beater, the binge shopper, the mule humper, the chocaholic, the failed anorexic, or the person suffering from bulimia envy (ravenous jealousy caused by all the attention that bulimics get).

But after the psychiatrist was found dead, who would be the central character in the movie? That was easy enough: someone who had suffered at the hands of the recovery movement. I decided that the protagonist of the film would be a cop whose wife and two children had been killed in a hit-and-run accident by a schizoid anorexic recovering alcoholic with Attention Deficit Disorder who got off with a suspended sentence because she claimed to be fleeing an abusive chocaholic husband who used to beat her up whenever he had one too many of the nougat caramels. Thus, the case would present the hero with a wonderful opportunity to avenge himself on the recovery movement, which had ruined his life. His predicament was something everyone in the United States could identify with. Except for all those weepy, self-pitying bastards in twelve-step programs.

Yes, I decided, this was the theme I would go with. *Jaws V* and *Cold Reception* and *The Seventh Seal II: First Blood* had a certain superficial appeal, but the initial joke didn't get any funnier just because you went out and made the movie. *Twelve Steps to Death*, on the other hand, would provide me with a wonderful opportunity to satirize the loathesome recovery movement and the appalling pseudoscience of psychiatry in a way that audiences might approve of and even enjoy. Surely I wasn't the only person out here who thought that most twelve-step programs were a farce and that recovering people in general were unbelievably annoying fuckheads. Surely I would find an audience for my film.

That's how *Twelve Steps to Death* was born. How much would it cost to make? I had no idea. How would I learn to direct it? Well, I guess I'd have to take a course somewhere. How would I learn how to write a screenplay? Well, I guess I'd have to take a course to learn that, too. Where would the actors come from? Good question. The cameraman? An even better question. Once I'd finished shooting the film, where would I edit it? Hey, don't bore me with the details, we could figure all that out later. For now, it was enough to know that I had a workable concept for a low-budget film. The rest would fall into place later.

Those early days were pretty heady times. Oh, sure, in the back of my mind, I worried even at this early date that my movie was going to cost more than $7,000 to make. But I didn't care. The way I had things sized up, I probably could get other people to underwrite some of the costs. Potential targets ranged from local banks, to rich industrialists, to committed philanthropists, to patrons of the arts, to venture capitalists, to gullible friends and greedy in-laws who thought they could smell money. To generate interest in my project, I even thought about hiring a friend to do public relations and make it known around town that I was looking for an "angel" for my project. At that point, I had such confidence in the ultimate success of my epic undertaking that I even considered launching a public offering via some small, crooked brokerage house that would enable investors to buy shares in my burgeoning media empire. Hey, I was pumped.

And even if these schemes didn't work out, there were many other revenue streams to consider. Product placement, for example. Even if all those potential investors turned me down, I still had the option of approaching various manufacturers of popular consumer products and asking if *they* would like to have their merchandise prominently featured in my film. For example, while watching *Alive* a few months earlier, I'd noticed a partially obscured cola carton visible in the background shortly after Ethan Hawke and the other survivors of the Andes crash had broken down and decided to start eating their dead compatriots. I had never been able to ascertain whether any soft drinks company had actually paid to have its trademark displayed in this fashion, but I kind of doubted it. This would not deter me from approaching the makers of Pepsi, Wheaties, and Minoxodil and asking if they would like to have their products prominently displayed in a film in which all of the murder suspects were people in twelve-step programs. Maybe they could all be *bald* recovering chocaholics. We could negotiate this.

Should Pepsi, General Foods, and Upjohn turn me down, I would point out that in *Sudden Impact,* Clint Eastwood hands a can of Budweiser to Sondra Locke, who is playing a rape victim who avenges herself on her attackers by luring them into her car and then shooting them in the genitals at point-blank range with a .38. It is very difficult for me to believe that Anheuser-Busch actually paid to have its products prominently endorsed by a neurotic actress playing a testicle-mangling vigilante. With this in mind, I would encourage my potential advertisers to provide generous financial support for my film. Otherwise, I'd have one of the main characters repeatedly urinate on their products throughout the film. Or brandish one of their soda containers while hacking off a man's nuts.

Obviously, at this date, it was too early to be thinking about casting, but I was thinking about it just the same. Because of my puny budget, logic would seem to dictate that my film would be studded with unknown actors and actresses I dredged up from Manhattan. But there were other possibilities, as well. Maybe I could take out ads in prominent industry publications announcing a massive casting call. Who knows? Maybe Art Garfunkel would show up. He could certainly use the work. I'd be sure to send him an invitation to come in for a screen test, and also send one out to that guy who used to play Illya Kuryakin on *The Man from U.N.C.L.E.* I'll also try to persuade some mildly famous athlete (Danny Ainge? Macky Sasser? Mugsy Bogues?) to appear in a cameo role in the flick. Or maybe I'd get Nina Totenberg to appear in a small role as a self-promoting superbitch journalist who works for National Public Radio. Oh, the possibilities were endless.

My blue-skying didn't end there. How about the novelization of the movie? Or tie-in merchandise? And what about foreign markets? Perhaps I'd dub my film into Spanish and Yoruban and Croatian and assorted other languages, jump on an airplane, and try to sell it in the direct-to-video overseas market. This would give me the opportunity to visit places I'd always wanted to visit. Like downtown Zagreb.

Then, of course, there was the little matter of publicity. Once I'd finished making the film, I would contact prominent, respected, intelligent films critics, as well as Jeffrey Lyons and Michael Medved, and offer them bribes to review my film in their influential newspaper columns or on their highly respected TV shows. I would put the bribes on my credit card. While I was at it, I would offer to take Vincent Canby to Lutèce. I'd call up my old friend Graydon Carter at *Vanity Fair* and ask him to plug my film. Last, I would shamelessly trade on my friendships with fellow journalists and call in chits and issue vague threats to get the word out about my film. Failing that, I could always go back to bribes.

Obviously, at this point, there was no way I could predict how my project was going to turn out. But one thing I *could* guarantee was this: It was not going to turn out as badly as Richard Brody's project. Who is Richard Brody? Richard Brody is a scholarly-looking guy who was profiled by *The New York Times* in early 1993 in a series entitled "Struggling Artists" ("a periodic look at the quest for success in New York.") This ominously titled series portrayed Brody as a *maverick* filmmaker who still needed another $50,000 before he could finish a film called *Liability Crisis*, which he had already spent several years and $36,000 trying to make. The film dealt with a frustrated young artist from Manhattan who was living with a woman from Yugoslavia—not unlike Richard Brody, a frustrated young artist from Manhattan who was living with a woman from Yugoslavia. According to the glowing report in the *Times*, the film was "studded with reflections on art, love and American culture."

Reading this, I flashed back to those formative Saturday afternoons in the surreal gloom at the Alden Theater in Philadelphia. I thought about *The Tomb of Ligea, Dr. Terror's House of Horrors*, and all those winsome virgins with alabaster white necks. And I promised myself one thing: No matter what happened in the coming months, there was no way in hell that I was going to make a film that was studded with reflections on art, love, and American culture. What's more, there was no way I was going to tell people I needed $50,000 to make my film. If anybody asked me about the budget for *Twelve Steps to Death*, I was going to tell them that the price tag was $7,000, tops. No, screw that, I was going to tell everybody that I intended to make this thing for $6,998, beating Rodriguez's *El Mariachi* record by two bucks.

And, so help me, I was putting the sucker on my Discover Card.

two

The Pride
and the Pity

Shortly after I announced my plans to make *Twelve
Steps to Death*, I began to receive a raftload of unsolicited advice from friends. The advice consisted of
two kinds: the positively horrifying and the merely in-
furiating. The horrifying advice came from people
who were already working in the film or television industry. They told me that my project, while courageous, was doomed to failure because it was based on
an idiotic premise: that a complete amateur could
make a watchable motion picture for just a fistful of
a few dollars more. They said that I would end up
making a hideous, unfunny, cinematographically dis-
orienting movie that would make me look like a buffoon, and, what's more, that it would bankrupt me.
My wife, Francesca, had virtually the same opinion,
save that she never thought the project was one bit

courageous and didn't think my coming off like a buffoon would be any major new development.

Typical was the advice I got from a dear old friend named Andy Aaron. Andy was a writer, producer, editor, and soundman who had written for *Spy*, done postproduction sound effects editing on films as varied as *Far and Away, Honeymoon in Vegas,* and *Ishtar,* and had briefly been employed as a segment producer and writer on the ill-fated *Chevy Chase Show.* In the seven years of our acquaintance, we had collaborated on a number of projects for *Spy* magazine and Comedy Central and had eaten many fine lunches together. I had also once taken him and his wife, Barbara, aside and told them that children weren't anywhere near as dreadful as they seemed at first glance, so it might be a good idea to have some. In short, ours was a relationship based on candor, trust, and the acquisition of very small amounts of money (*Spy,* Comedy Central, *The Chevy Chase Show*). Since Andy was a person whom I liked and respected, his advice was all the more chilling.

Basically, Andy thought I was a lunatic for telling everyone that I was going to make a movie for $2 less than *El Mariachi.* He told me that no matter what Robert Rodriguez or anybody else was going around telling people, it was impossible to make a feature-length movie for $6,998, or for any sum even vaguely approaching $6,998. Thirty grand was about the cheapest he'd ever heard of, and that was to make one of those artsy black-and-white student films where a bunch of pretentious, not especially good-looking assholes sit around in dimly lit rooms for ninety minutes discussing the meaning of life.

"Hey, I liked *Manhattan,*" I protested.

Andy cautioned me that the lingering financial fallout from *Twelve Steps to Death* could imperil my children's futures for years to come, ultimately making the difference between a collegiate career at Swarthmore and one at Central Connecticut State. I told him thanks for the tip, but noted that neither of my children were Swarthmore material, anyway.

Still, it scared me to think that a person who had worked on both *Ishtar* and *The Chevy Chase Show* should think that I was headed directly for the shoals of financial disaster. It was like hitting the high seas in a wooden dinghy and getting a small-craft warning about a coming squall from someone who had worked as entertainment director on the *Titanic* before landing a job as talent coordinator on the *Lusitania*. It wasn't the sort of warning you could just ignore cavalierly.

But I did just ignore it cavalierly: I had to ignore it and all advice of its ilk. The only way *Twelve Steps to Death* was ever going to get made was if I ignored the advice of my friends in the business. My friends had very fixed ideas about what a film should look like, how large the crew should be, how much should be spent on film, developing, equipment, and post-production, and what level of competence the actors in the film should achieve. Their favorite word was "No." Their favorite phrase was "No way." Half the time they opened their mouths it was to say "Boy, have you got a lot to learn." The rest of the time it was to say "Get a grip" or "Grow up." Every bit of advice they ever gave me was paternalistic, condescending, pitying.

I didn't blame them for treating me this way. They were in the business. They knew what they were talking about. I didn't care. I wanted to make my movie. So, very early on, I decided that *Twelve Steps to Death* could get made only if I deliberately avoided using seasoned professionals and instead depended on amateurs or callow youths. At that point, I made a vow to myself that if it was at all within my power, a prerequisite for working on my movie was that a person had to know less about making movies than I did. Otherwise, I'd have to listen to *his* advice.

I had another reason for adopting this credo. People who knew less about making movies than I did would never stop believing in the project. They'd never bore me with reveries about past grandeur—about how they'd once worked as a gaffer for Otto Preminger and never thought they'd end up like this. They'd never tell me that filming a two-and-a-half-minute sequence from a single camera angle was beneath their dignity. They'd never tell me that what I was doing in a particular sequence was too Cassavetesesque, too Sam Fullerish, too Andy Warholian. They'd simply do what I told them to do. They'd be grateful to be in the movie. What's more, I could get them to work incredibly long hours, or prepare large vats of lasagna for the cast, or baby-sit my ball-busting kids. Best of all, I wouldn't have to pay them.

Thus, from the very outset, I decided to freeze out the pros. But I also decided to freeze out the semipros: the legions of aspiring actors, actresses, editors, and directors who dreamed of stardom and who assumed, for some strange reason, that I could help them achieve it. Let me explain how I reached this decision. When I started out on my epic voyage of self-discovery, I thought the idea of enlisting the assistance of anyone willing to help me was just peachy. It didn't matter to me how I got my film made. I just needed to get it made. So the first thing I needed to do was to get on the horn and bang the drum slowly, casting a wide net to see who would come out of the woodwork after I was finished beating the bushes. If you see what I'm driving at.

Let me put it another way: When you come up with an idea for a film like *Twelve Steps to Death,* the first step you take isn't to write the script or cast the film or even line up the technical crew. The first thing you do is to hype it. This is also the second, third, and fourth thing that you do. The single most important element that goes into the making of a motion picture is hype. A lot of people starting out to make their first low-budget film naturally assume that their top priority is learning how to direct or write a script or set up camera angles or make storyboards. Get real. You can learn how to write a screenplay in a week, and you can learn to direct in an afternoon. But neither of these talents is likely to have a material effect on the success or failure of your motion picture, nor is the ability to storyboard. Robert Rodriguez did not get a fantastic deal at Columbia Pictures because anyone thought he was a terrific director. He got a terrific deal at Columbia because the powers-that-be in Hollywood were impressed by his talent for budgeting and hype. I realized this from the get-go. So once I started working on *Twelve Steps to Death,* my top priority was to spend the next six months hyping the project before I even thought about sitting down and learning how to direct or act or write a screenplay or do any of that other peripheral stuff.

One of my main objectives in hyping my film was to attract well-heeled investors who would help defray the cost of production. Although for public consumption I was telling anyone who would listen that I was making a movie for an anemic $6,998, I recognized almost immediately that this figure was fraught with incipient bogusness. Film costs a lot of money. Editing costs a lot of money. Postproduction costs a lot of money. Getting a print of your film made costs a lot of money. And $6,998 is not a lot of money.

Still, the hook for *Twelve Steps to Death* was the prospect of making the cheapest film in motion picture history, so that's the way I hyped it. But I didn't want to make the cheapest film in motion picture history with my own money. What I really wanted to do was to make the cheapest film in motion picture history with somebody else's money. So in the beginning, the idea was to scare up some money. That's why I set the hype machine in motion. I talked about it constantly on "Imus in the Morning," after I became a regular guest starting in February 1994, and Don himself rattled on about it endlessly. I discussed it on scores of TV and radio programs while I was going around promoting my book *If You're Talking to Me, Your Career Must Be in Trouble*. I talked about it on ABC Worldwide News, CNN, *Politically Incorrect*, assorted cable outlets. But my biggest break of all came when Janet Maslin of *The New York Times* wrote a story about my fool's errand on March 23, 1994.

Maslin, who happens to live in Pocantico Hills, the next village over from Tarrytown, where I live, wrote a lot of incredibly nice things about me in her article, but the best part of all was the headline "Next: Auteur of the Bad Movie," which, of course, drew attention to my upcoming film. Boy, did the phones start ringing off the hook after that. First, I got a call from Troma Pictures, the low-budget outfit that has produced such diabolically substandard films as *Toxic Avenger, Teenage Catgirls in Heat, Class of Nuke 'Em High III,* and *Surf Nazis Must Die.* They were interested in seeing my film. Fabulous. But then I got a call from a person named Deborah Jelin Newmyer, an executive at Amblin Entertainment, Steven Spielberg's company. Newmyer would be in town soon and wondered if she could talk to me about the project. She proposed that I meet her for breakfast at the Plaza Hotel. Confronted with a choice between Troma and Amblin, I chose Amblin. At some primal level, I probably realized that I was already well on the way to selling out. But at least I was selling out to the right people.

While counting the days, the hours, and the minutes until my meeting with the Amlin bigwig, whom I dearly hoped would have the wherewithal to make me rich and famous, I fielded the scores of phone calls and letters that came flooding in from people who had read Maslin's article and who wanted to help me make *Twelve Steps to Death*. Typical was the actress who had appeared in the Sidney Lumet film *Daniel* when she was just a little girl and who now wanted to be in my movie. She had worked with Mandy Patinkin on her way up, so it was probably inevitable that she should work with me on her way down.

She was not alone. An actor who had appeared in an episode of *Spenser for Hire* was interested in appearing in the film. So was a 125-pound actress with honey blond hair who had appeared in a community theater production of *Bye-Bye Birdie*. Because my home telephone number was listed at the time, my wife received several calls from an actress based in New Jersey who said she was prepared to work for "practically nothing." Practically nothing, of course, was a whole lot more than I was interested in paying.

There were many other calls, résumés, head shots. Some came from film editors, some from cameramen, some from musicians, some from dialogue coaches. There was even a letter from a Wynantskill, New York, man who offered to make a comic book version of *Twelve Steps to Death*. My, my, my, I thought, people were certainly getting worked up about my film. Everyone, it seemed, wanted a piece of the action.

Yet, for some strange reason, this Niagara of enthusiasm left me with an oddly muted feeling. First of all, I was disappointed that Nicholson hadn't called. Most of the calls I was getting were from nobodies or quasi-nobodies who wanted to piggyback on my operation. They'd seen the article in the *Times*; they saw that the movie had a chance of making a bit of a stir; and they wisely decided to put their two cents in. I didn't blame them for their pluck, their panache. But I wasn't sure I wanted to work with them. To tell you the God's honest truth, they kind of scared me.

They scared me because I wasn't sure they were the kind of people who would readily succumb to my low-budget/mav/indy charisma. When you're a 113-pound dumpling with dark brown eyes who's already worked with Mandy Patinkin, you're not going to take kindly to being bossed around by some zany Walter Mitty type from Palookaville (in this case, Tarrytown, New York, a quiet, affluent suburb of Gotham). When you've got that kind of background, you're going to want to throw your weight around. All 113 pounds of it. This was the kind of thing I wanted desperately to avoid. As soon as I got a bunch of people who'd already worked in films involved in my project, I knew that I was going to have to deal with egos, attitudes, expectations, angst. The last thing I wanted on the set of my movie was egos, attitudes, expectations, or angst. I could get that from my family.

But clearly, that's what I would be getting. Yes, what I detected in all these letters and phone calls was a sense that these people were professionals—of a sort—and that they, out of the goodness of their hearts, were ready to help me out of a tight spot. I didn't want that kind of help. I recognized that I was, in some sense, pathetic. But I wasn't as pathetic as they seemed to think. And I wasn't an idiot. I didn't want to find myself on the set of the movie having to argue with actors and actresses about whether we should do another take or not. I wanted to be in complete control of the operation from the very beginning.

Basically, my aversion to accepting help from outsiders came down to a question of dollars and cents. I already knew enough about film budgets to realize that the film had to be shot in less than ten days, meaning that every scene in *Twelve Steps to Death* would have to be shot in one or two takes. Otherwise, the film would take months to shoot and cost a fortune. Yes, I realized that making an entire movie out of a bunch of first and second takes would mean that in many cases I would be signing off on takes that were merely functional, but not especially good. But that was the only way I could bring the movie in anywhere near budget. I also realized that actors and actresses who entertained dreams of stardom, however flickering, however dim, would have a hard time accepting this policy. They'd want to keep doing each take until we got it right.

Well, not with my money.

I also didn't care for the highfalutin tone in some of the communications I was receiving. Editors and sound engineers and musicians who volunteered their services seemed to think that my movie was going to be one big hoot. That "Auteur of the Bad Movie" headline in the *Times* had encouraged them to think that this was going to be some kind of Ed Wood farce where we would be striving to make a deliberately awful movie. That wasn't what I had in mind at all. *Twelve Steps to Death* was going to be a cheap movie, an amateurish movie, a gerryrigged movie, but it wasn't going to be a stupid movie or a camp movie or even an artsy movie. It was going to be a serious attempt to make a conventional Hollywood movie on an extremely low budget without any real talent to speak of.

As the days passed and the phone calls continued to pour in, I solidified my resolve to spurn the offers of help made by these various professionals and semiprofessionals. If these people were so darned talented, why were they contacting a guy making a $6,998 movie up in Sleepy Hollow, New York? Wasn't Francis Ford Coppola hiring that week?

Most important of all, I didn't want to get halfway through the movie and then have some actor quit because he'd landed a part in *Spenser for Hire,* or get some actress pissed off at me because I wouldn't let her do a ninth take and then have her quit the movie, forcing me to reshoot all her scenes from the very beginning. I wanted to be in a situation where I was in complete and utter control, where no one had any option but to do my bidding. To achieve this, I knew that I must spurn aspiring thespians and instead draw from a vast pool of untapped talent whom I could rule with absolute dictatorial control, never doubting for a moment that they would submit to my raw, psychological dominion.

Neighbors.

NEIGHBORS HAVE ONE indispensable attribute that makes them infinitely preferable to real actors: You know where they live. Unlike aspiring actors and actresses who lead fly-by-night existences, constantly changing jobs, apartments, appearances, sex, neighbors tend to lead relatively sedentary lives. They find it extremely difficult to hide. This is particulary true of suburban neighbors, who usually live right down the street and have huge mortgages on expensive houses, and who have kids to support and who aren't going anywhere anytime soon. From the point of view of the low-budget filmmaker, neighbors are the single most valuable resource available to him, because once they're in, they're in for the duration. Neighbors can't walk off the set in a huff halfway through the movie because they know that you know where they live and they know that if they walk off the set, you'll come and punch their lights out or put sugar in their gas tanks or poison their golden retrievers. I realize that this is an unconventional and, in some ways, sociopathic way of approaching filmmaking, but that's the reason I decided to cast my film with neighbors.

But could my neighbors act? Sure they could. Or put it this way: They could act well enough for my purposes. The way I looked at it, acting was basically a case of keeping a straight face. If I could write them good lines, and if I could cast them in plausible roles, I was sure they could get the job done. They would do what I told them to do. They would be like putty in my hands. They were my neighbors.

Now, the big question was: Did I intend to use just any old neighbors, or would I make a concerted effort to seek out the people in my neighborhood who actually had some acting experience, who had actually strolled the boards in high school or college? This was a very tricky question. Tarrytown is a fairly cosmopolitan little community, a scant half hour from Manhattan, so it's filled with people who have appeared in collegiate and semiprofessional venues such as community theater. In fact, one of my best friends is a trained actor who I have every reason to believe is probably very good at what he does, or who at least used to be very good at what he did, since he doesn't do it anymore. So in theory I could have cast my film with locals who had some acting experience and perhaps even some acting ability. And for a short time, this was exactly what I planned to do.

Then, one evening at a barbecue, I had an unnerving experience that completely changed my ideas on this subject. The Saul at Tarsus incident took place at the home of T.J. Elliott, the aforementioned actor friend. Before getting married, having three children, and settling down to a dreary life in the suburbs, T.J. had appeared in a number of off-off-Broadway plays and once had a paying job in a public service commercial. I knew this, and he knew that I knew it. Since he was the only one of my close friends in Tarrytown with real acting experience, and since we played basketball together at least once a week, and since our families socialized together, and since he knew that I was making my own low-budget movie, it seemed inevitable that I should one day offer him a part in the film.

Then he said something that changed my mind. These were still early days in the proceedings; I hadn't started, much less finished, writing the screenplay and still hadn't learned how to direct or edit or storyboard or any of that other stuff. But I'd already made it known around Tarrytown that I would be using various Friends to Be Named Later as principals in my film. My daughter Bridget, age ten, who had once appeared in the coveted role of the Dew Fairy in the 1992 Winfield L. Morse production of *Hansel and Gretel,* had already nailed down one of the principal supporting roles, and my son Gordon, age seven, was also clamoring for a shot at screen stardom. Roles were going fast, so this was the moment of truth. While munching on some hamburgers, T.J. asked me how many takes I planned to do of each shot. I said one or two.

T.J.'s eyes grew wide as saucers. "Two takes?"

"That's right," I replied. "Three, if necessary."

T.J. chuckled with infinite disbelief. "Let me tell you a story, Joe. About fifteen years ago, I made a public service commercial for public television. I was playing a construction worker who was talking about cleaning up the Hudson River. I had one paragraph: "Even construction workers care about saving the environment, etc., etc." The commercial was thirty seconds long. Do you know how many takes that took?"

I didn't.

"Eighteen."

Now *my* eyes widened into vast saucers of incredulity. "Eighteen takes?"

"That's right."

"Eighteen takes to make a thirty-second public service commercial?"

"You got it."

I thought about if for a second, then spoke. "T.J., I don't think you're going to be in my movie."

To be perfectly honest, there was one other reason that I didn't want a trained actor like T.J. in my film. Let me use a labyrinthine musical analogy to explain why. Have you ever been to a party with a bunch of Baby

Boomers where there's an old Martin DC-35 guitar lying around? Of course you have. Inevitably, as the afternoon drifts on, each and every male attending the party will drift over to where the guitar sits and ritualistically begin strumming it. Five'll get you ten that the first contestant will play "Heart of Gold" or "Don't Think Twice, It's All Right." Then he'll put the guitar down and another male will come over and play a stripped-down version of the theme from *Forbidden Games*. After he's done, a third guy will play "Helpless" and the opening riff from "Layla." Then a fourth will come over and play "Hey, Joe." Then it's Male No. 5 with "Down By the River, I Shot My Baby," Male No. 6 with the opening riff from "Stairway to Heaven," Male No. 7 with "Fire and Rain," Male No. 8—a slight change of pace—with a tasty fingerpickin' version of "Freight Train," and so on and so forth until Male No. 20 finishes up with "A Horse With No Name."

Even though the music that these would-be Neil Youngs and Loudon Wainwright IIIs will bang out during the course of the party will be pretty objectionable, no one actually will complain about it, and some people actually will enjoy it. Live guitar music plays funny tricks on the brain. By the end of the afternoon, a small cluster of people, mostly neurotic females, will be kneeling around the guitarist, clapping their hands and waving their hair in the breeze, harking back to those halcyon days of yore, singing "Blowin' in the Wind" or "High Flyin' Bird." Even though the level of musical expertise will be quite low, the people listening to the songs will be quite happy.

Science has no explanation for this phenomenon.

This arcadian reverie will be shattered only if a real musician shows up on the scene. If a real musician, a professional musician, somebody who knows his ass from third base, shows up on the scene, the horrible musicianship of all those guys playing "Streets of London" will immediately be thrown into bold relief. This will ruin things for everyone: the amateurs, who will feel upstaged and embarrassed; the weepy hangers-on, who will resent the shattering of their illusion; and the professional musician himself, who will not be able to understand why everybody has decided to leave the room as soon as somebody who actually can play a guitar has entered it. The moral of this story: Professionals take things to another level, but not necessarily to a level everyone feels comfortable with.

This was precisely what I feared would happen if I used real actors in my movie. Real actors were going to want to *perform,* which was going to throw into bold relief how bad everybody else in the film was. Even if these actors weren't especially good, they would still have their basic acting chops down pat: furrowing their eyebrows, rolling their eyes, pausing deliberately, ceaselessly hyperventilating. Whether they were talented actors or hammy old hacks, their display of even the most rudimentary thespian skills was going to upset my $6,998 apple cart completely.

Real actors, like real professional musicians, were certain to have a disruptive influence on my film because they would draw the audience's attention to the fact that some people in the movie had real acting experience, while others did not. What I most feared was this deviation from the mean. I had already decided, as soon as I started this project, that all of the acting had to fall into the same general range of acting ability. Everybody had to be roughly as good as everybody else. In the back of my mind, I accepted the fact that once we started shooting, a couple of cast members probably would turn out to have real acting ability while several others would eat it raw. There was nothing I could do about this. But at all costs, I wanted to avoid a situation where I *deliberately* cast someone with real talent, because this was going to make everybody else stand out like a sore thumb. Thus, on a microlevel, I was trying to do what Geoff Murphy had done in *Young Guns II:* cast an entire movie with people of uniformly horrible acting ability like Emilio Estevez, Kiefer Sutherland, Christian Slater, and Lou Diamond Phillips so that the audience would never bother its pretty little head trying to figure out who sucked the most.

There was one final reason why I did not want to use people with real acting experience in my movie. Real actors, no matter how bad, had all started out as dreamers. Every actor, at the core, was a perfectionist of a sort, a person who possessed a platonic conception of the ideal way a scene should be played. I, by contrast, was not a perfectionist. I was a person with a very small budget. I was a person who didn't want any problems on the set. I was a person who had already made up his mind what he did and what he did not want on the set of his film. No perfectionists. No dreamers.

No actors.

THE DAY OF my meeting with the Amblin personage finally arrived. We hooked up in the elegant Palm Court at the Plaza Hotel in New York City. Deborah Jelin Newmyer was surprisingly nice for someone who worked in the film business. She had grown up in suburban New Jersey; perhaps this had enabled her to retain a veneer of human decency. For whatever the reason, I took an immediate liking to her. Newmyer asked how far along I was. Specifically, she wanted to know how the screenplay was coming. I said that I hadn't written it yet. She wanted to know what the holdup was. I said that I hadn't finished reading all the books I needed to read in order to write a screenplay.

"How many books is that?" she asked.

"About seven," I replied.

"Read three," she said. "As soon as you finish writing the screenplay, send it to me."

Wowie-zowie, I thought. Here was this big-time Hollywood talent scout from the most important production company of them all and she was actually interested in reading my not-yet-written script. This was just like Lana Turner getting discovered at Schwab's, or Bridget Fonda getting discovered at Henry Fonda's. I was on my way.

Newmyer and I talked for about thirty minutes. She wasn't really all that interested in the film per se; she was only interested in the script. If the script was good, she wondered aloud, what was the point of wasting it on a low-budget film filled with a bunch of nobodies and directed by a clown? (She did not actually call me a clown.) If the script was good, why not let the professionals handle it?

I told Newmyer that I understood where she was coming from. But making this movie was important to me. I had a point to make. I had promises to keep. I had miles to go before I slept. Besides, I'd feel like a schmuck if Janet Maslin had gone to all that trouble of writing that terrific story about Joe Average making a low-budget movie and then I never actually went out and made it. Newmyer seemed puzzled by my attitude. This wasn't the way things were done in Hollywood. This was perplexing behavior. I didn't care. I am not a nice man, but I am an honorable one. Well, sort of. For the most part, I keep my promises. Generally. One thing was certain: I was going to make this goddamned movie, come hell or high water. Probably.

We left it at that. Newmyer asked when the script would be ready. I estimated two months. She wanted a specific date. I gave her one. She said that if she hadn't heard from me by that date, she'd call to find out about the script.

Right then and there, I decided that I didn't need Troma in my corner anymore.

TOTALING UP THE ledger, I had much to be happy about. The *Times* article had piqued Amblin's interest. A major player in the industry was interested in reading my script. And Don Imus was already making noises about getting his friends at New Line Cinema to look at my film once it was done.

On the negative side of the scoreboard, I still had no script, I still didn't know how to direct a film, and I was now resigned to having to make my film with a cast of talentless neighbors. I was also face to face with the reality that none of my *Ishtar*-type friends was going to be much help in bringing the project to fruition. Finally, after all the phone calls and letters and meetings, no major player had come forward with an offer to bankroll my film. That public offering wasn't going to take place. No corporation had come forward with a proposal to have its products plugged in a super-low-budget movie about a cop whose wife and kids had been killed in a hit-and-run accident by a schizoid anorexic recovering alcoholic with Attention Deficit Disorder. If *Twelve Steps to Death* was ever going to see the light of day, it was going to have to be made with my money. I was still staring straight down the barrel of a $6,998 gun.

Make that $6,989.01. Yes, after all of the shameless hype I had engaged in for the past six months, I had managed to shake loose a grand total of

$8.99 in outside financing. After reading the article in the *Times*, a Gotham film buff named Laura Sinderbrand sent me a check for $6.99 to "support" my film, which she felt would be "the definitive antidote to the bilge pouring out of Hollywood lo these many years." She added: "My husband suggested that I offer you an investment of $69.98 and ask for artistic control, but I've never had any experience as a hairdresser and I'm not sure I want to interfere with your vision of the movie's mission or direction."

Personally, I wished that she'd listened to hubby's advice and sent me the rest of the money. To my way of thinking $6.99 was an insult. But $69.98, I could live with.

The other contribution arrived in an envelope that a woman named Lisa Kennedy dropped off at my local diner after reading about me in the *Times*. Ms. Kennedy said how much she enjoyed reading my articles in *Movieline* and munificiently contributed two dollar bills to my film budget. Ms. Kennedy, a mysterious sort, did not include an address or a telephone number, and indicated that she did not go to the movies and did not even have her house wired for cable. Nevertheless, she wanted me to have the $2 in case I went over budget, and ended up tying, rather than beating, Robert Rodriguez's *El Mariachi* record.

"It'll be our little secret, okay?" she wrote.

No, it won't, Lisa. For $2, I don't keep secrets. But thanks for the thought. And the money.

three

Our Crap Is
Twenty Times Better
than Their Crap

The most important question that a neophtye film-maker needs to ask himself is how much time and money he is willing to devote to learning how to direct a film. Ideally, an aspiring director should go to a film school like New York University or Southern Cal for four years and study at the feet of the masters. But I didn't have four years to spare, and besides, it would have seemed a little weird to spend $85,000 to learn how to make a $6,998 movie.

There *were* other options available to me. The New York Film Academy, a school that operates out of Robert De Niro's TriBeCa Film Center, was always running ads in *The New York Times* promoting an eight-week "hands-on," "total immersion workshop" taught by "award-winning instructors" that would teach me how to write, direct, shoot, and edit my own short (sixteen-minute) film. But shortly after I sent for the academy's brochure, *The New York Observer* published an article reporting that the school had nothing to do with Robert De Niro and that the courses it offered were no great shakes. On a particularly troubling note, the article suggested that the school was packed to the gills with students who had been rejected by New York University's prestigious film school, meaning that I'd be taking the course with a bunch of losers.

But that's not the reason I didn't sign up for the course. The reason I didn't sign up for the course is because it cost $4,500, and I didn't feel like spending $4,500 to learn how to make a $6,998 film. Forking over that kind of money would do unspeakable violence to the whole mav/indy/Joe-Blow-on-a-shoestring ethos that I was working so hard to cultivate. It would be like spending $4,500 to learn how to be a seamstress.

Price being such an overriding concern, my options kind of narrowed. One friend handed me an ad for "America's Oldest and Most Prestigious Film School's Newest Summer Program," run by the University of Southern California School of Cinema and Television, which came with an enthusiastic testimonial from Maximilian Gruber of Vienna.

"Sie werden fur jeden anderen Beruf verloren-sein!" Gruber declared in the ad. Fact is, I wasn't interested in film schools that got unsolicited testimonials from people named Maximilian *Gruber*. I was interested in film schools that got unsolicited testimonials from people named Peter *Guber*. And I wasn't interested in waiting until the summer to learn how to direct a film either. Also, I don't speak German, so I had no idea what Maximilian Gruber was actually saying about the course.

Disappointed at what was available to me, I decided that I'd have to adopt an autodidactic approach to the situation and teach myself how to direct. I had a two-pronged strategy. First, I would read a bunch of books on the subject. Second, I would spend all my free time watching movies that had really impressed me over the years and then steal all the really good shots. By doing so, I figured I could teach myself how to direct in about six weeks.

First, I read *Feature Filmmaking at Used-Car Prices: How to Write, Produce, Direct, Film, Edit and Promote a Feature-Length Film for Less than $10,000* by Rick Schmidt. This had a lot of technical information about cameras and editing equipment and microphones and such but wasn't much help in the directing department. Then I read *Independent Visions: A Critical Introduction to Recent Independent American Film* by Donald Lyons. This book discussed the backgrounds and work of such mav/indy/Joe Blow directors as Quentin Tarantino and Jim Jarmusch, but didn't provide much advice of a technical nature, because Lyons is a critic and critics don't know anything about making movies.

Next I read *The Movie Business Book: The Inside Story of the Creation, Financing, Making, Selling and Exhibiting of Movies As Told By Mike Medavoy, David Puttnam, Mel Brooks, William Goldman, Sydney Pollack, Lee Rosenberg and 34 Other Leaders in the Movie Industry,* which was edited by Jason E. Squire. This was an extremely interesting book that explained how the motion picture industry works, but it wasn't much help to low-budget people like me because it didn't concern itself with low-budget movies. What's more, it didn't have much to say about the craft of directing. Finally, an artsy-crafty friend lent me *The Films of John Cassavetes: Pragmatism, Modernism and the Movies,* written by Ray Carney. This was largely a book about how Cassavetes got the most out of his actors, something I didn't really need to worry about, since I would be using my neighbors. This book was no help at all.

The whole time I was hacking my way through these books, I was simultaneously watching hundreds of films and making crude drawings of interesting shots I wanted to steal. *A Farewell to Arms* contains a beautiful sequence where Gary Cooper stares up at a bare ceiling and then the camera plunges directly into Helen Hayes's eyes as she swoops down to give him a kiss. I made a note reminding myself to hijack this shot. *Of Human Bondage* has a number of fascinating shots of feet shuffling up the sidewalk. I also decided to lift these. *Lilies of the Field* opens with a great shot of Sidney Poitier's car heading down an empty ribbon of highway toward the towering mountains, the human speck in the awesome panorama symbolizing man's search for meaning in a large, sophisticated universe, or something. And *Reservoir Dogs* has that great scene where Michael Madsen cuts off a cop's ear. Every time I saw a terrific shot like this, I would mark it down in a notebook and keep it on file for when I got around to directing the movie. Basically, I already had decided that my directorial philosophy would be to simply steal a couple of hundred shots from other people's movies and then integrate them into my screen-play. This would save me the cost of going to film school.

I do not want to create the impression that I adopted a completely hoity-toity attitude toward the films of the past, limiting myself to stealing shots from great movies. Far from it. All movies, even bad movies, are di-rected by people who learned how to direct by looking at good films and stealing the best shots. So even in a horrible movie like *Rudy* or *Dennis the Menace,* you can find shots that are eminently stealable, because the directors of *Rudy* and *Dennis the Menace* probably stole them from some-body else first. *Rudy* had a nice shot of a kid talking on a public telephone while the camera remains riveted on an empty hallway behind him. Nat-urally, the rest of the movie sucked, but that shot was worth lifting. And in *Dennis the Menace,* when director Nick Castle first introduces the vil-lainous Christopher Lloyd, the camera focuses on a full moon poised in the distant heavens, then pulls away as Lloyd's profile is superimposed on the shimmering lunar oval. This image was Castle's way of symboliz-ing mankind's tragic predilection for screwing up a perfectly wonderful universe by letting people like Christopher Lloyd into it. I wanted that shot in my movie.

There were numerous other shots that I was absolutely determined to get into the picture. Although *Twelve Steps to Death* was not intended as an out-and-out parody, it would definitely contain a number of parodic elements—the hard-boiled cop, the brain-dead sidekick, the obviously framed murder suspect, the *femme fatale*—that paid tribute to the great conventions of the genre. So even before I had written an outline of the screenplay, I began to compile a list of generic shots that would pay homage to great movies of the past:

- A head butt
- A car chase
- Handwriting done in blood
- At least one good kick in the nuts
- A crucifix juxtaposed with the image of an evil man
- The camera entering a room through a window
- A Cops in the Shithouse scene

- A gun in somebody's mouth
- A camera looking out from under a bed at a woman's legs as she takes off her panties
- Two men sitting on a park bench whispering
- A diner shot
- A camera looking over the murderer's shoulder
- The murderer's feet descending from a car
- A blind person
- A bare butt
- Light protruding from underneath a door, behind which is concealed a killer
- A corpse in a trunk
- A shot of a person getting into a car, not knowing that a bad person is already hiding in the backseat
- A shot of an elevator door opening to reveal the killer
- A woman dressed up as a French maid, preferably poised seductively on a hotel bed

At this point, I still wasn't quite clear on which one of my neighbors was going to get dressed up as a French maid poised seductively on a hotel bed. I'd get back to that.

BY THE TIME February of 1994 rolled around, my crash course in low-budget filmmaking had come to an end. I'd read all the books, listed all the shots I wanted to steal, begun to sketch an outline of the screenplay. Yet, despite all this information that I had assimilated, I still didn't feel that I knew what the hell I was doing. I was pretty clear on the setting-up-the-shots side—steal everything—but the technical side had me baffled. Who was going to film this thing? Where would I get the camera from? Where would I buy the film? What kind of sound equipment should I use? How many days would it take to shoot the picture?

I was also starting to feel external pressure from friends and business associates. After I told my friends that Janet Maslin had a *New York Times* profile in the works, everybody and his brother started assailing me with questions. How far had I gotten with the screenplay? When was shooting scheduled to get underway? Where was I going to edit the film? Was *Twelve Steps to Death* still under budget?

One day, I confided in a friend that after months and months of laborious research, I still didn't have the foggiest notion of what I was doing. He suggested that I sign up for a course at The Learning Annex. He'd read about a $29 guerilla filmmaking course taught by a guy named Jefferson Davis, who for $8,000 had made a film so good that it won awards at film festivals all around the country and had even been shown at the Kennedy Center in Washington.

For $29, this sounded like just the ticket. But when I picked up a copy of The Learning Annex's latest catalog, I was crushed to discover that Davis had made an $8,000 *videotape* with a home video camera that he had then blown up and transferred to film. That didn't do me any good. *Anyone* could make a cheap old movie on videotape and transfer it to film. But that wasn't the same as making a movie. That was super-low-rent bullshit that was bound to look atrocious. I hadn't come this far to make a cheesy home movie on videotape. Doomed tots who grow up in rat-infested, crime-ridden, disease-plagued housing projects in the nation's worst inner cities don't spend their childhoods dreaming of growing up to direct, produce, write, and star in their own *videos*.

Then just when all hope seemed lost, salvation manifested itself in the most unlikely of places: the classified advertising section in the back of *Movieline* magazine. One afternoon, as I was paging through the magazine for which I had written so many articles making fun of the motion picture industry, I spied an advertisement for something called the Hollywood Film Institute. Each year, the Hollywood Film Institute sponsored a series of two-day crash courses in filmmaking given by a man named Dov S-S Simens, who had, in fact, founded the Hollywood Film Institute. According to the ad, Simens would be in San Diego on January 29, in Las Vegas on February 12, and in Nashville on February 26. No help to me. But on March 5 and 6, Simmons would be bringing his Hollywood Film Institute Course to New York City. What's more, the course cost only $279, right in my price range.

I didn't even wait to get the brochure or find out who Dov S-S Simens was, or what the "S-S" stood for. I called the 800-number and booked a place right away.

I LIKED DOV SIMENS from the moment I met him, and not just because he was only charging me $279 to learn the tricks of the trade he had picked up while working as a "producer, director, production manager, and line producer" of a bunch of films that were never actually identified in the Hollywood Film Institute catalog. Simens was a short, muscular, intense man in his mid-fifties who looked like he had worked his entire life in the garment district. There was absolutely nothing artistic or effete about him. He did not look like a man who was interested in discussing the waterlily imagery in Pasolini's *Canterbury Tales*. He did not look like a man who could spell the word *cahiers* or pronounce the word *auteur*. From the moment Simens opened his mouth that Saturday morning in the Millennium Film Workshop, a dark theater on the Lower East Side of New York, I knew he was my kind of guy.

Right off the bat, Simens indicated that he would spend the next two days doing all the talking, and that he would prefer not to be interrupted too often because any possible questions that might be asked he had been asked a million times before. He was a font of priceless wisdom; we were mere putty in his hands. We would have to deal with it.

"I have scanned the list, and you are all nobodies," he remarked as he strolled back and forth in front of us. There were perhaps sixty of us in the room, roughly seventeen women and forty-three men, of whom I was probably the second or third oldest. Many of the class members seemed shocked by his abruptness and condescension. But I liked this approach. Dov wasn't here to be my friend. He was here to show me how to make a film.

For the next eight hours—and all of the next day—Simens stalked back and forth in the front of the room, ranting and raving about the motion picture business, only stopping for two ten-minute breaks and a very short lunch. During that time, Simens almost never stopped talking about money. He started off by saying that 60 percent of our efforts as filmmakers should be devoted to marketing. You could feel a *frisson* in the room as he said this with his tough, street-smart accent: The artsy types were already wondering if that $279 hadn't been misspent. But I responded enthusiastically to this declaration, because it made me feel smarter than the rest of them. Up until this point, approximately 99 percent of my efforts as a filmmaker had been devoted to marketing. And I'd been worried that 99 percent might be a bit on the low side.

Simens laid out the game plan. First, he would show us how to make a film for between $180,000 and $300,000. Then he would show us how to make a film for $150,000. Then he would show us how to make a film for $120,000. Finally, he would show us how to make a film for $5,000. With that out of the way, he now asked us to identify the seven steps to making a movie. Somebody in the back of the room hollered out that you needed talent.

"That's right," said Simens, scrawling the numbers 1 through 7 on a blackboard. "You need talent. Talent is very important. Talent is number seven on the list."

He then enumerated the six other sine qua nons of filmmaking in declining order of importance. They were:

1. The script. Not the concept, but the actual screenplay.
2. Get the money.
3. Get organized.
4. Get on the phone to get more money.
5. Learn to say no.
6. Energy.
7. Talent.

Simens stressed that the script was all-important. It had to be good, it had to be tight, it had to be ready to shoot. If it ain't on the page, he noted, it ain't on the stage. And so on. Beyond that, he didn't go into specifics about the screenplay. Did we want to shoot a monster movie? Fine. A murder mystery? Terrific. A coming-of-age classic? Hey, whatever floats your boat. Whatever movie we planned to make, it made no difference to him, because all movies got made exactly the same way. They cost money. Lots and lots of money. For the rest of the day, for all intents and purposes,

Simens would talk about nothing but money. The next day, when we came back, he did the same thing.

One of Simens's key points was the importance of hyping your budget, rather than your film, to the press. He said that if you didn't have enough money to lay a legitimate claim to having made the most expensive film of the year, then by all means tell everyone that you'd made the least expensive film in the history of motion pictures, because this was good marketing. He said that several of these films were made each year, of which the latest was *El Mariachi*. If you were going to engage in hype, engage in real hype.

"It's no miracle to make a movie for $20,000," he explained. "So say that you made it for $3,500."

He also said that whenever anybody asked how far along we were in making the film we were presently hyping, we should come back with the all-purpose reply: "I am currently in preproduction." This meant absolutely nothing because it could mean positively anything. At this point, he stressed, the product didn't matter. Only the hype was important.

When we took our first break at 11 A.M., I could tell that a lot of the people taking the course were flustered by Simens's bluntness. Most of them were twenty-something bohos committed to making poignant, delicate movies that addressed broad human issues, thoughtful films that spoke to the human heart. But all Simens seemed interested in talking about was ruses, ploys, gambits, and moolah, all of which would help us to make movies with names like *Goliath Had a Mother*.

"The secret to making films is learning how to write thirty-eight checks," Simens said at one juncture. To get the money to write those checks, it might be necessary for us to suck a few people off. Thus, in discussing the annoying editorial control exercised over films by philistine producers, he said, "The Golden Rule is: He who makes the gold makes the rules." In short, if the producer's son wanted a co-producer's credit, give it to him. In fact, if anybody was willing to give you money, give their son a credit. Or their daughter. Or their unborn nephews. That's what the term "associate producer" was invented for.

At one point, somebody in the audience tried to cut in on his presentation. Simens quickly cut him off, remarking: "I don't want to hear your ideas. They're great."

Then another intrepid seminar participant asked our course moderator about the difference between U.S. films and foreign films. As always, Simens had a canned response. "Right now, everyone in this room is better than 80 percent of those French froggy filmmakers." He sneered. *"Our* crap is twenty times better than *their* crap."

The burgeoning Truffauts in the audience clearly didn't care for these kinds of generalizations. But I loved it. While growing up in a rat-infested, crime-ridden, disease-plagued North Philadelphia housing project, I'd met lots of guys like Dov Simens and had always admired their swagger. They shot from the hip. They cut to the chase. They didn't waste your time. That day I filled an entire copybook with notes. An awful lot of the material I injested was extremely useful further down the line. For starters, the difference between shooting on film and shooting on videotape. Simens said to forget about making a movie on videotape. "Tape looks like tape, and film looks like film," he said with a sneer. "Nobody in this room knows anyone who's going out tonight to see a feature tape."

Simens wasn't that much more enthusiastic about films shot in 16mm ("It'll look like a dressed-up student film") but said it was okay to shoot in 16mm if your film had a budget under $120,000. Mine did. So it was 16mm all the way. 35mm would simply be too expensive.

Simens was short on theory, strong on specifics. He gave us the names of places we could buy film cheap. He told us it was possible to buy recanned film (reels that had been opened, but only the first few feet had been used) that had been left over from big shoots. He told us to buy Kodak if at all possible because "your cinematographer will prefer it." And he said to always be on the lookout for cameramen with stolen film they were happy to unload.

"Film stock is gold; it gets stolen from every shoot," he noted. "It's an unwritten rule of the industry; we all take home a couple of cans. It's called *liberating* film."

To be economically feasible, Simens said that a low-budget film had to be ninety minutes long—a ninety-page script—and shot in three weeks, shooting an average of five pages of script per day, and shooting at a ratio of four to one (four feet of film shot for every foot of film actually used). The easiest way to do this was to shoot in one location.

"Take twelve kids to a house and chop them up" was his coarse suggestion. "There's your movie. Twelve actors. One building. One fusebox."

Next, he went into details about equipment, saying it was possible to rent a high-quality camera for $150 a day, regardless of what the official rate card said. He strongly recommended hiring a sound person who had his own equipment, because then you wouldn't have to worry about dud rentals. He also advised us to run a nonunion shoot.

"I like the union and I like the guild," he proclaimed. "But I like filmmakers better. Use scabs."

Not all of the advice that Simens threw out that day was going to be useful to me. He spent a lot of time talking about hiring directors on the cheap. But I had no plans to use a director. He also explained how to hire someone to write a screenplay for you for next to nothing. Again, I was planning to write my own screenplay, so I daydreamed through this section of the presentation. Finally, he talked about hiring actors, and again advised paying union scale for a low-budget flick. How could we do that, somebody asked. Wouldn't the scabs lose their union memberships?

"In the entire history of the Screen Actors Guild," Simens explained disdainfully, "only one guy has ever been thrown out. And that was after doing about nine hundred non-Guild shoots. Just promise them a big credit. Any actor who's been around knows: Just screw the Guild. They don't do anything for us anyway."

Simens strongly intimated that for the right price, all but the most famous movie stars would be willing to do a nonunion shoot for a few days. I was pleased to learn this. But I had no plans to use shop worn movie stars, no matter how tarnished their luster, in my film. Yes, I had long since given up any hope of luring Art Garfunkel to the set of *Twelve Steps to Death* through an ad in *Backstage*. My film would be made by and with people who were even bigger nobodies than me.

Simens repeatedly stressed the importance of bending or breaking the rules when making a low-budget movie. Take the subject of permits for shooting in public places. Although better municipalities everywhere insist that obtaining a film permit is "free," they still require filmmakers to take out lots of insurance, and insurance is not free. They also shake down filmmakers for $75 an hour to cover the cost of the police and the fire department in case there are mishaps on the set. Simens said that the way to get around this was to send away for a permit application and fill it out, but never actually file it. Then, when the cops showed up and asked to see your permit, you could simply wave the application in their faces. Most of the time they wouldn't bother to read it. If they did, you could say you were on your way over to City Hall to file it that very afternoon. The odds of them coming back to check were not great.

"Cops have other things to do," Simens noted. "They have rape, murder. Filmmakers are very low on their list." He added, parenthetically, "There is no filmmakers' prison."

What I most enjoyed about Simens's course was his ability to demystify the filmmaking process completely. Most of the callow youths attending the program that weekend had come here with the idea that moviemaking was an art, or at the very least a science. Simens thought of it as a job. This being the case, he forced his audience to part with their illusions and admit to themselves that making a film was going to be one long series of compromises—and they'd better get used to it.

"You're not a perfectionist," he snapped when asked how many takes a director should film before calling a wrap. "You thought you were a perfectionist, but now you're a realist. You don't care how; you just want to get it done. Get it done. You hope it's perfect, but get it done."

Simens insisted that the director had to learn how to be a dictator. He demonstrated for us how to fold our arms tightly around our bodies so that when people came to us asking for more money, our body language would make it transparently clear that there was no more money available. Not now; not ever. So wrap those arms tight.

This technique was also useful whenever actors or cameramen wanted to put in their two cents about the film's progress. "The worst thing is when they come in and say, 'Dov, can I tell you something about filmmaking?' Ignore them. That's what I teach here. Film schools teach communication. I teach no communication."

As I mentioned before, an awful lot of Simens's course wasn't going to be of much help to me because so much of it was intended for people making movies with budgets of more than $100,000. But I wrote down everything he said anyway, in case *Twelve Steps to Death* was such a huge success that I then went back and made a film with a much larger budget. For example, Simens suggested that a low-budget director walk around with a wad of $100 bills in his pocket to be used to pay off anyone who complained about the filming.

"The first day a film crew shows up to make a movie, everybody is excited," he explained. "But after three days, everybody hates film crews. Even if you're shooting in your own backyard, even if you're shooting in your own house, your neighbors will hate you. Give them all hundred-dollar bills."

By adamantly refusing to spend more than a few seconds here and there answering questions from the peanut gallery, and by sticking to an amazingly tight schedule, Simens was able to compress an unbelievable amount of information into a two-day, sixteen-hour course. He talked about workmen's comp and the various other forms of insurance a filmmaker would need. He discussed the vital importance of getting Errors & Omissions Insurance Coverage, a policy that made sure that no unauthorized product plugs or libelous statements made their way into the film, and provided money for reshoots in case offensive or trademark-infringing elements had to be taken out after the film was edited.

"If you shoot a film at a place called Al's Grill, make sure that Al's Grill doesn't exist," he told us. "Make sure the street addresses you use don't exist. Always use a phone number beginning with the numbers 555, because there are no phone numbers that begin with the numbers 555. And remember: You can't use a Coke can to kill somebody."

At one point, somebody in the audience asked about the cost of including special effects in a low-budget movie.

"How do you budget special effects?" Simens asked himself rhetorically. "I don't know. Nobody knows. Here's how you do it. You make a movie. Somebody chops off somebody's head. The head falls on the floor, sprouts two legs, and runs away. So you go to a special effects person and ask: 'What's the going rate for that in Manhattan?'"

During the breaks in the course, some of the participants would wander outside, smoking cigarettes, grumbling about the course. Most of the participants in the class had come here with the mistaken assumption that Simens was going to spend two days talking about camera angles and how to get the best possible take from your actors. Instead, he talked about money. Whenever somebody would put up his hand and ask a question about the creative process, Simens would look at his watch and say, "We'll talk about that around twenty to five this afternoon." Then he'd go back to talking about money, insurance, distribution deals.

As it turned out, everything Simens had to say on the subject of directing got compressed into one forty-five-minute segment at the end of Day One.

"Every movie I've ever seen, the first two minutes are good and the last two minutes are good," he noted. "It's the middle eighty-five minutes that are the problem." He now showed us how to get around this. First, he explained how to deal with actors. "Acting is nothing more than the ability to read and talk." So that took care of that. Then he told us how to set up a wide master shot. Then he told us about closeups. About medium shots. Then he explained cutaway reaction shots, and he told us that each scene must have tension. He said that if we wanted to indicate the passage of time, we should keep cutting away to a clock on the wall. Then he held up a couple of books we could read to learn more about directing. And that was the end of that.

With directing out of the way, we got back to the really important stuff: hype. Simens reckoned that a good publicity campaign would cost $10,000, but that even a super-low-budget publicity campaign would run at least $1,000, if only to cover the cost of press kits and postage. He then told us everything we needed in the press kit—a folder with an embossed gold title, five to ten photos of the shoot, a one-page, double-spaced synopsis of the film, and a one-page bio of the filmmaker himself.

"Compare yourself to George Lucas in your one-page bio," he counseled. "Compare the film to *The Rocky Horror Picture Show* or *sex, lies and videotape,* then say why it's better. But no buttons! Buttons went out with Eisenhower."

Above all, he noted, we should never lose sight of the miraculous power of exaggeration and outright duplicity.

"*Isn't it amazing?*—that's the marketing concept you want to go with," he said. For a low-budget film to warrant attention, it had to have a hook. It had to be the cheapest movie ever made. Or the fastest movie ever made. Whenever a filmmaker went out to pitch his product, he had to be able to describe his movie as the _____est film ever made.

Simens also said that we should hire our own publicists to do most of the hyping to the press.

"You can't hype yourself," he reasoned. "You have to hire a publicist to do it for you. That way it doesn't seem like you're blowing your own horn."

Simens also said that for a press kit to work, it had to contain at least one photograph of the director pointing off into the distance.

"The press kit must have a photo of you with script in hand, pointing in the direction where the actors should be looking," he explained. "Camera right, pointing left. On the actual set of a movie, you would never see a director doing this. But all publicity stills must show the director with the script in hand, pointing left. It's a tradition."

Naturally Simens talked to us about editing. Naturally he told us about adding music and sound effects, strongly advising that we use public domain compositions for the soundtrack. Naturally he talked about film festivals, agents, selling the movie directly to video, selling to cable, selling to foreign markets. He said that when it came time to show a screening of the film for movie executives at a film festival, it was a good idea to fill the room with clamorous friends, but warn them not to applaud during the opening credits. Otherwise, the executive would know the entire room was filled with ringers. And naturally he talked about how we should deal with distributors.

"The term 'honest distributor' is an oxymoron," Simens hissed late on the second day. "When you meet a distributor, he will immediately tell you something like this: 'You, the emerging filmmakers, are our lifeblood. We need you. We're looking for you.' "

Simens paused, then added: "What he's just said is: 'We are vampires. We're gonna suck you dry.' "

On the practical side, Simens stressed the importance of catering. "It ain't food—it's fuel," he declared. "If you can't make coffee on time, you can't make your movie." He told us to budget between $9 and $14 per day for each cast and crew member, and to have coffee, fruit juices, soda, muffins, bagels, and schmears of cream cheese ready by the time the crew arrived in the morning.

"For lunch, have a real catered meal," he said. "And before you start shooting, find out who are the Zen macrobiotic people in your crew."

On an even more practical note, Simens said to never close your eyes on the set.

"When you call a wrap, keep your wits about you to make sure stuff doesn't get stolen," he warned us.

After Simens had finished his presentation on Saturday, I went up to the front of the class and bought a couple of hundred dollars' worth of books he was selling. They included four books about screenwriting. I then asked Simens what was the best way to learn how to direct and he sold me a book called *The Grammar of the Film Language*. It had diagrams of all the shots and setups I needed. While I was there, I asked Simens what he thought about Robert Rodriguez. He told me that the *El Mariachi* that played in theaters was not the *El Mariachi* that Rodriguez had originally made, because by the time the film was released commercially, Columbia Pictures had spent at least $100,000 to clean up the sound and transfer it from 16mm to 35mm. I'd already heard scuttlebutt to this effect from other course participants at lunchtime. I was impressed by Columbia's sagacity. I suspected that they'd spent the $100,000 but hadn't made a big fuss about it because they knew that doofus film critics all around the world would continue to describe the *El Mariachi* being shown in theaters as a $7,000 movie. Why? Because the public likes heartwarming stories, and stories about Tex-Mex kids who work as lab rats and get their leading man's relatives in Guadalajara to do all the catering so they can make $7,000 movies are heartwarming, whereas stories about studios that remake $7,000 movies into $107,000 movies are not. Still, his point was not lost on me: You could not make a film like *El Mariachi* for $7,000. Not a film that could be released anywhere. Somebody had to spend big bucks on postproduction and cleaning up the sound. Somebody had to transfer the print to 35mm. Somebody had to turn a work-in-progress into an authentic motion picture.

Simens said that the only way I could make a movie for $7,000 was if I worked like a young Henry Jaglom, the no longer young director who had made a bunch of movies about people sitting around talking about their problems. That is, if I made a film that literally required no editing. Simens's advice?

"Get twelve actors in a single room. Rent a camera for one day. Buy ten thousand feet of film, and tell the actors to talk for ninety minutes. No script, just talk. There's your $5,000 film. It can be done, but it must be done in one to two days. So rehearse on Saturday and shoot on Sunday."

I came out of my two-day experience at the Hollywood Film Institute with a curious mixture of elation and disappointment. I already knew that the film I had in mind could not be shot in one day or even two days in a single room with a stationary camera, so I could not make a film for $5,000. I was also disappointed to learn that the $7,000 El Mariachi that everyone was talking about was not, in fact, a $7,000 film, or anything like a $7,000 movie. I knew that my film was going to be a murder mystery requiring numerous set changes, that it was going to take at least a week to shoot, and that it was going to cost a lot more than the $6,998 I had projected.

On the other hand, I now knew everything I needed to know to make a film. Okay, so I couldn't make it for $6,998. But I still had hopes of making it for around $10,000. After all, directing was no big deal. And, armed with the books Simens had sold me, I could teach myself how to write a screenplay in a couple of weeks. Most important, Simens had confirmed my suspicions that the single most important element that went into making a film was a tremendous amount of hype. That, plus a good script. So, *Twelve Steps to Death* was going to cost more to make than I had originally budgeted; now at least I had the confidence to make it. Before I'd taken Simens's course I was winging it. Now I had a game plan. Thus, I was very grateful to Dov Simens and his itinerant Hollywood Film Institute for teaching me the ropes. At long last, I could get rolling.

ONE OF THE most important things that I learned from Dov Simens was to get my technical crew together early and get into preproduction as quickly as possible. As soon as I'd graduated from the class—yes, a few days later, I received my official-looking diploma in the mail—I started wrestling with the question of who was going to operate the camera and the sound equipment on the movie. At this point, I still expected the production to be a very primitive operation, so I figured I'd hire a couple of kids from a local film school and pay them a few bucks to work the equipment. Then John Domesick entered the picture.

I'd met John Domesick at the Democratic National Convention in New York in August 1992. I was covering the convention both for *Barron's* and for Comedy Central, admittedly an unusual combination, and was sitting in the media hospitality suite when a very funny video clip appeared on an overhead monitor. There, just a few yards away, I was treated to the spectacle of a fresh-faced, twenty-something kid claiming to be a reporter for an outfit called The People's Network, who was constantly sticking his puss into the faces of such notables as Ed Bradley and Andrea Mitchell and getting them to act tongue-tied and befuddled. The kid had lots of chutzpah and possessed a very engaging on-screen presence. Also, it was great to see the media powers-that-be get put on the spot for a change.

The clip was so entertaining that I started asking other journalists in the immediate vicinity what cable station we were watching. I finally found out that the People's Network consisted entirely of Ted Carleton and John Domesick, two recent college graduates who were wandering around the country pretending to be journalists. They'd asked the manager of the media hospitality suite if he would show their amusing footage, and he had graciously agreed to do so. And it just so happened that the two of them were sitting in a booth over in the corner of the room.

I went over to the booth, introduced myself, told them how much I'd enjoyed the clip, and then spent the next year or so trying to get someone I knew to give them a job. Tragically, I have zero clout, and nobody— not Comedy Central, not *Spy* magazine, not anybody—ever let them get their feet in the door. Ted, the on-air reporter, eventually drifted off to Nevada to become a newspaper reporter, but John, who worked the videocam and did most of the editing for The People's Network, stayed in the New York area, crashing at his brother's apartment. For the next eigh-

teen months, John would regularly check in to let me know how his career was progressing. Most of the time, it wasn't progressing.

One day, John told me a useful bit of information about himself. Several years earlier, he'd attended film school at the University of Southern
California. He hadn't graduated, or let's just say, he hadn't graduated with
a major in film, dropping out of the full-time program after one year, but
he knew more than a little bit about making movies. In fact, he remarked,
he'd once made a short feature film of his own, though I never actually
saw it. In any case, since he wasn't doing much of anything at the time,
he would be more than ready to help me make my movie.

Now, operating a movie camera and operating a videocam are two entirely different things, and John made no claims to being an expert cinematographer. But, seeing that I was only making a low-budget movie, his
talents would probably be more than adequate for the production. What's
more, he had a friend named Mike Berman, who had once supported himself as a professional balloonologist in Hawaii, but who was currently
studying film at NYU, alma mater of such luminaries as Martin Scorsese
and Oliver Stone and Jim Jarmusch and the guy who directed *Adventures
in Babysitting*. Mike, too, would be happy to work on the film, perhaps as
the soundman, but, if not, as a gofer. What did I think?

At this juncture, John seemed like the answer to my prayers. He was
young, he was enthusiastic, he would work for practically nothing, and
he'd been to film school for a year. What's more, he had a balloonologist
friend who also wanted to work on the movie. So I told him he was hired.

Immediately after that, John and I started crunching the numbers.
While I started gearing up to write the screenplay, John visited a bunch
of equipment rental outfits in Manhattan and solicited estimates. On the
theory that you could rent a camera for $1,500 for a ten-day period span-
ning two weekends, plus $500 for insurance, plus $500 for sound equipment rental, plus film, plus catering, plus whatever I paid John, we figured we should be able to get the film actually in the can for around
$5,000 or $10,000. Here was a preliminary budget that John drew up.
This makeshift budget eventually would serve as a symbol of my ambiva-
lent relationship with John Domesick. On the one hand, I liked the idea
of having at least one person working on the movie who knew his ass from

Twelve Steps to Death: Budget Estimate/ Containment

Summary: All fat eliminated, what must be spent to physically make movie with no personnel and no unnecessary materials in one week's shoot.

Materials/ Services	$Cost

FILM STOCK:
Film Exchange, 1133 Broadway, 255-0445.
Color 16mm. $90.00 for 400' roll. 10 min. =3600'
$90 x 9 = $810 (can't use every second on roll)
810 x 2 = $1620 = realistic amount of film 1,620
(We want 93, 200 ASA, or 96/98, ASA for inside.)

FILM LAB:
DuArt Lab, 245 W55th 757-4580 #637, David Fisher
Develop: 7200'@12 1/2 cent/ft = $900 900
Work Print: 7200' @ 19 1/2 = $1,404. 1,404
[Synch dailies: $43 per hr. 5 x $43 = $215 215
3 hrs for 800' — not essential, we can do it]
"Mix mag" 3 tracks to one optical track
Optical Sound Track = $1,000 1,000
AB rolls: Negative Cutter: $5.00 per cut
150 cuts x $5.00 = $750 750
1st answer Print 80 cent/ft x 3600' = $2,880 2,880
16mm Release Prints $1,000 each (we need at least one) 1,000
{35mm Release Prints 80 cent/ft x 3600' = $2,880 ....2,880}

CAMERA RENTAL:
Film Friends, 16 E17th St., @5th/Broadway 620-0084
Arriflex SR1, 16mm camera, 10-100mm lense, 2 mag, 2 batt.
1 week rental 1,300

POST HOUSE:
Sound One, 1619 Broadway, 765-4757. @49th 8th Fl
Edit Room with supplies = $800/month 800
DAT Transfer to Mag, $100/hr. 3 hrs. x $100 = $300. 300
Edge Numbering, 1 cent/foot x 7200ft = $72 72
Mixing $160 per hour if done in one day or less. Minimum
possible 5 hours 5 x $160 = 800 (If longer, $225 per hour) 800
Phone, $50 per month, plus charges ....(est) 75

EDITING INSTRUCTION FOR STEENBECK TABLE, ETC.:
Kenna at Sound One, 947-1684, $100 100

AUDIO EQUIPMENT:
ASC, 326 W48th St., 977-5151 - Kenny in
Sony DAT Pro II Recorder, $120/wk 120
Boom $35/wk 35
Sennheiser 415/6 Super Cardiod $80/wk
$80 x 2 (mikes) = $160/wk 160
Deposit: Credit Card

	*Total: $13,316

*Does not include $2,880 for each 35 mm Blowup Print. W/Blowup $16,196

third base. On the other hand, when he handed me a budget like this, I had to wonder if he wasn't veering a wee bit on the optimistic side in preparing the numbers. His projected budget for postproduction seemed a mite on the low side, and I wondered if he wasn't fudging the numbers out of the fear that I might get spooked and call off the whole project, and he'd never get to work on a feature film. Throughout our relationship, I worried that John might secretly have me pegged as a deep-pockets idiot who wouldn't mind getting caught holding the bag for what could turn out to be a very expensive film, a low-budget *Heaven's Gate*, as long as I got some kind of film out of the experience. On the other hand, I welcomed his obvious enthusiasm for the project. And at that point in the undertaking, I really needed his help.

Whatever illusions John may have had about our relationship, my conception of his role in the making of *Twelve Steps to Death* was always clear. Right from the beginning, I envisioned John as a resourceful sidekick whom I would plunk down in a chair right beside me while I directed the film. The way I planned things, I would periodically turn to him and say: "You went to one of those ritzy film schools, John; how do you think we should set up this next shot?" I really liked the idea of paying an assistant director $5 an hour to share the secrets it had cost his parents $65,000 for him to learn at Southern Cal. It appealed to my highly developed sense of irony. One develops a keen sense of irony growing up in the rat-infested, crime-ridden, litter-strewn housing projects of North Philadelphia.

But I also had other plans for John. Right from the get-go, I constantly warned my frat-house assistant director that eventually I would have to fire him, because that's the way things always happened in real-life movie situations, and this, too, would appeal to my highly developed sense of irony. We used to joke about this all the time. We used to crack up. We used to go to Harry's Bar in the Sherry Netherland Hotel in midtown Manhattan, the hotel where movie industry executives always cut their deals, and joke for hours about my eventually having to fire him, perhaps after a heated dispute over the artistic direction of the film. As we bantered back and forth this way, regaling one another with outlandish dreams of glory, I think he half thought that I was serious.

I was serious.

four

Don't
Get It Right—
Get It Written

I learned how to write the screenplay to *Twelve Steps to Death* the same way everybody else learns how to write a screenplay: by stealing as much good stuff as I could from movies like *Vertigo, Blue Velvet, Reservoir Dogs, sex, lies and videotape, Blow-Up, Blowout, The Maltese Falcon, Charade,* and *The Conversation,* and by reading Syd Field's famous book *Screenplay: The Foundations of Screenwriting.* In recent years, it has become quite fashionable to heap criticism on this book and say that it sucks because it reduces screenwriting to a rigid set of mechanical rules that give screenplays a cookie-cutter quality. That doesn't change the fact that everybody in the movie business basically adheres to these rules—because screenwriting *is* a cookie-cutter art form—and that all the other famous books about screenplay writing are little more than rehashed Syd Field.

After I read Field's book, I also read Linda Seger's *Making a Good Script Great* and Michael Hauge's *Writing Screenplays That Sell,* but they didn't tell me a whole lot about screenwriting that I hadn't already learned from Syd Field. I am not saying that Syd Field is an especially great writer, nor do I consider him a particularly innovative thinker, and I am certainly not going to argue that he is a force for positive good in the motion picture industry. All I'm saying is that everything a layman would ever need to learn about writing a screenplay he can find in Syd Field.

Sure, there are computerized screenplay writing courses that you can send away for, and yes, there are crash screenwriting courses that you see advertised in movie magazines all the time. But Syd Field's book has one huge advantage over these other approaches: It costs only $9.95. Given the choice between paying $400 for a screenwriting course taught by a man who can't get his own screenplays produced, $79.95 for a computerized screenwriting course taught by a man who can't get his own screenplays produced, or $9.95 for a book written by a man who can't get his own screenplays produced, I'm sticking with Syd every time.

Field's theory is basically this: Learn how to write like the guy who wrote *Chinatown* and you're on your way. The way Field sees it, all successful films—*Network, Three Days of the Condor, Raiders of the Lost Ark*—adhere to an incredibly simple formula that gets repeated over and over again in the motion picture industry. First off, the screenplay must be divided into three distinct acts, cleverly titled "Beginning," "Middle," and "End." According to Field, the screenwriter must introduce the main character and explain what his problem is in the first ten minutes of the film. Otherwise, he's lost the audience for good.

At the end of Act I—roughly twenty-five minutes into the film—the writer must insert a "Plot Point," which Field describes as "an incident, or event, that hooks into the story and spins it around in another direction." In Act II, the writer must set up the big confrontation, usually between Good and Evil, and then insert a second Plot Point, which occurs about three-quarters of the way through the film. Then, in Act III, the writer must deliver the big payoff when the disparate strands of the story all come together: Indiana Jones finds the Ark of the Covenant, Keanu gets all those people off the bus, the shark eats the boat.

The example Field uses to make his case is Roman Polanski's memo-rable, albeit complicated, film *Chinatown*, written by Robert Towne. At the beginning of the movie, we learn that Jake Gittes (Jack Nicholson) is a sleazy private eye who has been hired by a mysterious woman named Mrs. Mulwray (Diane Ladd) to trail her philandering husband. The first Plot Point occurs twenty-five minutes into the movie when Gittes learns that Ladd is not the real Mrs. Mulwray—Faye Dunaway is. Gittes now wants to find out what the hell is going on here, so he spends most of the second act trying to get to the bottom of the case, until he reaches the second Plot Point, when he stumbles upon the eyeglasses of the now-dead Mr. Mulwray in a swimming pool, and realizes that they must either be-long to him or to his murderer. From here, the film races toward its thrilling conclusion when Gittes discovers all that neat stuff about water rights and incest.

As soon as I'd finished reading this material, I pulled out a pen and paper and started diagramming the plot of *Twelve Steps to Death* to see if my sketchy outline could be superimposed on Fields's ideal screen-writing template. True, there was a part of me that rebelled against the notion of adhering to a mechanistic literary formula. But that rebellion didn't last long. From the moment I'd started thinking about making *Twelve Steps to Death*, I knew that I wanted the movie to be entirely con-ventional in theme and structure: a traditional murder mystery. Yes, the movie was intended to be a black comedy, but I didn't want the film to have an artsy or idiosyncratic quality. I didn't want it to seem impres-sionistic or surreal in any way, and I didn't want it to have a loose, ram-bling structure. I didn't want it to be like one of those movies they show at the Film Forum in New York.

No, I wanted *Twelve Steps to Death* to be a straightforward Hollywood black comedy, with a beginning, a middle, and an end, and a plot that was easy to follow. Except for the fact that the protagonist of the film would be a cop whose wife and two children had been killed in a hit-and-run accident by a schizoid anorexic recovering alcoholic with Attention Deficit Disorder who was fleeing an abusive chocaholic husband who used to beat her up whenever he had one too many of the nougat caramels, *Twelve Steps to Death* would be exactly like *The Maltese Falcon*.

With this in mind, I began stretching *Twelve Steps to Death* on the scaffold that Field had supplied. By this point, I had already decided that the movie would deal with a wealthy but unpleasant psychiatrist named Peter Thorpe whose forty-five patients are all in twelve-step programs. One day, Thorpe is found brutally murdered, and the police suspect that one, or several, of his disgruntled patients did him in. But which one? The lush? The woman who loves too much? The credit card addict? The chronic gambler? The sexaholic? The abusive shopper? Or was it perhaps the man who claimed to be suffering from bulimia envy? (He is insanely jealous of all the attention that his bulimic wife gets because of her condition, and constantly beats her, which causes her to puke, which makes her even more bulimic.)

The setting for the movie would be a small town in semirural America, because that way I could shoot the entire movie in the place I lived: a small town in semirural America. Well, a small town in suburban America, but close enough. The town would be called No Quarter, and it would be located in the wilds of Wisconsin because Wisconsin seemed like a state that you could say anything about without having to worry about people going out and checking to see if what you'd said was true.

For the purposes of my movie, No Quarter had to be a town marooned in a region so desolate that there was not another psychiatrist within seventy-five miles, so all the dysfunctional people in the community had to go to the same shrink. Due to this therapeutic monopoly, the shrink could treat his patients anyway he wanted. The shrink I had in mind would choose to treat them badly.

Charged with investigating Thorpe's murder is Turk Bishop, formerly a detective on the Los Angeles Police Department, who has returned to his native No Quarter in a state of shock and grief. Two years earlier, we quickly learn, his wife and two children had been killed in a hit-and-run car accident by a schizoid anorexic recovering alcoholic with Attention Deficit Disorder who did not remember committing the crime. The killer got off with a slap on the wrist: eighteen months counseling senior bulimics in the Beverly Hills program Scared Plump. Desperate for revenge on the American recovery movement, the vindictive cop began beating up recovering chocaholics until he was finally apprehended by Internal

Affairs and thrown off the force. After that, he returned to downscale No Quarter, where he quickly landed a job as Chief of Detectives. Saddled with this tragic, violent history, Bishop really wants to nail one of the loathesome twelve-steppers and perhaps even prove that a whole bunch of them colluded in Peter Thorpe's murder. After the death of his wife and kids, his heart has turned to stone.

At the outset, the case looks like an open-and-shut affair: Bishop discovers sixteen Devil Dog wrappers and a crate of Diet Pepsi at the scene of the crime, all bearing the fingerprints of an obscenely fat patient who was being treated by Peter Thorpe as part of a court-mandated program for chronic overeaters who used their enormous girth to force their spouses to perform a wide assortment of repugnant sex acts. To make matters worse for the spatially challenged murder suspect, Bishop also unearths a videotape of the patient threatening to kill Thorpe on the day that he died. At this point, it looks like curtains for the loathsome chunkster.

But then Bishop finds out that the meanspirited shrink has a twin brother. Bishop now has reason to believe that the shrink feigned his own murder, killing his brother instead, so that he could get out of the psychiatry business for good and dump his nagging wife and useless, whiny children in the process. In short, to kill two birds with one twelve-step stone. Now Bishop finds himself confronted by a profound moral dilemma: whether to nab the real murderer, whom he kind of sympathizes with, or to simply pin the crime on one of the odious twelve-steppers.

Herein lay the general outline of my screenplay. Now it was time to apply Field's principles of screenwriting structure to see if everything would fit into place. First, I decided, the audience would have to see Thorpe interacting negatively with his patients. This would establish that he was a complete prick. The scenes would take up the first seven minutes of the movie. Then the audience would see Thorpe being murdered, though they would not actually see the face of his killer. This scene would take less than a minute. Then the audience would be introduced to Turk Bishop, also a bit of a prick, who would be seen abusing his partner on the phone while aiming a gun off into the distance. This scene would occur about eight minutes into the movie, and would establish that he was a trigger-happy son of a bitch. Thus, in the first ten minutes of the joe queenan

movie, the audience would learn that Turk Bishop, a hard-nosed police
officer, had been called in to investigate the murder of Peter Thorpe, a
vicious, unsympathetic psychiatrist, one of whose patients had already
threatened to kill him. And, since Thorpe was already out of the way, the
audience would recognize that Bishop was the main character in the film.

So far, my outline adhered perfectly to Sid Field's first principle of
screenwriting: that the writer had ten minutes in which he must answer
these questions:

1. Who is your main character?
2. What is the dramatic premise?
3. What is the dramatic situation?

Beyond a shadow of a doubt, I had already answered these three questions, though technically speaking I had not yet written the screenplay.
Watching thousands upon thousands of movies in the past few years had
provided me with an intuitive sense of how to construct a workable
screenplay. I was pleased. This was really going quite well.

After I'd outlined the first ten minutes of the movie, I sketched out the
remainder of Act I. In the remaining twenty minutes of the opening act,
the audience would learn the sordid, tragic story of Turk Bishop's past.

Then, at the end of Act I, we'd hit the first Plot Point. During an otherwise unproductive conversation with Thorpe's pouty, know-it-all daughter Courtney, Bishop would find out that Peter Thorpe had a twin brother
named—what else?—Paul, who had not even bothered to attend his own
twin brother's funeral. *Creepy.* The brother, it would soon be revealed,
was a wacked out dish-dryer in a greasy-spoon restaurant seventy-five
miles up the road in Dutchman's Prairie, a complete airhead who'd taken
too much blue acid at Woodstock. In short, a loser. But—and here was
the key point, the Plot Point, if you will—a loser who looked exactly like
his murdered brother. For the first time in the film, the audience would
be confronted with the possibility that Thorpe had not been murdered by
one of his patients but by his own brother. But why would Paul Thorpe
want to murder his own twin brother? Good question.

In Act II, the plot would thicken, as both Bishop and the audience learned more about Thorpe's patients, and gradually came to appreciate what a revolting bunch of self-pitying screw-ups they were—so revolting that an unhappy psychiatrist might do almost anything to get away from them. Little by little, inch by inch, second by second, Bishop would start considering the possibility that Peter Thorpe had murdered his own twin brother and switched places with him so that he could get away from his horrible patients. Which is what most people in the audience, put in precisely the same situation, would have done.

The key to cracking the mystery would be the fact that Peter Thorpe was a lifelong Cubs fan, while Paul Thorpe was a dyed-in-the-wool White Sox fan. This would lead to the second Plot Point at the end of Act II, when Paul Thorpe makes a fatal error when discussing the exploits of the famed ChiSox slugger Bo Jackson, an error proving that he is not really a White Sox fan after all. This would be like those scenes in World War II movies where the Nazi spy gives away his Kraut identity by not knowing who Babe Ruth is. All this drama would lead inexorably to Act III, where Bishop solves the mystery of Thorpe's murder and comes to terms with his own feelings about truth, justice, revenge, and the American Way.

I now had the skeletal outline of *Twelve Steps to Death* in place. I also knew which scenes from famous movies that I wanted to parody or steal: the handwriting in blood from *Charade,* the serene opening shots from *Blue Velvet,* the ear mutilation scene from *Reservoir Dogs.* But I hadn't written any of the dialogue, and I also hadn't finished sketching out the characters' personalities. So now I returned to Fields's book for more guidance. Going back to the first ten minutes of the movie, I learned that the opening scenes must hook the reader and let him know immediately what was going on. So I decided that in the first scene, Dr. Thorpe would make fun of one of his fat patients, who would then threaten to kill him, and that the shrink would secretly videotape the conversation, making sure that the tape fell into the hands of the police. In short, Peter Thorpe, having planned to murder his brother Paul and switch places with him, was now going to frame one of his patients for the murder.

Field also said that the entire plot of the movie must be established in the first thirty minutes, so that's what I got working on next. First, I would introduce all the horrible twelve-step people who made up Dr. Thorpe's practice. Then I would introduce Peter Thorpe's widow, Brittany, and make it clear that she was absolutely horrible, and that the insane desire to get away from her and their awful kids may have strengthened Thorpe's motivation to murder his brother. By the time thirty minutes had elapsed, the audience would have a pretty good idea what was going on here.

Although *Screenplay* is 244 pages long, that was basically all I got out of Syd Field. True, the book has some useful stuff about screenplay format and camera angles and what-not, but it's not much help in creating characters or writing dialogue. Like all authors of books about how to write screenplays, Field himself is a pretty terrible screenplay writer; he includes the first nine pages of his own unproduced screenplay *The Run*— which deals with speedboat racers—in the book, and you could tell from reading his cardboard dialogue why the screenplay had never been produced. The only other information I got out of Syd Field that was useful was his suggestion that you construct your screenplay fragment by fragment by writing down the idea for each scene or sequence on 3×5 index cards and carrying them around with you. That's what I did for the next three months or so until I was ready to sit down and actually write the screenplay. Every time I got an idea for a sequence in the movie, I would jot it down on an index card, complete with notes about locale, time of day, and even tiny snippets of dialogue. All told, I used fifty-two cards for the fifty-two scenes in the movie. Three months later, I was ready to rip.

Before I could write the screenplay, though, I needed to learn a bit more about character development. For help in this department, I turned to Michael Hauge, author of *Writing Screenplays That Sell*. Hauge is a screenwriting expert who has taught at UCLA, USC, and the American Film Institute. He says that the way to write a successful screenplay is to "enable a sympathetic character to overcome a series of increasingly difficult, seemingly insurmountable obstacles and achieve a compelling desire." Well, that was Turk Bishop in a nutshell, so clearly I had no problems there.

Structurally, Hauge says that a good screenplay needs a hero, a nemesis, a reflection, and a romance. I already had a hero—Turk Bishop—and

I already had his nemesis—Paul Thorpe, who might actually be Peter. Now I needed a reflection—a character who is in the same basic situation as the hero, but who isn't as smart or handsome or likable or important. In short, the Morgan Freeman character. For the reflection of Turk Bishop, I went right down the middle of the plate with a sidekick. The sidekick would be Tom Stoddard, a decent, honest cop who is not nearly as intelligent or resourceful as Bishop, but who, like him, wants to get to the bottom of the mystery. I also decided that Tom would be a stay-at-home type who has worked his entire life on the pitiful No Quarter Police Department, and who would therefore provide a sharp contrast to the more glamorous, successful Bishop, who had once worked for the super-high-profile L.A.P.D. before getting thrown off the force.

That left only the romantic element. Hauge says that good screenplays usually need a romantic lead to provide meaningful counterpoint to the dramatic action at the center of the film. But I had a problem here. Because I would be shooting *Twelve Steps to Death* in my own small town using my neighbors as actors, I couldn't afford to have a lot of sex in the screenplay, because none of my neighbors would feel comfortable with that, even if I would. Look at it this way: If Turk Bishop, played by one of my neighbors, had a bunch of torrid sex scenes with another neighbor, the neighbor playing Turk Bishop might get complaints from his wife. Or vice versa. Especially if I included a lot of garter belts and gooey sticks of butter in the screenplay.

The obvious solution to this problem was to cast both a male neighbor *and* his wife as Turk Bishop and his romantic partner in the film. On first glance, this seemed like a perfectly fine suggestion. Unfortunately, I had already decided which of my neighbors would be perfect for the part of Turk Bishop, but when I approached his wife about being in the film, she absolutely refused to get involved. There was a fallback solution—I had another neighbor in the back of my mind who would be perfect for the lead role—but I was afraid his wife would be uncomfortable in front of the camera. So I found myself in a bit of a pickle.

And then it hit me: Why not use a nun as the romantic lead? By introducing a nun who used to be Bishop's main squeeze years and years earlier, I could inject an element of simmering romance into the screenplay but wouldn't have to risk outraging everyone in staid, suburban Tarrytown by having the two romantic leads go down on each other. That's how I came up with the idea for Sister Wilhemina des Portes de Saint Denis. Sister Wilhemina (née Veronica De Fonzini) had once been Turk Bishop's girlfriend, but she was now a nun, so as an object of desire she was completely hands-off. But she would serve a valuable dramatic function in the film, in addition to being the statutory old flame, because it was during Bishop's conversations with Veronica about his deceased wife and kids that the audience would come to understand why he was such an incredible prick. Otherwise, I would have to do all this with flashbacks to Bishop's days on the L.A.P.D., and every screenplay book ever written warns you not to use flashbacks because they're hokey and cheap and annoying, and show that you don't know the first thing about writing a screenplay. Even though *Maverick,* one of the biggest-grossing films of 1994, which was released the week I started writing my screenplay, and was written by William Goldman, one of the most talented and successful screenwriters in history, opens with a flashback.

But never mind.

Now that I had all the major characters in the film lined up, I went back to Hauge's book to make sure I was adhering to all the important rules about characterization. Hauge, whom I now trusted implicitly, says that no script can succeed unless it contains the five following elements:

1. The story must have a hero who is on screen most of the time and whose "visible motivation drives the plot."
2. The audience must identify with the hero.
3. The hero must have a clear objective that he hopes to achieve by the end of the movie.
4. The hero must be courageous.
5. The hero must overcome a bunch of serious obstacles before achieving his objective.

I started checking off the points one by one. Bishop would be on the screen most of the time, and his motivation would drive the plot, so we were all squared away on Point No. 1. Next, Hauge said that "the reader must identify with the hero." Well, Turk Bishop was a hardworking cop and family man whose life had come crashing down around him after his wife and two children were killed in a hit-and-run car accident by a schizoid anorexic recovering alcoholic with Attention Deficit Disorder who did not remember committing the crime and who got off with a slap on the wrist—eighteen months counseling senior bulimics in the Beverly Hills program Scared Plump—because she said she was fleeing an abusive chocaholic husband who used to beat her up whenever he had one too many of the nougat caramels. Clearly everybody in the audience would be able to identify with that, so Point No. 2 was out of the way.

Point No. 3 was making sure that the hero had a clear objective. Bishop did: finding out who murdered Peter Thorpe and then bringing the murderer to justice. Point No. 4, the one about being courageous, was a given, so that only left Point No. 5, that business about the hero having to face a number of serious obstacles. Here I had obstacles in spades. Bishop faced one set of serious external obstacles because Peter Thorpe had seemingly committed the perfect crime and set up a perfect fall guy for the crime: the porculent overeater whose fingerprints were found all over those sixteen packages of Devil Dogs found at the scene of the crime. But a second, more serious set of obstacles were those that Bishop had himself erected: Every fiber of his being being cried out for him to pin the crime on a member of a twelve-step program because it was a person suffering from a spectacularly pop dysfunctionality who had ruined his life. This, then, was the central dramatic tension in *Twelve Steps to Death*: Would Bishop, once he had discovered the truth about Peter Thorpe's murder, bring the real murderer to justice? Or would he allow his insatiable desire for revenge on the recovery movement to lure him into criminal complicity with a murderer whose motivation he understood only too well?

Satisfied that my outline fulfilled all the basic criteria of successful screenwriting, I was now ready to write the script. In fairness to Hauge, I should point out that *Writing Screenplays That Sell* contains many other charts and lists and graphs and hints, not to mention a step-by-step analysis of the script from *The Karate Kid*. But to me, most of this material seemed like padding. Just about everything Hauge has to say that is really useful is contained in the first three chapters of the book. The only other points that are even vaguely helpful are when he says that all of the action in the film must advance the hero's quest in some way—no gratuitous sex scenes, no bullshit cameos, no star turns—and when he says that a movie must establish its own set of rules and stick to them.

This was one thing I was absolutely determined to do in *Twelve Steps to Death*. I recognized that the story line I was advancing here was a tad macabre. But once I had established the parameters of lunacy in the screenplay, I wanted all the characters in the movie to remain locked inside this hermetically sealed universe of rampant dyfunctionality. Otherwise, the whole premise of the movie would fall apart.

I wrote the screenplay to *Twelve Steps to Death* in eight days over a three-week period in July 1994, working as hard as I could for a single day, then taking at least one day off before going back to work. I would put in between ten and sixteen hours, then spend the next twenty-four to forty-eight hours writing articles or book reviews or op-ed pieces or screaming at my kids, then go back to the screenplay with fresh inspiration on the third or fourth day. The fewest pages I ever wrote was four, the most was twenty-six. By the last day in July, I had the screenplay ready to hand out to my cast. How good was it? I had no way of knowing. The only thing I knew was this: It was done. Hauge has a terrific cliché that he uses at several points in the book, and it was a cliché that, in a slightly mutated form, would stand me in good stead in the weeks and months to come. The cliché to which I refer is Hauge's first rule of screenwriting: "Don't get it right, get it written." By July 31, 1994, I had it written.

Twelve Steps to Death

by

Joe Queenan

CHARACTERS

Amber Duggan

Dr. Peter Thorpe

Turk Bishop

Sister Wilhemina

Sister Damian Barabbas

Miguel Feneiro

Sherman Krebs

Tom Stoddard

Joey Bellini

Jim Franklin

Nathan Schwartz

Father John De Fonzini

Courtney Thorpe

Butch Thorpe

Brittany Thorpe

Paul Thorpe

Dysfunctional Person 1

Dysfunctional Person 2

Dysfunctional Person 3

Dysfunctional Person 4

Dysfunctional Person 5

Dysfunctional Person 6

Dysfunctional Person 7

Dysfunctional Person 8

Dysfunctional Person 9

Dysfunctional Person 10

Dysfunctional Person 11

Seamus Fogarty

Bingo Tyson

Ext.—Suburban Street—Midmorning.

Reassuring images of prosperous suburban life: Friendly homeowners wav-
ing to passersby, a young woman helping an old man across a busy street, a
yipping terrier wagging its tail in the shadow of an American flag, a grand-
father with his grandson waving a toy sword, a lovely, tree-lined street where
a man is watering his lawn amid a forest of white picket fences. We see a
massive, gorgeous white house worth at least $1.2 million in any market—
up or down. A van pulls up in front and AMBER DUGGAN, *an obscenely fat*
woman of indeterminate age, gets out. She struggles up the steps to the
house, and disappears inside.

Int.—Psychiatrist's Office—Midmorning.

We see Duggan sitting in a chair. Behind her are some bookcases, some pro-
fessional diplomas, and a Chicago Cubs banner, plus some other Chicago
Cubs regalia.

AMBER: I think that my problem—caloric
intolerance—derives from my need for
space. As a child, I had to share a room
with three sisters. I think maybe my
inclusion in the ranks of the spatially
challenged is the physical expression of
a subconscious desire for more space.

We see DR. PETER THORPE, *a laconic, rail-thin, middle-aged psychiatrist.*
He is working his way through a Whitman's Sampler while guzzling a 32-
oz. container of Pepsi. His feet are positioned atop an old desk, beside a
Chicago Cubs cap, with a mountain of cookies, donuts, Twinkies, and even
a strawberry shortcake poised on an end table to his right.

THORPE: Well, you certainly take up a lot of it.

AMBER: Come again?

THORPE: I said, "You certainly take up a lot of
it." Space. You certainly take up a lot of
space.

He stuffs three chocolates into his mouth simultaneously.

THORPE: (Cont.) Most fat people do.

AMBER: *Fat* is a judgmental term.

Thorpe gets to work on a pepperoni pizza, pouring himself another glass of soda and eyeing a milk shake covetously.

THORPE: I practice judgmental therapy. My teacher in Vienna moonlighted as a soccer ref. Also, he was at Auschwitz. But we've been through this before. The point is: You're fat, and I'm not. And I'm here to remind you of that. One day, you won't need to be reminded anymore. That's the day you stop being fat.

AMBER: Do you also remind your substance-abusing patients that they're quote, unquote "alkies" and quote, unquote "cokeheads"?

Thorpe, now slamming away a package of Tastycakes, produces a large bottle of whiskey, a hypodermic needle, a six-pack of beer, and a vial of crack yanked from beneath his desk.

THORPE: Boy, do I ever.

AMBER: Has anyone ever told you that you're a heartless human being?

THORPE: *Heartless* is a judgmental term.

AMBER: This makes no sense. I come here every week to work through my food disorders, and you sit there mocking me.

THORPE: You come here every week because you're in a 12-step program for chronic overeaters, and part of your court-appointed therapy is private counseling.

> You come here because your ex-
> husband had you arrested when you
> repeatedly used your body to suffocate
> him because he wouldn't perform
> certain repugnant sex acts.

AMBER: *Repugnant* is judgmental.

THORPE: You come here because failure to
attend these sessions could result in
your parole being revoked, at which
time they'd slam your butt in jail, where
it would be impossible for you to
continue your life of dietary crime.
Now, would you care for a Twinkie?

AMBER: You're disgusting.

THORPE: I haven't bitten into it yet.

Amber gets up to leave.

AMBER: I think we better call it a day. You
know, I come here every week, trying to
grow as a person, and all I get is abuse.

Thorpe studies her, gnawing on a Snowcone.

THORPE: If you grew any more as a person, you
couldn't fit through that door.

Amber now turns and rivets Thorpe with a malevolent stare.

AMBER: You deserve to die a slow, painful
death.

THORPE: Yeah, don't we all?

Amber closes the door behind her.

Int.—Psychiatrist's Office—Midmorning

We see SHERMAN KREBS, *a spindly man in his mid-thirties wearing a T-shirt that reads:* DON'T DISS THE DYSFUNCTIONAL.

KREBS: Last week, I called my ex-wife Cindy to apologize for betting my daughter Caitlin's Harvard endowment money on a basketball game back in 1983.

Thorpe is seen playing dominos on the top of his desk, which is piled high with playing cards, a roulette table, a canasta board, a dozen bocci balls, and some Mah-Jongg tiles.

THORPE: That was big of you. Who'd you bet on?

KREBS: Kentucky. They were playing Georgetown in the NCAA's.

THORPE: Kentucky? That team had three of the biggest stiffs in history: Bowie, Walker, Turpin. Cadavers. What the hell did you bet on Kentucky for?

KREBS: That's not relevant now. What's relevant is that I made that important first step. I reached out and tried to make up with Cindy.

THORPE: How many points did you get?

KREBS: Well, I *gave* eight. But that's not relevant now. What's relevant is . . .

THORPE: You *gave eight*? And Georgetown was favored by three. Christ, that's the story of my life. The shrinks on Park Avenue get the guys who bet on Jordan and Alcindor. I get the schmucks who *give* Georgetown and eight.

KREBS: The spread isn't important. The game isn't important. The bet isn't important. What's important is that I've finally admitted that betting the 27 Gs on Kentucky was nobody's fault but my own. And now that I've got that off my

chest with Cindy, I'm ready to do the
right thing with Caitlin.

Thorpe is now seen shuffling a deck of cards.

THORPE: After you lost the Harvard money,
           where did Caitlin end up going to
           school?

KREBS: Uhh . . . Central Connecticut State.

THORPE: I'd hold off making that phone call,
           Sherm. I don't think Caitlin's going to
           be all that happy to hear from you.

KREBS: Caitlin is in denial. She can't be healed
           until I'm healed. Nursing a grudge
           turns the heart into a stone. It's like
           that John Prine song where he goes:
           "You can gaze out the window, and get
           mad and get madder . . ."

Thorpe cuts him off with a decisive hand gesture.

THORPE: Sherman, I'm going to level with you
           here. I don't think you should call your
           daughter after all these years and tell
           her how sorry you are that you blew her
           Harvard scholarship money on a
           Kentucky-Georgetown game. I don't
           think she's going to be real happy to
           hear from you. I think she might come
           gunning for you with a mortar
           launcher.

KREBS: Well, I think you're wrong.

Thorpe extends his hand, which he then opens to reveal a shiny silver dollar.

THORPE: You wanna bet?

Krebs hesitates several seconds, watching the therapist flip the coin back and forth from palm to palm. Then he speaks.

        KREBS: All right. But we use my coin.

Int.—Same Office—Midmorning

We see JOEY BELLINI, *a randy stud, lying on Thorpe's couch. Bellini is dressed like a man who sleeps with a lot of women, though most of them are the kind who wear Philadelphia Flyers bomber jackets to church. He is cocky, even arrogant.*

        BELLINI: When I was growing up, I never got the feeling that my mom ever really loved me. Could that explain my insatiable desire to dominate women?

        THORPE: I don't know. Did you ever fuck her?

        BELLINI: Fuck who?

        THORPE: Your mom.

Bellini looks shocked, like a man who has had his psychic space violated.

        BELLINI: Hey, Doc, I feel like you're violating my psychic space here.

        THORPE: Sorry. Good point.

        BELLINI: So why this obsession with women? I screw six, seven women a day. They're more addictive than Marlboros.

        THORPE: I didn't know you smoked.

        BELLINI: I used to. Two packs a day.

        THORPE: What made you quit?

        BELLINI: The Surgeon General's Report.

        THORPE: And that scared you?

        BELLINI: It did. I felt like I had a gun cocked at my head.

Thorpe slides up his right pants leg to reveal a knife sheath from which he produces a very sharp Bowie knife. As Bellini continues to stare at the ceiling, Thorpe sneaks up behind him and plunges the blade directly between his thighs. The knife lands, shaft upward, scant inches from his client's genitals.

BELLINI: Jesus, you fucking lunatic! You could have cut my nuts off!

Bellini attempts to yank the shaft loose but has no luck. Thorpe serenely returns to his seat and begins paging through a magazine.

THORPE: I'll grant you this is an unorthodox therapeutic technique. But the next time you're thinking about screwing the baby-sitter, think what it would be like if her dad cut your nuts off and made you testicularly challenged, urologically voided, gonadally gone, penilely neutralized. Now get the hell out of here.

Int.—Same Office—Midmorning.

We see JIM FRANKLIN, a certified public accountant.

FRANKLIN: It's bad enough when you have a rare disease, but what could be worse than having a rare disease in a town that's too small for anyone else to have the same disease?

THORPE: Why don't you just move to New York?

FRANKLIN: New York is 1,200 miles away. My roots are here in Wisconsin. My friends are here. My career is here. My neuroses are here.

THORPE: Neuroses are a movable feast. Hey, it looks like I've misplaced my notes.

> Could you remind me what your
> problem is again? Are you a gin
> monkey? A cokehead?

FRANKLIN: I'm an addictive, bulimic, abusive
codependent.

THORPE: I'm sorry, I've forgotten what that
means. Is that when you constantly barf
and encourage your significant other to
barf with you?

FRANKLIN: No. It means that I live with a bulimic,
but I'm jealous of all the attention she
gets. So I beat her, and it makes her
puke. Our relationship literally makes
her puke. Her bulimia contributes to
my abusiveness, and my abusiveness
contributes to her bulimia.

Thorpe studies his patient, then reaches into a desk drawer and produces a custard pie, which he throws directly into Franklin's face. With a stone-faced expression, he watches Franklin disbelievingly scrape the custard off his face.

THORPE: Mr. Franklin, I don't think I can help
you.

Ext.—The Battlements of a Famous Local Castle—Dusk.

Thorpe is peering out at the landscape with a pair of high-powered binoculars. He is dressed quite nattily—sports coat, dark turtleneck, expensive sunglasses.

THORPE: This look works. It works for me.

A shadow closes in on him. Thorpe turns slowly.

THORPE: Hey.

Thorpe turns back to his birdwatching.

THORPE: (Cont.) Look at the canopy those trees form over the town. From here, you can't even tell there's a town down there.

The camera moves to ground level, as we see a screaming body fall from the highest rampart in the castle. Thorpe lays face down on the ground, his body ruined. The camera tightens on the gaping cataract of blood pouring from Thorpe's body. We see a finger scrawl a message in blood on the driveway macadam. It reads:

D...O...C...E...P...A...S...

The camera pulls away. Some time passes. The sun comes up on the corpse. A car pulls up several feet away. The car door swings open, and a pair of feet descend. They march slowly, resolutely, toward the corpse. The camera looks up into the face of SEAMUS FOGARTY, *the groundskeeper at White Castle.*

FOGARTY: Mister, are you all right?

Getting no answer, he scurries off.

Ext.—Street—Early Morning.

Police Lieutenant TURK BISHOP *is seen pointing his gun directly at the audience. He is in his late thirties, perhaps early forties: alert, intelligent, but world-weary. Suddenly the cellular phone in his back pocket rings.*

BISHOP: Bishop. What do you want? The station house burned down? When? How did that happen? A Bunsen burner in July? What were they doing with a Bunsen burner in July? Making cappuccino? Fucking Yuppie cops. All right, so what do I do? I work out of my car until a new station house is built? Jesus.

Bishop aims his gun off into the distance, still listening on the phone.

BISHOP: (Cont.) What's that you said? Where? When? White Castle? He fell? Nobody falls off a castle. Hey, this sounds tasty. I'm on my way. Ten–four.

Ext.—White Castle—Midmorning.

Bishop stands above the shrouded corpse that has landed in the parking lot of White Castle. Next to him is his partner, SGT. TOM STODDARD, *a stocky, intense type. Stoddard wears tinted sunglasses, extremely cheap polyester clothes, and a longshoreman's tam. They are joined by* NATHAN SCHWARTZ, *town coroner, a bland bureaucrat who carries a laptop computer in addition to his medical bag.*

SCHWARTZ: Did this guy Thorpe actually live here?

STODDARD: He was loaded. He had his own home and he used the castle just for birdwatching.

SCHWARTZ: Amazing.

Stoddard stares down at the coroner, seated in a folding chair, fiddling around with his laptop.

STODDARD: Did he jump or was he pushed?

Schwartz ignores him, punching some data into his laptop. Stoddard becomes visibly annoyed.

STODDARD: Let me rephrase that. Did he jump or was he pushed?

BISHOP: I think he was pushed. Nobody would jump with his binoculars still on.

Stoddard looks confused.

STODDARD: Why not?

BISHOP: He could get his hands caught in the straps, and then he'd land on his face.

Even suicides aren't into that. Think it
through, Tommy.

*All the time they have been talking, Schwartz has been studying the video
display screen on his laptop computer.*

SCHWARTZ: Shh. It's coming up on the screen now.

STODDARD: What's coming up on the screen?

SCHWARTZ: I'm not really a coroner; I'm a
gynecologist. But the nearest coroner is
forty-five miles away in Harlot's Fork.
So I subscribe to Coroner/Net, the on-
line, interactive coroner's network. It
tells me everything I need to know.

BISHOP: Yeah, well what's it telling you now?

SCHWARTZ: It's telling me that this man was
probably pushed to his death. He's
wearing a $5,000 Rolex, a $1,200
Armani suit, and a $875 pair of Gucci
loafers. He's got a nifty pair of antique
binoculars which must go for $3,600
wrapped around his neck. Nobody
planning to take his own life would leap
from a castle parapet with an expensive
set of binoculars wrapped around his
neck while dressed in his best suit and
sporting a Rolex.

Stoddard and Bishop gaze inquisitively at the coroner's laptop computer.

STODDARD: No shit?

SCHWARTZ: He'd change into sweats before he
jumped. Suicide victims are very
conscientious about leaving expensive
haberdashery behind for their loved

ones, in case they need extra cash for the funeral.

STODDARD: You got all that off that computer screen?

Schwartz passes him the laptop.

SCHWARTZ: Be my guest.

Stoddard studies it, cocks his head, whistles. He hands it to his partner, but his partner signals "No" with an annoyed movement of his head. Bishop saunters away to inspect the corpse.

STODDARD: Pretty impressive.

Bishop gestures with his foot at the message scrawled in caked blood on the ground.

BISHOP: Hey, what's this? Does that mean anything to you?

SCHWARTZ: D-O-C-E-P-A-S? Docepas. Sounds Greek. Could be the murderer's last name?

BISHOP: Could be. We'll check. One other thing, Doc. Could a person who fell or was pushed from that height still have the energy left to write a message in his own blood?

Schwartz punches some data into his computer.

SCHWARTZ: One hundred fifty feet, forty-three-year-old man, lands on his kneecaps, fall cushioned by binoculars between face and macadam. Let's just run the numbers.

Schwartz waits several seconds, then nods and hands the laptop to Bishop.

SCHWARTZ: It's stretching it, but it could happen. It says here on Coroner/Net that if he came up clean with a dead-cat bounce, he might still have a minute or two to scrawl a message. But what the message means, I have no idea.

BISHOP: We'll be in touch.

Schwartz leaves as Bishop continues to stare at the message.

BISHOP: "Docepas"? "Docepas"? What the fuck does that mean?

Stoddard sidles over to the corpse, shaking his head.

STODDARD: Where's the ice truck? This guy's getting a little ripe.

THORPE: Oh, that's a nice touch, Tommy.

STODDARD: We'll run a check through Milwaukee on everyone named Docepas. It does sound kind of Greek, doesn't it?

Bishop stares at him icily.

BISHOP: Oh, you studied Greek now?

STODDARD: No.

BISHOP: You know who Aeschylus was?

STODDARD: No.

BISHOP: You ever heard of the Oresteia Trilogy?

STODDARD: No.

BISHOP: Can you tell me what was decided at the Battle of Thermopylae?

STODDARD: No.

BISHOP: Can you tell me the causes of the Peloponnesian War?

STODDARD: Listen, Turk . . .

BISHOP: Look, can you tell me the causes of the
Peloponnesian War?

STODDARD: No.

BISHOP: Then shut the fuck up.

BISHOP walks way.

Ext.—A Cliff Overlooking the River—Noon.

*A small crowd of mourners surround a table on which sits an urn contain-
ing the remains of Peter Thorpe. BRITTANY THORPE, a tall, cold woman,
weeps softly as a dour priest, FATHER JOHN DE FONZINI, delivers her husband's eulogy entirely in cryptic sign language, which is then translated into
English by a NUN standing to his right. Meanwhile, off to the side, Thorpe's
two children, COURTNEY, age ten, and BUTCH, age seven, play hand-held
video games. We see Bishop staring resolutely at the NUN. His expression
strongly suggests that he recognizes her. He shakes his head, confused, then
mutters to himself.*

BISHOP: Veronica? Veronica De Fonzini? It can't
be.

*The nun studies Father De Fonzini's strange hand gestures for a few sec-
onds, then speaks.*

NUN: He walked with a high head and a low
heart.

The nun turns back to study the next hand signals.

NUN: (Cont.) And the angel of the Lord said
unto him, 'Wherefore hast thou smitten
thine ass these three times?'

Father John DeFonzini continues his odd gesticulating.

NUN: Take a pot and put an omer full of
manna therein, and lay it up before the
Lord, to be kept for your generations.

The crowd looks a bit confused. The nun turns to the priest for more details. Then she nods her head, smiles, and resumes translating.

NUN: It will be used in its bountiful glory for all to enjoy. And for generations to come, the world will abound in happiness and health, as well as sadness and death.

The crowd continues to look confused.

NUN: Now an omer is the tenth part of an ephah.

The assembled mourners nod to one another, happy to have this matter cleared up.

NUN: Eli, eli, lama sabachtani?

Britanny Thorpe slowly walks away from her husband's final resting place. Bishop approaches her, notepad in hand.

BISHOP: Mrs. Thorpe, I know this is a bad time, but could I talk to you for a few minutes about your husband?

MRS. THORPE: Yes, but make it quick. Courtney has ballet class and Butch has a skeet-shooting lesson.

BISHOP: Courtney and Butch is kind of an unusual combination, Mrs. Thorpe. Butch is short for what?

MRS. THORPE: Butch is short for Butch. My husband let me name our first child; he named the second. As you can see, I'm kind of WASPy.

BISHOP: Is there a third child?

MRS. THORPE: There might have been. There *would* have been.

BISHOP:	And the third child's name would have been?
MRS. THORPE:	Sandy, if it was a boy, Brie, if it was a girl. It would have been my turn to name the child. Whomever murdered my husband made sure there was one less Sandy in the world. Or one less Brie.
BISHOP:	Do you think that could have been a motive for the murder?
MRS. THORPE:	Come again?
BISHOP:	Nothing—just thinking out loud. Mrs. Thorpe, I know this is a difficult time, but can you think of anyone who would have wanted to see your husband dead?

Brittany Thorpe yanks opens the trunk of her van and produces two massive filing cabinets, piles of notebooks, and a gargantuan Rolodex.

MRS. THORPE:	These are the confidential files of all of my husband's patients for the last ten years. You'll find all the shocking, intimate details about their sexual deviancies and fetishes right here. Technically speaking, it's against the law for me to give you these files. But technically speaking, it's also against the law to kill my husband. So they're all yours.

Mrs. Thorpe drags the filing cabinets out of the car.

BISHOP:	Mrs. Thorpe, I appreciate your being so helpful with these files, but they probably contain hundreds and hundreds of his patients' names. What

I really need to know is whether there's anyone in particular you can think of who would have wanted to see your husband dead. Did he have any enemies? Had he ever been threatened? I noticed that the turnout to the funeral was kind of sparse.

Mrs. Thorpe studies Bishop quizzically.

MRS. THORPE: Lieutenant, are you at all familiar with the therapeutic process?

BISHOP: I am. I underwent therapy myself a couple of years ago. It didn't work.

MRS. THORPE: It rarely does. Psychotherapy is a process, but there's never really an end product. Peter used to compare the professions to baking. Law, he used to say, is like preparing a pot roast. Medicine is like salvaging a defective stew. Psychotherapy is like preparing Jell-o: Your dessert may settle, but it never really hardens.

BISHOP: And dentistry? Did your husband ever mention dentistry?

MRS. THORPE: My husband was very good at creating analogies. His favorite word was "like." But he never finished things. When he gave speeches, people used to say: "What about certified public accountancy?" "What about forestry management?" He never had an answer.

BISHOP: I'm still a bit confused.

MRS. THORPE: It's simple. You go to a lawyer because you want to sue somebody. You might

win, you might lose, but there's a
definite outcome. But psychotherapy
isn't like that. You can spend years
working through your neuroses and
never get to the bottom of your
problem.

BISHOP: You think that bothered his patients?

MRS. THORPE: I think some of Peter's patients thought
that psychotherapy was like boat repair
or SmokeEnders. But it isn't like that at
all. Psychotherapy is like repairing a very
old rattan lawn chair. You can replace
all those broken canes, but that's no
guarantee that it will stay fixed forever.
If you sit in that chair long enough, it's
going to break. This would also be true if
you stood on it while hanging pictures.

BISHOP: So you think the person who murdered
your husband may have been a
disgruntled patient?

MRS. THORPE: Let's just put it this way, Lieutenant. My
husband was a pillar of the community,
the salt of the earth. My husband was a
prince among men, the flower of
Christian manhood, a bright beacon of
sanity in a raging sea of madness.
Whoever killed him was a very sick
person. Here are two filing cabinets
filled with sickos.

BISHOP: But you have no specific suspect?

Mrs. Thorpe studies him glacially, shaking her head.

MRS. THORPE: You've got your work cut out for you,
Lieutenant. They were *all* sick fucks.

Mrs. Thorpe walks toward a tiny cluster of friends a few yards away. Bishop turns back to the table with the urn, where COURTNEY *and* BUTCH *are enthusiastically playing hand-held video games. Bishop approaches them.*

BISHOP: Sorry about your dad, Cour . . . Brittan . . .

They turn as one, putting the video games behind their backs. Courtney, age ten, is pretty, if a bit on the plump side. She radiates intelligence and sophistication, but, like her mother, lacks warmth. Butch, age seven, looks like a jock.

COURTNEY: Courtney.

BISHOP: Sorry. I need to ask you a few questions about your father.

COURTNEY: Our father was the salt of the earth.

BISHOP: Was he now?

The two children nod simultaneously.

BUTCH: Our father was the flower of Christmas manhood.

BISHOP: So I heard.

COURTNEY: Our father was—

BISHOP: No, let me guess. Your father was a pillar of the community?

The children nod.

BISHOP: (Cont.) Your father was a prince among men?

They nod again.

BISHOP: Now, let me ask you one more question. Was your father also a bright beacon of sanity in a raging sea of madness?

The children look at one another and shake their heads.

COURTNEY: That sounds more like our uncle Paulie.

BISHOP: Your uncle Paulie? Your father had a brother?

BUTCH: Yeah.

BISHOP: I didn't see him at the funeral today.

BUTCH: He lives upstate and couldn't get off work or something.

BISHOP: Well, wouldn't you think he'd make an exception for his own brother's funeral? Especially after a murder?

COURTNEY: Uncle Paulie's kind of wacked out. He was at Woodstock and stuff.

BISHOP: Interesting family. Well, like I said, my deepest condolences in your hour of grief.

Bishop walks way and is joined by his partner, Stoddard. Bishop glances over in the direction of a black car, into which Father John DeFonzini and the nun are disappearing. His eyes reflect a mixture of recognition and disbelief.

STODDARD: The lab report just came in; it looks like he was pushed. There were scratches around the nape of his neck, where the killer must have grabbed him from behind.

BISHOP: You know, this was a personal thing. They left the Rolex, the binoculars, the wallet. This was not just a routine mugging that got out of hand.

STODDARD: You're a fucking whiz, Turk. Eight years on the L.A.P.D., it was worth it, huh?

BISHOP: Yeah, it was worth it. Eight years on the L.A.P.D. and they throw me off for

rolling a couple of recovering
chocaholics. She's got some files up
there; check 'em out. And don't ever
mention the L.A.P.D. again or you and
me are going to do it right here.

Ext.—Holy Innocent Bystanders Church—Early Afternoon.

*We see Father John De Fonzini enter, followed by the nun. Seconds later,
Bishop pulls up in his car and walks into the church. He is greeted by a
second, older nun, SISTER DAMIAN BARABBAS.*

SISTER DAMIAN BARABBAS: May I help you?

BISHOP: That nun who just went through that
door there—I thought I recognized her.
Veronica De Fonzini?

SISTER DAMIAN BARABBAS: Sister Wilhemina des Portes de St.
Denis—Sister William of the Gates for
short. But yes, Sister used to be
Veronica De Fonzini before she
embraced the wimple. Would you like
to speak with her?

BISHOP: Yes, I would.

SISTER DAMIAN BARABBAS: Your name?

BISHOP: Turk Bishop.

SISTER DAMIAN BARABBAS: I'll just be a second.

*Bishop stands waiting in the archway. Seconds later, Sister Damian Barab-
bas reappears and gestures down the hallway.*

SISTER DAMIAN BARABBAS: Third door on the left. She's waiting.

BISHOP: Thanks.

*Bishop walks down the hall and enters a tiny cell furnished only with a
cheap desk and a massive crucifix on the wall. On the desk in the center of
the room sits a personal computer, a modem, and a phone. Behind it sits
SISTER WILHEMINA DES PORTES DE SAINT DENIS, SISTER W. for short.*

She is about twenty-eight, very attractive, despite her drab nun's clothing. Her face explodes in a radiant smile.

SISTER W.:　Turk-man.

BISHOP:　I heard you'd taken the vow. But seeing is believing.

SISTER W.:　It's been a long time.

BISHOP:　Ten years.

SISTER W.:　Is it that long? Seems impossible. I heard about your wife and children.

BISHOP:　Life is a bitch.

SISTER W.:　Did they ever find the driver? I heard it was a hit-and-run.

BISHOP:　Yeah, we found the driver. She was a schizoid anorexic recovering alcoholic with Attention Deficit Disorder who was fleeing an abusive chocaholic husband who used to beat her whenever he had one too many of the nougat caramels.

SISTER W.:　The Twinkies Defense?

BISHOP:　It was more like the Whitman's Sampler Defense. She got off with two years suspended sentence doing community service because she says she can't remember doing it.

SISTER W.:　What kind of community service does a recovering alcoholic schizoid anorexic with Attention Deficit Disorder do?

BISHOP:　She lectured senior bulimics as part of the Beverly Hills Negative Role Model Program called Scared Plump.

SISTER W.:　You said she was a schizoid anorexic? What is that?

BISHOP: A schizoid anorexic is a fat person who keeps vomiting so she'll have more room for more food. She was actually about 215 pounds, which is a lot on a five-foot-five frame. She was a beast.

SISTER W.: I'm so sorry. But if it's any consolation, on the Last Judgment Day, God will not accept Attention Deficit Disorder as an excuse for vehicular homicide. If it's not covered in the Bible, it doesn't count up there.

BISHOP: It isn't any consolation. But thanks for the thought.

SISTER W.: And after the accident?

BISHOP: I lost it. It started to affect my work. One day, I went over to her house and trashed it. I trashed the car, the pool, the whole bit.

SISTER W.: And they caught you?

BISHOP: Nah, they could never prove anything, but my career out there was over. There were a few other incidents—Internal Affairs caught me pistol-whipping some recovering chocaholics—

Flashback: Ext.—A Los Angeles Alley—Night

Bishop is seen leaning against a wall next to a door with a sign reading OVEREATERS MEETING TONIGHT. *Two obese men exit the building furtively.*

BISHOP: Got an Armagnac soufflé you can spare?

THE MEN ignore him, as Bishop goes into kick-boxer mode, beating the men senseless. The flashback ends.

Int.—Sister W's Cell—Midday.

BISHOP: The department put me on ninety-day suspension. Finally, I just packed it in and came home to No Quarter. They needed a real detective; the force up here is a bunch of losers. It's been two years.

SISTER W.: Again, Turk, I don't want to get all touchy-feely about this, but remember what the Good Book says: Vengeance is mine.

BISHOP: Does that mean that God's going to nail this bitch? Pardon the expression.

SISTER W.: God writes straight in crooked lines.

BISHOP: That's good to know. But what about you? What are you doing back in town? Last I heard, you were still in Rome.

SISTER W.: I'm on leave. There were some problems over there. They sent me home . . . to rest.

BISHOP: To rest?

SISTER W.: You probably heard about Johnny's accident?

BISHOP: I heard he was in a car accident in Portugal or something.

SISTER W.: Spain. He was on a Jesuit bike trip. A tractor-trailer hit him full-bore. He lost his hearing; he'll never speak again. He was too banged up to ship home so they kept him over there in Madrid.

BISHOP: So that's where he learned sign language?

SISTER W.:   Yes, but he can only sign in Spanish.
                Nobody can sign in a place like No
                Quarter, so he has to have a translator.
                That's what I was doing at the funeral
                today. It's a shame about that poor
                man.

BISHOP: A wife and two kids. Sound familiar?

SISTER W.:   The world can be a terrible place.

BISHOP: Especially a dump like No Quarter. But
                come on, Veronica . . .

SISTER W.:   Sister Wilhemina.

BISHOP: Jesus, Veronica, I took you to see Ozzie
                Osbourne.

SISTER W.:   That was a long time ago, Turk. It's
                Sister Wilhemina now. They don't like
                us to use the names we had before we
                took the veil.

BISHOP: Okay, fair enough. But you didn't come
                all the way home from the Vatican to
                translate sign language for your
                brother. I heard you were a huge hit
                over there. And God, what kind of cell
                do they have you living in here? A
                crucifix, a futon, and a computer.
                What's this laptop business you got
                going on here?

SISTER W.:   I'm in data management now, Turk.
                You've heard of the Society of Jesus?
                I'm in the Paperless Society of Jesus.
                They've got me working as an electronic
                missionary, healing heathens through
                the Internet.

BISHOP: You've lost me.

SISTER W.: Once upon a time, missionaries toiled in far-flung places like the Congo. We lost a lot of people that way. These days, the church has had to downsize. So we do our proselytizing on-line, converting pagans through electronic bulletin boards.

BISHOP: Sounds wild.

SISTER W.: Everyday I interface with headhunters, cannibals, snake worshippers, the whole bit. It's the same work that Christ did. I just do it on a laptop. If He were here today, He'd be on the Internet.

BISHOP: Hmmm. But if you can do this kind of work anywhere in the world, why'd they send you back to No Quarter? Why not keep you in Rome?

SISTER W.: I had a breakdown, Turk. Or, let's say, my superiors think I've had a breakdown.

BISHOP: You wanna tell me about it?

SISTER W.: I was in Lourdes eight months ago. I was gathering data about miracles. There'd been this strange report that sixteen blind people were cured in one week, and all of them were wearing Cleveland Indians jerseys.

BISHOP: We're talking megamiracle here.

Sister W. now turns very somber and introspective.

SISTER W.: I was in the grotto. I was all alone. It was noon on a Tuesday. You know how the French are—they were all off having lunch. There was a radiance on my laptop screen. There was a shimmering light. And then I saw her.

BISHOP: You saw who?

SISTER W.:   I saw the Virgin.

BISHOP: France is a funny place to go looking for virgins.

SISTER W.:   Not *a* virgin. *The* Virgin. The Blessed Mother of God.

BISHOP: You saw the Blessed Virgin Mary?

Sister W. nods.

BISHOP: (Cont.) The Blessed Virgin Mary appeared to you in the same grotto that she appeared to St. Bernadette?

SISTER W.:   Yes. She did. But not in person.

BISHOP: Again, you're losing me here.

SISTER W.:   She appeared on my computer screen. *This* computer screen.

Bishop eyes the laptop. His eyes find Sister W's.

BISHOP: Could you show me this?

Sister W. plunges her face into her hands.

SISTER W.:   She's gone. I was such an idiot. She was right there on the screen, gesturing to me with Her rosary beads. And I talked to Her. I really talked to Her. I mean, She was there.

BISHOP: So why isn't She there now?

SISTER W.:   I heard people coming. She must have heard them, too. The image started to

BISHOP:

fade. I saved the file She'd appeared to me in. It was titled LOURDES. FIL. Then I rushed back to my hotel room. I opened the file. She was still there. She wasn't saying much, but She was still there. So I took a floppy disk and inserted it into the floppy drive, and then . . .

BISHOP: And then?

Sister W. is now practically hysterical.

SISTER W.: The phone rang. Somebody knocked at the door. There were all these distractions. And you know how I am. Somehow I must have copied over the file on the laptop. I copied over the file with the Blessed Mother in it. And now She's gone! She's gone forever! And it's all my fault.

Bishop grimaces.

BISHOP: Have you told other people about this?

SISTER W.: My superiors. They were . . . understanding. But they felt I should have some time off. So they sent me back here to be with Johnny.

A knock is heard at the door. The door opens. Bishop looks out into the hallway at Father John De Fonzini.

BISHOP: Excuse me, Veronica, but your brother is signing to me.

Bishop makes an extravagant gesture with his hands.

BISHOP: (Cont.) What does this mean?

SISTER W.: Your partner needs you.

BISHOP: Okay, I gotta get rolling.

Bishop puts his hand on Sister W.'s shoulder.

BISHOP: (Cont.) Get some rest, Veronica.

SISTER W.: But you believe me, Turk? You believe She was in there?

BISHOP: I believe you, Veronica. But hey, I'm a Catholic. I believe all kinds of things.

Ext.—Outside Bishop's Car—Day.

STODDARD: We found sixteen Devil Dog wrappers in the trash can up on the castle tower. We also found a couple of Diet Pepsis.

BISHOP: Thorpe was a pretty fit guy, so it would have taken a fair-sized person to push him off that roof. That means we can rule out all the anorexics and all the bulimics. So what's that leave us with?

STODDARD: This is starting to look like an open-and-shut, Turk.

Stoddard now consults his notebook.

STODDARD: (Cont.) Thorpe had forty-five active patients: thirteen juicers, four cokeheads, two junkies, four pill-poppers, two sexaholics, three chronic gamblers, one woman who loved too much, two credit card addicts, one mule-humper, one codependent, one guy suffering from bulimia envy, one man who had a thing for teenage boys, one woman who had a thing for prepubescent girls . . .

BISHOP: You almost done there?

STODDARD: Not quite. There was a seventeen-year-old boy who liked to see senior citizens dressed up in diapers, two welfare loafers suffering from—get this—Chronic Lateness Syndrome—and one chocaholic with Attention Deficit Disorder: She could never remember whether she was working on her third or fourth box of Russell Stover's Dark Milk Chocolates.

BISHOP: Jesus.

STODDARD: Forty-four of these clowns have the same airtight alibi—they were all attending a twelve-step meeting that didn't break up until midnight.

BISHOP: All of them? Together? Why would they all be at the same meeting if they have different addictions?

STODDARD: Do the math, Turk. No Quarter only has 350 people. Forty-five of them are in recovery, about the national average.

BISHOP: So the town's too small to have a twelve-step program for each of them.

STODDARD: You got it. They all attend twice-weekly umbrella meetings. Mondays, the boozers, pill-poppers, and sex maniacs get to talk; Thursdays, it's the gamblers, porkers, and your more exotic nutcases.

BISHOP: Sounds like a fun-fest to me.

STODDARD: You can see why Thorpe lived in a house like that, with a castle for a hangout. He was loaded. There's not another shrink for seventy-five miles around, so he had

every nutcase in the northern corner
of the state. Plus, he had 'em coming
and going: He got paid directly by
the insurers, but the state also paid
him to take all the court-appointed
whip-offs. The guy was loaded.

BISHOP: You checked the will?

STODDARD: The wife and kids get everything.

BISHOP: No other relatives?

STODDARD: He had a brother upstate somewhere.

BISHOP: Yeah, the kids told me. He wasn't at the
funeral.

STODDARD: If he was, you would have noticed. He's
a twin.

Bishop studies him with a glazed expression.

BISHOP: An identical twin?

STODDARD: You got it.

BISHOP: A brother not coming to his own
brother's funeral I can understand; you
know how families have falling outs. But
a fucking twin? A fucking twin didn't
come to his own twin brother's funeral?

STODDARD: The wife asked him to stay away.
Apparently, it's pretty common for
twins to duck the funeral. A surviving
twin really spooks people.

BISHOP: You check this guy out?

STODDARD: He's a dish-dryer up in Dutchman's
Prairie. He works in a diner. His boss
swears by him.

BISHOP: Where was he the night his brother
caught the bus?

STODDARD:	Drying dishes. Dry, dry, dry.
BISHOP:	Is he clean?
STODDARD:	Some Mexican was there with him. Funny thing, life. One brother's this big-time shrink with loads of dough; the other brother's a dipshit menial. You'd think the brother would at least be a veterinarian or something. Something classy.
BISHOP:	Let's suppose you had a twin, Stoddard. Would he be a cop, too? And if he was a cop, would he be the kind of cop who hangs around with his finger up his ass when he should be upstate checking out an alibi?
STODDARD:	I don't have a twin.
BISHOP:	Neither do I.

Bishop slides into his car and drives off.

STODDARD:	But if you did have a twin, I'd bet he'd be a prick.

Int.—A Meeting of the No Quarter Twelve-Step Program—Night.

We see twenty-five DYSFUNCTIONAL TOWNSPEOPLE *in a large meeting hall festooned with enormously inspirational banners of a maudlin, somewhat revolting variety. In the corner, at the rear, sit Bishop and Stoddard, watching the proceedings. Sherman Krebs, still wearing a white T-shirt that reads* DON'T DISS THE DYSFUNCTIONAL, *strolls to the front of the room to address the crowd.*

SHERMAN KREBS:	Hi, my name is Sherman. I'm an addictive gambler and I haven't placed a bet for thirty-three days.
EVERYONE:	Hi, Sherman.

KREBS: I want to tell you about an experience I just had with my daughter, Caitlin. Eleven years ago, I placed a bet on a college basketball game. I bet my daughter's entire Harvard scholarship fund.

Joey Bellini interrupts.

BELLINI: Who'd you bet on?

KREBS: It doesn't matter who I bet on. What does matter is, I lost the money. All of it.

BINGO TYSON, a man suffering from the chronic inability to arrive anywhere on time, interrupts.

TYSON: How much did you bet?

KREBS: I bet $27,000.

A roar of disbelief from the crowd, who all begin to mutter.

EVERYBODY: Twenty-seven thousand? Did he say $27,000?

TYSON: And you lost it?

KREBS: I lost it all. I was doubling up.

BELLINI: Then it *does* matter who you were betting on.

KREBS: No, it doesn't.

EVERYBODY: Yes, it does. You bet your ass it does.

KREBS: All right. I bet on Kentucky.

EVERYBODY: Kentucky? You bet on fucking Kentucky?

BELLINI: Was that the game where Georgetown kicked the shit out of them? The '83 regional finals? You bet $27,000 on Kentucky against Georgetown?

KREBS:	That's right.
BELLINI:	You fucking schmuck.
KREBS:	Look, dickhead, the bet doesn't count.
EVERYBODY:	Oh, yes it does!!
KREBS:	You're not a very supportive group. In fact, you've never been a very supportive group. Coming here and talking to you is a waste of time.

Bishop watches the proceedings with a cold mask of scorn written on his face.

AMBER:	Can we get on with this? Sherman has problems; we all have problems; so let's hear his problem, give him our support, and proceed. Besides, we all agreed: ten minutes per dysfunction.
KREBS:	All right. I haven't spoken to my daughter for eleven years, since the night I placed the bet. Her mother threw me out. I can accept that. But I'm never going to be able to close the circle unless I can make things right with my daughter.
BELLINI:	So after you blew her Harvard scholarship money, where'd she go to college?
KREBS:	Central Connecticut State.
EVERYBODY IN UNISON:	Central Con-nec-ti-cut State???
KREBS:	You got it.
BELLINI:	I'll bet she was glad to hear from you.
KREBS:	She wasn't glad to hear from me. She despises me. She hung up the phone. I

called again. She hung up the phone.
I called again. She hung up the phone.
I called again. Then she called the
police.

BELLINI: Smart girl. Even if she went to Central
Connecticut State.

KREBS: Hatred breeds hatred. The refusal to
forgive makes a stone of the heart. It's
like that John Prine song: "You can
gaze out the window and get mad and
get madder."

TYSON: You quote that John Prine song again
and I'm gonna whip your ass.

KREBS: This is my time. I have the floor.

Amber Duggan rises from her chair. She is, if possible, even fatter than the last time we saw her.

AMBER: He's right. Hey, show some
compassion. We've all been in that boat
before. Remember: Don't cower;
empower.

BELLINI: I never bet twenty-seven large on
Kentucky against Georgetown.

AMBER: Stop with the jock talk, already. What is
it with you guys anyway, the way you
freeze the rest of us out. Especially the
women. I don't even know what twenty-
seven large is.

BELLINI: It's your dress size.

AMBER: Bastard! You heartless bastard!

Stoddard whispers to Bishop.

STODDARD: She's the one. She threatened Thorpe
last week. She says she was home with

	her cat the night of the murder. She's the only one with no alibi.
BISHOP:	She's hefty enough to have done it.
BELLINI:	Hi, I'm Joey Bellini. I'm a man who loves too much and I haven't had any for forty-six days.
EVERYONE:	Hi, Joey.
BELLINI:	You know, most of my life I've gone around thinking of myself as a predator. I couldn't keep my hands off the young stuff. Then, just recently, I've come to realize that in a funny way, I'm kind of a victim myself. Women check out this laser gun down here and they're all over me. This baby's a twenty-seven large.
AMBER:	That's not a twenty-seven large. That's a six Petite.
TYSON:	Maybe.

The crowd grows restless. One by one, individuals begin to rise from their seats.

A.D.D. PERSON:	Hi, I can't remember who I am and I can't remember why I'm here. But I need love and understanding. Whoever I am and whatever I've done, I'm not a sick person getting sicker, but a forgetful person getting less forgetful.

By this point, everyone in the room is out of control. Chaos breaks out as people start jumping up without being called upon to speak about their problems.

DYSFUNCTIONAL PERSON NO. 1:	Hi, I'm Chuck and I drove thirty-three miles here tonight with a credit card addiction like you wouldn't believe.

I charged two shotguns, a Glock 9mm, and a bow and arrow. And I don't even hunt. It's just that the gun shop was the only place that was still open.

DYSFUNCTIONAL
PERSON NO. 2:

I surrendered to my Higher Power and my Higher Power said it was okay to have four margaritas.

DYSFUNCTIONAL
PERSON NO. 3:

I haven't screwed a mule in thirteen days.

DYSFUNCTIONAL
PERSON NO. 4:

I am powerless before my mint-flavored Higher Power.

DYSFUNCTIONAL
PERSON NO. 5:

I ain't looked up a little girl's dress since July.

DYSFUNCTIONAL
PERSON NO. 6:

Hi, I'm Jerry and I'm a bulimic. But get this—I haven't barfed in twenty-three days. Spit up a bit, and gagged a little, but I haven't barfed in twenty-three days.

The meeting now degenerates into a free-for-all, with everyone on their feet declaiming this or that.

DYSFUNCTIONAL
PERSON NO. 7:

Can't you see? The glass is half full, not half empty.

DYSFUNCTIONAL
PERSON NO. 8:

I've worked hard to eliminate car clutter.

DYSFUNCTIONAL
PERSON NO. 9:

So have I.

DYSFUNCTIONAL
PERSON NO. 10:

Don't take that shot, Greenie.

DYSFUNCTIONAL
PERSON NO. 11:

Be punctual, not dysfunctional.

DYSFUNCTIONAL
PERSON NO. 4:

I am powerless before my mint-flavored Higher Power.

Bishop and Stoddard exchange concerned glances, then exit, as the pandemonium continues.

BISHOP: These were all Thorpe's patients?

STODDARD: Every last one of them.

BISHOP: I think this may have been a suicide after all.

Int.—Stoddard's Apartment—Early Morning.

STODDARD: This guy Thorpe wasn't the world's most caring guy. No wonder nobody came to his funeral. He's got all his patients' files arranged by nickname: Mrs. Lardbutt, Mr. Boozehound, Mr. Jolly Roger, Mrs. VisaGold.

BISHOP: So he called a spade a spade. I can relate to that. But if he had thirteen gin monkeys, how did he keep track?

STODDARD: Mr. Gin Monkey, Ms. Lush, Mrs. Smashface, Mr. Hipflask, Mrs. Boilermaker, Mr. Depth-Charge, Mrs. Tom Collins.

BISHOP: The guy must have had some memory.

STODDARD: He could treat 'em like shit because he's the only shrink from here to Milwaukee. And he did treat 'em like shit. Here, get a load of this.

Stoddard loads a videocasette onto his VCR. A black-and-white videotape of Peter Thorpe's final session with Amber Duggan appears on the TV screen.

AMBER: You know, I come here every week, trying to grow as a person, and all I get is abuse.

THORPE: If you grew any more as a person, you couldn't fit through that door.

AMBER: You deserve to die a slow, painful death.

THORPE: Yeah, don't we all.

Cut back to INT. of Stoddard's apartment.

STODDARD: The guy was a piece of work.

BISHOP: His patients were scumbags. They got what they deserved. Hey, who's taking over his practice?

STODDARD: Nobody. Nobody wants them. The town council took out an ad in the *Chicago Tribune* for a psychiatrist, but so far, no takers. Whoever killed him didn't kill him to get his practice.

BISHOP: You check out the wife?

STODDARD: She was with the kids all night.

BISHOP: Could she have hired someone to do it?

STODDARD: Not the type. She's a WASP. WASPs aren't into confrontational stuff. If the wife was going to do him in, she would have set up a kayak disaster or a skeet-shooting mishap.

BISHOP: Troubles in the sack?

STODDARD: Friends say they were a team. No passion, but after fifteen years, what the fuck? It was her money that put him through medical school; her father's president of *American Collie* magazine.

BISHOP: No fucking around on the side?

STODDARD:	The marriage wasn't on the rocks. They just weren't that close.
BISHOP:	So she didn't kill him, no rival for his practice, no gambling debts, no lawsuits, no drugs. That leaves his patients.
STODDARD:	And it doesn't look good for Mrs. Duggan.
BISHOP:	That's . . . Miss Porkface?
STODDARD:	Mrs. Lardbutt. She's separated from her husband. He got a restraining order because she kept pouncing on the poor bastard and forcing him to go down on her. A beast like that could give cunnilingus a bad name.

Bishop hesitates a second before speaking.

BISHOP:	It already has a bad name.
STODDARD:	Maybe for Catholics. Anyway, Mrs. Lardbutt wasn't at the twelve-step meeting that night.
BISHOP:	Where was she?
STODDARD:	Home with the cat. Eating a crate of Devil Dogs. The same kind we found up at the castle. You want a drink?

Bishop nods.

BISHOP:	You know, this is too neat. It would be leaving a bloody glove at the scene of a murder and having another bloody glove matching it at your own home. What kind of moron would do that?

Stoddard hands him a large tumbler.

STODDARD:	O.J.?
BISHOP:	Forty-five potential suspects, all of them with alibis, and she's the only one who's home alone the night of the murder. What is she, an idiot?
STODDARD:	All that sugar plays a tune on your thinkbox. Maybe she just lost it. Crime of porky passion. He sure put her through the wringer that morning. Should I bring her in?
BISHOP:	Bring her in where? The station burned down. No, just keep an eye on her, don't let her go anywhere. I've got a little trip to make this morning.

Ext.—Bellas' Diner—Early Morning.

We see a cigar-boxed, greasy-spoon restaurant. BISHOP enters.

Int.—Back Room—Early Morning

BISHOP enters the dishwashing area in the rear. As he walks in, he sees MIGUEL FENEIRO, clad in a dirty T-shirt, black jeans, and pink-and-yellow sombrero passing a pile of dishes through a lazy susan into the next room. He walks into the room and confronts the obviously terrified menial.

BISHOP:	Turk Bishop, N.Q.P.D.
MIGUEL:	I am legal.
BISHOP:	I understand you were here the night Paul Thorpe's brother was murdered. Where was Mr. Thorpe?
MIGUEL:	*Sí, sí,* he was in the dish-drying area, and I was in the dishwashing area. And he was in the dish-drying area, and I was in the dish—
BISHOP:	Yeah, I'm starting to see a pattern here. He was in the dish-*drying* area?

111

MIGUEL: *Sí.*

BISHOP: You were in the dish*washing* area?

MIGUEL: *Sí, señor.*

BISHOP: Where is Mr. Thorpe now?

MIGUEL: Well, he is in the dish-drying area and I
            am in the dishwashing area, and we are
            separate because of the old people and
            because of the germs. *Sí.*

Bishop studies the dishwasher malevolently.

BISHOP: I'll get back to you.

MIGUEL: *Sí.*

Bishop wanders into a room several yards down the hall and sees PAUL
THORPE, *the spitting image of his dead brother, drying a pile of pots and
pans. Bishop flashes his badge.*

BISHOP: Turk Bishop, N.Q.P.D.

Unlike his dour brother, PAUL THORPE *is a radiantly happy human being
who flashes a vast, headlight smile as he looks up from the mountain of dishes
he is drying.*

THORPE: N.Q.P.D.?

BISHOP: No Quarter Police Department.

THORPE: Far out.

BISHOP: I'm investigating your brother's murder.
            I noticed you weren't at the funeral.

THORPE: Twins flip people out, especially at
            funerals. Besides, Peter and I never had
            much to do with each other. Mom
            pretty much separated us at birth.

BISHOP: How'd she do that?

THORPE: Mom was a sociologist. She wanted to
            find out if personality traits were

inherent or culture-based. So she used us as guinea pigs. Peter went to private school, Princeton, medical school. I went to public school, the navy, the school of hard knocks. Mom was right: It's cultural.

BISHOP: And Dad?

THORPE: Dad disappeared when we were about six. Mom's experiments freaked him out. She died two years later.

BISHOP: A broken heart?

THORPE: Schoolbus hit her.

BISHOP: You don't seem too upset about it. In fact, you don't seem too upset about your brother's murder.

THORPE: We were twins. Twins are under all this pressure to connect. That's not my scene. That's not my philosophy. This is my philosophy.

THORPE turns all the way around to display a white T-shirt bearing the legend HAPPY TO BE HERE.

THORPE: (Cont.) Happy to be here. Happy to be here. We come this way but once. Better enjoy it while it lasts.

BISHOP: You're a jaunty guy, aren't you, Thorpe? Your brother didn't seem to be such a jaunty guy.

Thorpe is still whaling away on those dishes.

THORPE: Better jaunty than dead, Lieutenant.

BISHOP: Meaning?

THORPE: My brother was a success by the world's standards. Somebody murdered him.

I'm a dish-dryer. Nobody's coming around to murder me.

BISHOP: You don't think this could be one of those serial twin murder–type things?

THORPE: Lieutenant, my brother practiced extremely hostile, confrontational therapy. He was always in people's faces. They didn't like that. They weren't happy campers. Neither was he. Now somebody's murdered him, and I think you have a pretty good idea who did it.

BISHOP: One of his patients?

THORPE: Maybe all of his patients. Maybe they all joined in and covered for each other. He wasn't a very nice man.

BISHOP: But you are. You're Mr. Happy Face. I've never seen a guy get such a rush from drying dishes.

THORPE: You should try it some time, Lieutenant. Humbles the psyche but elevates the spirit.

BISHOP: One other thing. Your mom—did she have a favorite?

THORPE: Mom was a big Summerhill buff. She thought the goal of human life was personal happiness, not financial reward. Just happy to be here—till the bus hit her.

BISHOP: So you were the favorite?

THORPE: Except when I pulled those pranks.

BISHOP: Pranks?

THORPE: You know, switching fingerprint records, switching girlfriends. Peter once did three weeks in the navy for me; I substituted for him in the lab at the Mayo Clinic. Twin stuff.

BISHOP: Sounds like you and your brother were pretty tight for a while.

THORPE: We were until he got married. His wife hated me. I dropped acid at their wedding. She's a WASP; they don't go for that shit.

BISHOP: So she froze you out?

THORPE: Yeah. He did, too. I guess he was ashamed of me. Can't really blame him, though. Still . . .

As Bishop turns to leave, he notices a huge Chicago White Sox banner in the corner of the room.

BISHOP: Sox fan, huh? Your brother was a Cubs fan, right?

THORPE: Huge Cubs fan. Yeah, that was Mom again. He got the Cubs uniform, I got the Sox outfit. He played hockey, I played lacrosse. He took Spanish in high school; I took German. Flunked it, too.

BISHOP: German's not much help in a profession like this, is it, Mr. Thorpe?

THORPE: I'm just happy to be here, Lieutenant. I'm just so damn happy to be here.

Ext.—Outside Bishop's Apartment—Early Afternoon.

Stoddard pulls up in his Previa van.

STODDARD:	Good news, buddy. We lifted prints off those Devil Dog wrappers and all of them read Mrs. Lardbutt. We also did a NEXIS search on the message Thorpe scrawled in his own blood. Get this. "Docepas" is actually one word and the beginning of a second. "Doce" means "twelve" in Spanish. And "pas" could have been the first three letters of the word "pasos," which means "steps." He was telling us that one of his patients did it.
BISHOP:	Why would he write it in Spanish?
STODDARD:	Good question.
BISHOP:	That's why I'm asking it. What about this Duggan character. Has she made a move yet?
STODDARD:	We've got the house staked out. She's holed up in there. Porking out. Fucking whale.
BISHOP:	What's the address?
STODDARD:	278 Wormwood.
BISHOP:	I'm on my way.

Ext.—The Backyard of Amber Duggan's House—Afternoon.

The house is opulent, seated on a hill overlooking the river. Amber Duggan is lounging in an armchair at poolside, feasting on several bags of marshmallows positioned to her left on a small iron table. In the pool bob a flotilla of inflatable ducks that look like they are about to explode. Off to the side can be seen the remnants of a gigantic plastic stegosaurus that has, in fact, exploded. Bishop enters through the garden.

AMBER:	This is it, isn't it? ¿El momento del verdad?
BISHOP:	You speak Spanish?

As Bishop reaches for a marshmallow, Amber protectively yanks the table away and jams a couple more down her gullet.

> AMBER: Pig Spanish, so to speak. I read a couple of Cormac McCarthy novels. And I saw *The Three Amigos.* So, have you come to slap on the cuffs?

> BISHOP: It doesn't look good, Mrs. Duggan. We found sixteen Devil Dog wrappers all with your fingerprints on them up at White Castle. We also found a videotape of you threatening him the day he died. You did threaten him, didn't you?

> AMBER: I threatened him every week. It was role-playing, Lieutenant. Dr. Thorpe practiced Revulsion Therapy; I pretended to hate him, he pretended to hate me. It was Abusive Role Playing.

> BISHOP: He was abusive to a lot of his patients, Mrs. Duggan, but you're the only one we have on tape threatening to kill him the day he died.

Bishop stares across the pool at the defunct stegosaurus as Amber forces another handful of marshmallows into her mouth.

> BISHOP: (Cont.) Incidentally, is this creature supposed to look as dead as it looks right now?

> AMBER: It's a stegosaurus. It got too fat. As part of my therapy, Dr. Thorpe told me to deflate my toy stegosaurus as I lost weight and to reinflate it as I gained weight. This one was here the night of

117

a Twinkie binge. But I guess I shouldn't
be telling you this.

BISHOP: It doesn't look good, Mrs. Duggan. And
I'm sorry to do this, but it's extremely
difficult to conduct this interview
while you're fooling around with these
guys . . .

*He yanks one package of marshmallows off the table, then when Amber
makes a move for the second bag, grabs it and tosses it into the pool. Amber
leaps from her chair and plunges into the pool in fast pursuit, splashing
water all over the police officer. Bishops looks on in disbelief.*

BISHOP: Jesus.

*Amber, now half submerged in the pool, opens the second bag of marsh-
mallows and resumes the conversation.*

AMBER: Lieutenant, every single person who
consulted with Peter Thorpe hated his
guts. He was an unbelievably cruel
human being without an ounce of
human decency. Any one of us could
have killed him, not just me.

BISHOP: But you don't have an alibi. And their
fingerprints aren't on the sixteen Devil
Dog wrappers we found up at White
Castle. And none of them are on
videotape threatening to kill him the
day he died.

AMBER: Let me ask you a question, Lieutenant
Bishop. If I'm the one who murdered
Peter Thorpe, how did I sneak up on
him at the castle? How did I even get
up the stairs? You think I had a
helicopter airlift me there? I know what

I am. I'm a pig. I'm a wild beast. So how did I haul all this blubber up those stairs?

BISHOP: There's an elevator to the next-to-last floor, Mrs. Duggan. You could have negotiated that last flight of steps, even in your . . . condition. The observatory up there is a high platform that sits back from the parapet—one good bump from that gut of yours and he'd go right over the side. You could have done it, Mrs. Duggan. You are not a defenseless woman.

Amber feasts on a huge handful of marshmallows.

AMBER: Could you prove that in court?

BISHOP: Juries hate fat people, Mrs. Duggan. Thin people like the Menendez boys and John De Lorean will occasionally walk, but generally speaking, fat people get the gas. If Rush Limbaugh ever killed his wife, they'd fry his fat butt.

AMBER: Am I under arrest, Lieutenant?

BISHOP: No, because we don't have a cell big enough to hold you in. We're still investigating this case, Mrs. Duggan. But don't go anywhere.

Ext.—Outside Amber Duggan's House—Late Afternoon.

Bishop is joined at his car by Stoddard.

STODDARD: Listen, Turk, we bringing her in?

BISHOP: Where would we put her? The jail's burned down and the next town with a cell big enough to hold her is forty-five miles down the road in New Jaundice. The strain of the ride might kill her.

STODDARD: I don't get it, Turk. We got the tape and the Devil Dogs. She wasn't with anybody that night but her cat. Why don't we just lock her in a grain silo or something till the state troopers come?

BISHOP: You ever see a picture of Attila the Hun?

STODDARD: I can't say that I have.

BISHOP: The amazing thing is that in all the pictures of Attila the Hun, he always looks exactly like Attila the Hun.

STODDARD: I don't get your drift.

BISHOP: You ever put anyone on Death Row?

STODDARD: No.

BISHOP: I've put thirteen people on Death Row, and every time I knew I had the right person. They were always from Central Casting: missing teeth, missing ears, fangs, tattoos. This one doesn't feel right. This is the perfect murder. But that lady doesn't look like the perfect murderer.

STODDARD: What's she look like?

BISHOP: She looks like a person with a very serious weight problem.

Int.—Sister W.'s Cell—Late Evening

Sister W. is working away on her laptop with her back to Bishop. She turns and looks up, startled.

BISHOP: Thought it might be the Virgin?

SISTER W.:   We know not the day nor the hour.

BISHOP: Nor the ZIP Code. What's up with the computer?

SISTER W.:   I'm logged onto VISION QUEST. It's a bulletin board for people who claim they've had extraterrestrial visitations on their computers. Unfortunately, most of them claim to have been visited by Satan.

BISHOP: I guess that's not much help to you.

SISTER W.:   You'd be surprised. Apparently, quite a few people have had the same problem as me. One man in Decatur, Illinois, said he was visited by both St. George *and* the dragon. But when he reopened the file the next morning, only the dragon's tail was still left.

BISHOP: You don't say.

SISTER W.:   He thinks that extraterrestrial visitors use up a lot more RAM than ordinary files. That would explain why I lost the Virgin. Maybe the Virgin disappeared off the screen because my laptop doesn't have enough memory.

BISHOP: It's a real drag to think that the only verifiable apparition of the Blessed Virgin Mary in this century got screwed up because of a computer glitch. Don't you think the Virgin would know that? Wouldn't somebody up there warn Her about appearing to somebody on a laptop?

SISTER W.: This is one area where IBM is right: Personal computers will never completely replace Big Iron.

BISHOP: Big Iron?

SISTER W.: Mainframes. If the Virgin had appeared to me on a mainframe, or even a midi, the whole world would know about it now.

BISHOP: What did She say to you that day?

SISTER W.: Pray for the starving children of Armenia.

BISHOP: Sounds a bit Eisenhower era–ish. Nothing about Rwanda? Somalia? Ethiopia? Newark?

Sister W. shakes her head.

SISTER W.: She said: "Pray for the starving children of Armenia." She must have said it a dozen times.

Sister W. now looks very downcast.

SISTER W.: Turk. I think this could have been a rogue apparition.

BISHOP: You lost me.

SISTER W.: There's a lot of mental illness in Heaven. A lot of martyrs went bonkers while they were being tortured. So the creature that appeared to me on my screen may have been a saint who thought she was the Blessed Virgin Mary, who got dressed up just like the Virgin Mary, but who was really just a loony. Now that I think of it, her appearance was a little weird.

BISHOP: Why's that?

SISTER W.:   She had lots of freckles. Lots. That doesn't jibe with what we know about Her from the Bible.

BISHOP: The Bible doesn't mention freckles?

SISTER W.:   It doesn't. Of course, three of the evangelists missed that stuff about the man getting his ear cut off on the Mount of Olives. I guess if they could miss that, they could have missed the freckles.

BISHOP: Actually, it seems like the sort of thing that would be kind of hard to miss.

SISTER W.:   The freckles?

BISHOP: The ear.

SISTER W.:   You're telling me. Another thing that really worries me: There's no record of Jesus having freckles on the Shroud of Turin. Now, you'd have to figure that if Mary had freckles, and she was Christ's only human relation, Jesus would have freckles, too. But from what we know about the Shroud of Turin, Jesus didn't have any freckles.

BISHOP: Have you told any of this to your superiors?

SISTER W.:   Turk, they already think I'm fried. They'll farm me out to the Cistercians for good if I start in with this freckle business. I'm going to let it go.

BISHOP: It's incredible, though, these bulletin boards. I never knew they were so specialized.

SISTER W.:	There are bulletin boards for everything. You'd be amazed.

Bishop grows very pensive. He strokes the right side of his face nervously.

BISHOP:	Is there a bulletin board for handwriting experts?
SISTER W.:	I assume. Probably several.
BISHOP:	Is there a bulletin board for experts in handwriting done in blood?
SISTER W.:	There you might be pushing it. I could check for you, though. But why don't you just check it down at the station house?
BISHOP:	The station house burned down the same night Dr. Thorpe was murdered. The computers are all gone. Anyway, you know what it's like in No Quarter. They're all idiots up here.
SISTER W.:	If the Lord loveth not the idiot, why did He make so many of them?
BISHOP:	You got me there, Sister. But if you could check out this handwriting thing for me, I'd be grateful.
SISTER W.:	Anything for an old Ozzie Osbourne fan.

Ext.—The Thorpe Home—Early Afternoon.

Bishop walks up the front path to the huge house. From inside can be heard the sound of raucous music, laughter, joyous celebration. Bishop tiptoes into the house, inches his way along the corridor, and looks inside to see:

Int.—Thorpe House—Early Afternoon.

More than a dozen children are cavorting merrily in the living room, whopping it up to the ebullient sounds of a Zydeco record, having a grand old time. In their midst, Bishop spies Courtney and Butch, who seem to be having the best time of all. Bishop knocks on the wall and is greeted by Courtney, dressed as a rabbit. As soon as she recognizes him, Courtney, now joined by her brother, Butch, dressed as an Arab sheik, turns very somber.

COURTNEY: You rang?

BISHOP: I need to ask your mother a few questions.

COURTNEY: She's in Monte Carlo. Can I help you?

BISHOP: You guys seem to be bearing up pretty well under the strain of all this.

COURTNEY: I'm sure we're both probably suffering from a form of posttraumatic stress. You know, happy on the outside, but inconsolable on the inside.

BISHOP: That go for you, too, Butch?

BUTCH: Our father was the flower of Christian manhood.

BISHOP: So I keep hearing. How about this uncle of yours?

Courtney and Butch exchange nervous glances.

COURTNEY: Our uncle Paulie is kind of downscale. We never had much to do with him. Mom doesn't think the classes should mix.

BISHOP: What did your dad think of his brother?

COURTNEY: He didn't talk about him much. He said he was kind of whifty.

BISHOP: Kind of whifty?

COURTNEY: Whifty. Like . . . out there. He was at Woodstock and stuff. He did drugs.

BUTCH: He liked Frank Zapata.

COURTNEY:	Zappa. Frank Zappa.
BISHOP:	Did you *ever* see him?
COURTNEY:	Zappa?
BISHOP:	Not Zappa, your uncle.
COURTNEY:	Once in a while at a baseball game.
BISHOP:	The Cubbies?
BUTCH:	The Sox. Uncle Paulie hated the Cubs. He said they were for Yippies.
COURTNEY:	Yuppies. He called them Yuppy Puppies. He'd never go to Wrigley. Never.
BISHOP:	Did you like seeing the White Sox?
COURTNEY:	No way. They had that crummy stadium on the South Side. It was barf-er-if-ic.
BUTCH:	It was scary. There were too many ethics.
COURTNEY:	Ethnics. Mommy didn't want us going down there. She doesn't like ethnics. She's a WASP, you know.
BISHOP:	And that was the only time you ever saw your uncle?
COURTNEY:	He'd call every once in a while with tickets to the White Sox. If Dad was around, he'd take us. But if Mom was around, she wouldn't let us go. I think Uncle Paulie had season tickets.
BUTCH:	He had a twenty-game plan.
COURTNEY:	But he got the cruddy games—the Mariners, the Rangers. He never had tickets to the Blue Jays or the Yankees. Who needs the Texas Rangers?

BUTCH: Who needs the Seattle Mariners?

BISHOP: And, aside from those few occasions, your dad never went to games with his brother?

COURTNEY: Dad thought the White Sox sucked.

BISHOP: The White Sox won their division last year.

COURTNEY: Dad didn't care. He said they had no tradition. They tanked the 1919 World Series. Dad said you couldn't learn anything about life from the White Sox. He said being a Cubs fan built character.

BISHOP: So you guys are Cubs fans?

Courtney and Butch exchange their trademark conspiratorial glances once again.

BUTCH: Dad was the flower of Christian manhood, but he had weird ideas.

COURTNEY: I like the Braves.

BUTCH: I like the Blue Jays. They stomped the Phillies. That guy Kruk is a pig.

COURTNEY: Big-time white trash.

BISHOP: Tell your Mom to call me when she gets back from Monte Carlo.

Int., Bishop's Apartment—Night.

Bishop is at home in his dowdy apartment, drinking a beer, studying the videotape of Amber Duggan's last visit to Peter Thorpe's office. The sound is turned up loud so that even a person in another room could hear.

THORPE: Now, would you like a Twinkie?

AMBER: You're disgusting.

THORPE: I haven't bitten into it yet.

127

AMBER: I think we better call it a day. You know, I come here every week, trying to grow as a person, and all I get is abuse.

THORPE: If you grew any more as a person, you couldn't fit through that door.

AMBER: You deserve to die a slow, painful death.

THORPE: Yeah, don't we all?

Bishop continues to stare blankly at the screen.

Int.—Bellas' Diner—Morning

We see Paul Thorpe removing his yellow dish-drying gloves. The camera zooms in on his hands, which do not look especially working class. He is singing "Keep Your Sunny Side Up."

BISHOP: How long you been in this line of work, Mr. Thorpe?

THORPE: A few years. But I've done other things. Carpentry . . . woodworking . . .

BISHOP: You guys who were at Woodstock were all really into that carpentry thing, weren't you? By the time we got to Woodstock, we were half a million strong. And every last one of us was a fucking woodworker.

THORPE: I like to work with my hands.

BISHOP: So did Jack the Ripper.

THORPE: Are we having a problem here?

BISHOP: Those don't look like dish-dryer's hands, Mr. Thorpe. And those don't look like woodworker's hands.

THORPE: What kind of hands do they look like?

BISHOP: Psychiatrist's.

THORPE: You have interesting theories, Lieutenant Bishop. You have an active and an inquisitive mind. Are those prerequisites for a job with the N.Q.P.D.?

BISHOP: That's a very snide comment, Mr. Thorpe. That's not the kind of comment I'd expect to come from you. It's the sort of thing that I'd expect to hear from your brother. And there's an interesting thing: Can you tell me how many hundredths of a point Dick Allen missed winning the Triple Crown by in 1973?

THORPE: You got me.

BISHOP: Eight hundredths of a point. He led the league in RBIs, he led the league in home runs, but on the last day of the season, he lost the batting title by eight hundredths of a point.

THORPE: That's the trouble with you jocks. You're all hung up on stats. Why can't you just appreciate the beauty of the game?

BISHOP: There's nothing beautiful about losing the Triple Crown on the last day of the season because you came in eight hundredths of a fucking point behind somebody else.

THORPE: I'm still not following you.

BISHOP: I don't think you're such a big White Sox fan. I think that's the sort of thing your brother would have known.

THORPE: My brother is dead.

BISHOP: One of you is dead.

THORPE: Meaning?

BISHOP: Peter Thorpe had a life he couldn't handle anymore. He had an iceberg wife, a pair of jerked-off kids, and forty-five patients who all deserve to be shot. On the other hand, he had this New Age, hippy-dippy dish-dryer brother spouting happy-face tripe because he took too much blue acid at Woodstock. Or maybe it was Altamont. So, maybe he decided to kill his brother, substitute the body, and take his life.

THORPE: Unconventional career move, wouldn't you say, Lieutenant? He'd rather be a five-dollar-an-hour dish-dryer than a psychiatrist with a thriving practice, a $1.2 million mansion, a lovely wife and kids?

BISHOP: You ever met his patients?

Bishop and Thorpe exchange serious glances for a long, long time. Then Thorpe puts his gloves back on and gets ready to leave.

THORPE: I'm just happy to be here, Lieutenant. This is the first day in the rest of my life.

As Thorpe leaves the room, Bishop meticulously examines a mountain of pots and pans that sit on the table, largely obscuring the view of the dish-drying area. Miguel Feneiro, nervously carrying a large stack of plates, enters from the left, trying not to make eye contact with the police officer. As he tries to leave, Bishop obstructs his path.

BISHOP:	Excuse me there, Miguel.
MIGUEL:	*Sí, señor,* I am legal.
BISHOP:	Yeah, we've established that already. I'd like to ask you a few questions.
MIGUEL:	*Sí.*
BISHOP:	This is, in fact, the dish-drying area, correct?
MIGUEL:	*Sí.*
BISHOP:	This is the area where Paul Thorpe works?
MIGUEL:	*Sí.*
BISHOP:	On the night that Peter Thorpe was murdered, Paul Thorpe was here for the entire evening except for one hour?
MIGUEL:	*Sí,* one hour for the din-din.
BISHOP:	When he came back from the din-din, as you so colorfully put it, did you see him return?
MIGUEL:	No, no, I didn't see him return, because the dishes were very high. The dishes were very high because we had lots of moussaka. Lots of moussaka.
BISHOP:	How high were the dishes, Miguel?
MIGUEL:	The dishes . . . they were very high.
BISHOP:	How high were the dishes, Miguel?
MIGUEL:	They were . . . they were . . . as high as the hills of my rolling country.
BISHOP:	Miguel, you're going to have to be a little more specific. If I may be so bold?

Bishop takes Miguel's left hand and lifts it into the air until it is even with his chest.

BISHOP: (Cont.) Were the dishes this high?

MIGUEL: Oh, no.

Bishop the dishwasher's lifts the hand a foot higher, almost to shoulder level.

BISHOP: Were the dishes this high?

MIGUEL: No.

BISHOP lifts MIGUEL's hand so high that it is even with the brim of his sombrero.

BISHOP: Were the dishes this high?

MIGUEL: Oh, yes, very high. About as high as the hills of my rolling country.

Bishop lets go of Miguel's hand.

BISHOP: Thank you. In other words, it's possible that Paul Thorpe could have left a tape recording of himself drying the dishes behind this mountain of pots and pans, and been invisible, disappeared for two hours, driven down the highway, murdered his brother, and come back here without you noticing it?

Now Miguel looks unbelievably frightened.

MIGUEL: *Sí*, I am legal.

BISHOP: Thanks, Miguel.

Int.—Sister W.'s Cell—Night.

SISTER W.: I've got something for you, Turk.

BISHOP: Shoot.

SISTER W.: There's an on-line bulletin board called the International Association of Coagulative Calligraphers. They're experts in handwriting done in blood.

BISHOP: Are they based in L.A.?

SISTER W.:   Santa Monica. I've networked with them this morning and they say that the word "twelve" is extremely hard to write when you're only seconds away from death.

BISHOP: Why's that?

SISTER W.:   Forming the letter "w" in blood is hard enough under normal circumstances, but when you've just fallen 150 feet and every bone in your body is broken, it'd be tough. Also "doce" has fewer letters than the word "twelve."

BISHOP: Why wouldn't he just write the number "12," then?

SISTER W.:   The murderer probably came down from the castle walls to make sure he was dead. By the time he—or she—got there, Thorpe would have been dead. If the killer saw the number "12" he—or she—would have known it was a clue and might have erased it.

BISHOP: Meaning that the killer couldn't read Spanish.

SISTER W.:   Or, at least, that the killer couldn't read Spanish in blood. Which is a whole different thing. Turk, did the fat lady know Spanish?

BISHOP: She did. But there's sixteen Devil Dog wrappers with her fingerprints all over them up on the castle ramparts, so it might not even be relevant.

SISTER W.:   This is a very difficult case, isn't it?

BISHOP: It's the worst case I've ever been involved in. Every suspect had a motive to kill this guy. Every person he ever came into contact with had a reason to kill him.

SISTER W.: But you kind of like him. I mean, retroactively. If he were alive today, you'd be friends with him, wouldn't you?

BISHOP: Let's just say he hates the same people I hate.

SISTER W.: *Hates?*

BISHOP: Hated. Hates. Whatever. Our values are similar. He despised whining assholes. So do I. Pardon my French.

SISTER W.: Turk, anger makes a stone of the heart.

BISHOP: I read that somewhere. But I can understand what might be going on here. I can see where Thorpe could get to a point where he might consider a desperate act. I've been in that boat.

SISTER W.: You think this is a suicide made up to look like a murder? To get back at one of his patients?

BISHOP: That's one possibility. He could have framed Mrs. Duggan to get back at all these mopey porkaholics. Or he might have hoped we'd book the forty-four other patients on a conspiracy rap.

SISTER W.: Turk, how did you ever get so bitter?

BISHOP: I lost the only thing that ever mattered to me. Though living in Los Angeles for eight years was certainly a contributing factor.

SISTER W.:   The world can be a horrible place.

BISHOP: Especially rural Wisconsin.

SISTER W.:   Turk, let me tell you about a dream I
had. Because I understand the way you
feel. And I understand your rage. Listen
to this, though. In the dream, there was
our world. And the world was dark
because there weren't any squirrels.
And the squirrels represented love. And
so along this time there was just this
darkness, and all of a sudden thousands
of squirrels were set free and they
scurried down and brought this
blinding light of love. And it seemed
like that love would be the only thing
that would make any difference. And it
did. So I guess it means there is trouble
in the world till the squirrels come.

Bishop studies her intently.

BISHOP: Thanks for being there, Veronica.

Int.—Bishop's Apartment—Night.

*Once again, Bishop is seen playing the Thorpe-Duggan videotape back and
forth. He plays the tape, listens carefully, then rewinds, and plays it again.*

AMBER: Has anyone ever told you that you're a
heartless human being?

THORPE: *Heartless* is a judgmental term.

AMBER: This makes no sense. I come here every
week to work through my food
disorders, and you sit there mocking
me.

BISHOP fast-forwards to another part of the tape.

AMBER:	You know, I come here every week trying to grow as a person, and all I get is abuse.
THORPE:	If you grew any more as a person, you couldn't fit through that door.
AMBER:	You deserve to die a slow, painful death.
THORPE:	Yeah, don't we all?

Suddenly, something clicks. Bishop recues the tape and plays the last sequence again.

AMBER:	You know, I come here every week trying to grow as a person, and all I get is abuse.
THORPE:	If you grew any more as a person, you couldn't fit through that door.
AMBER DUGGAN:	You deserve to die a slow, painful death.
THORPE:	Yeah, don't we all?

Bishop turns off the VCR and dials Stoddard.

BISHOP:	It's me. Did you ever measure the doors at White Castle?
STODDARD:	I didn't measure them personally. But somebody did.
BISHOP:	Did you take Amber Duggan's measurements?
STODDARD:	Whew, gross.
BISHOP:	Look, get Duggan's file and meet me at White Castle, top floor, in two hours.
STODDARD:	Can I ask what this is all about?
BISHOP:	Just meet me at White Castle, top floor, in two hours.

Int.—White Castle—Night.

Bishop is seen with a yardstick, measuring the width of the door leading to the ramparts of White Castle. He is accompanied by Stoddard.

BISHOP: This door is twenty-four inches narrower than any other door in this castle.

STODDARD: So what's your point, Turk?

BISHOP: This door is part of a Scottish castle built in the thirteenth century and transported to Wisconsin in the late nineteenth century by a prosperous cheese tycoon named Angus McDougal.

STODDARD: So what's the point?

BISHOP: In the thirteenth century, gluttony was still a sin.

STODDARD: So what's the point, Turk?

BISHOP: What kind of person would walk through a door this narrow leading to the ramparts of a thirteenth-century Scottish castle?

STODDARD: You got me.

BISHOP: An archer. Have you ever heard of a fat archer?

STODDARD: So what's the point?

BISHOP: Amber Duggan couldn't have fit through this door.

STODDARD: You're a fucking whiz, Turk. Eight years on the L.A.P.D.; it was worth it, huh?

BISHOP: As soon as this is over, you and me are going outside.

Int.—White Castle—Midmorning.

We see Amber Duggan standing a few feet from the archway of the tiny door leading to the ramparts of White Castle. She looks even fatter than the last time she was seen.

AMBER: If I can't fit through this door, it means I'm home free?

BISHOP: Something like that. You could have still hired someone to push Thorpe, but then why would you have left the sixteen Devil Dog wrappers with your fingerprints all over them? No, I'm going to give you the benefit of the doubt and assume that you're not a complete idiot. If you can't fit through this door, we can close the books on this case.

AMBER: I'm a lunatic for doing this. If my lawyer finds out . . .

BISHOP: Save yourself a fortune in legal fees, Mrs. Duggan, and walk up to that door.

He taps her gaping stomach with the yardstick.

BISHOP: (Cont.) Even from here, I can see that the good money's on you.

Amber frowns at this left-handed compliment. She takes a huge breath, puffs out her gargantuan form, and approaches the door.

BISHOP: No cheating, Mrs. Duggan.

Amber stares at him coldly, then sucks in her jowls in an attempt to make herself thinner. This is not a pretty sight. She hesitates. She doesn't really want to move.

STODDARD: Take that long walk to freedom, Mrs. Duggan.

Amber takes a last breath and approaches the door. As soon as her massive body is framed in the doorway, it becomes obvious that she cannot fit through it. *Not even close. She tries again. Same result. Beaming, she tries to give Stoddard a high-five. He does not reciprocate. She turns her head to sneer at a very disappointed Turk Bishop.*

AMBER: Satisfied?

BISHOP: Look, Mrs. Duggan, I want this to be over just as much as you do. But I'm going to have to ask you to do one more thing for me. Please turn sideways.

Amber does as she is told. The same result. No matter how her body is contorted, it could not possibly fit through the tiny aperture. Bishop shakes his head.

BISHOP: (Cont.) Okay, back the way you were.

Bishop now stretches a yardstick across Amber's massive shoulders.

BISHOP: Hey, Tommy, think we should try it with a crowbar?

Amber now wheels around to face Bishop, anger radiating from every fiber of her being.

AMBER: Is this really necessary, Lieutenant? Can't we put an end to this hideous charade?

Stoddard looks directly at his partner.

STODDARD: Turk, that's no thirteenth-century Scottish archer.

Ext.—The Town Reservoir—Afternoon.

Bishop and Sister W. are seen strolling at the side of the town reservoir.

SISTER W.: So, was the fat lady grateful when you told her she was in the clear?

BISHOP: Not particularly.

SISTER W.:	I guess you don't get much gratitude in your line of work, do you?
BISHOP:	Not a whole lot.
SISTER W.:	So where does it stand?
BISHOP:	It's still possible that one of his other patients did it. It's still possible that all of his patients were in on it.
SISTER W.:	But you don't really believe that, do you?

Bishop breathes heavily and sighs.

BISHOP:	No. I think that he murdered his brother, and I think that he switched places with him.
SISTER W.:	But why?
BISHOP:	Because he couldn't stand dealing with assholes any more.
SISTER W.:	Isn't that kind of a desperate act?
BISHOP:	He was a desperate man. Everybody in his life was the scum of the earth. Including his wife and kids. So I think he sees his brother, this New Age dish-dryer up there in Dutchman's Prairie, happy as a clam, and he figures he'll take his shot. Maybe, after all these years, he figured that his mother was right. He saw an opportunity to start a new life and he took it.
SISTER W.:	You sound almost sympathetic.
BISHOP:	I know where he's coming from.
SISTER W.:	But he killed his brother, Turk.
BISHOP:	There is *that*.

SISTER W.: You can't condone murder, Turk. You're sworn to uphold the law.

BISHOP: I don't condone murder. I accept it.

SISTER W.: Does that mean you're just going to let him get off?

BISHOP: I don't have much choice. These guys were always switching fingerprints when they were kids, so we're not going to nail him on that. The case against him is entirely circumstantial.

SISTER W.: But you know he did it.

BISHOP: Yeah, I know he did it. And I wish to hell he knew more about Chicago White Sox history so I could just walk away from this thing. If there was any justice in this world, Amber Duggan would have been able to squeeze through that door and we could just pin the whole thing on her. Or we could send up one of the cokeheads. Or the guy who gave Georgetown and the points.

SISTER W.: Can I tell you something, Turk?

BISHOP: Shoot.

SISTER W.: Turk, there's a big difference between an asshole—to use your term—

She blesses herself as she says this.

SISTER W.: (Cont.)—and a murderer. Amber Duggan is an asshole. Even the Lord will give you that. Joey Bellini is an asshole. Sherman Krebs is an asshole. They're all assholes in that twelve-step program.

BISHOP:	So what's your point?
SISTER W.:	They're assholes, Turk. But they're not murderers.

Bishop is now gazing longingly across the lake.

BISHOP:	I still don't have a case against this guy.
SISTER W.:	But if you let him walk, let it be because you don't have a case against him. Don't hold back, Turk.
BISHOP:	Look, this guy has committed the perfect crime.
SISTER W.:	You keep saying "this guy." But you mean *Peter* Thorpe. And Peter Thorpe is dead. He doesn't exist anymore. He's been replaced by some wacked-out dish-dryer who did too much blue acid at Woodstock.
BISHOP:	Yeah, I hate people like that.
SISTER W.:	So if you let him walk, don't think you're doing yourself any favors.
BISHOP:	Are you trying to tell me something here?
SISTER W.:	He's an asshole, Turk. He's just a different kind of an asshole.

Int.—A Urinal—Late Afternoon.

Stoddard and Bishop are seen taking a piss in the men's room of a diner.

STODDARD:	We followed our pal Thorpe every day this week. He made every White Sox game. Drove all the way to Chicago—290 miles round-trip.
BISHOP:	Imagine how much this guy must have hated his patients if he was willing to

give up season tickets to the Cubbies and go see the fucking White Sox every day.

STODDARD: They're gonna win the fucking pennant this year.

BISHOP: They're still the fucking White Sox. No class. No tradition. Remember, they tanked the World Series in 1919.

STODDARD: You're never going to be able to use this stuff in court, Tommy. So what do we pin on him?

BISHOP: This guy don't know shit about the White Sox. He couldn't even tell me how much Dick Allen missed winning the Triple Crown by in '73.

STODDARD: Neither can I.

BISHOP: The guy's a fake.

STODDARD: You think he'll bolt?

BISHOP: I don't know. I've never dealt with a guy like this before. Most murderers are morons.

Ext.—An Open Field—Twilight.

We see Paul Thorpe playing with a Frisbee.

BISHOP: The sound of one Frisbee clapping, huh, Thorpo?

THORPE: Different strokes for different folks.

BISHOP: Hey, listen, I want to talk to you about something.

THORPE: You got a warrant?

BISHOP: Warrant, schmarrant. You Deadhead fans aren't into that kind of stuff. Hey, I've been meaning to ask you: Is there a

trade magazine for people in your line
of work? You know—*Dish-drying
World? Modern Middle-Management
Plate Cleaner*—something like that?

Thorpe flashes his headbeam smile.

THORPE: I am what I am, and that's all that I am.
I'm just happy to be here.

BISHOP: I hear you. Shit, I shouldn't be ragging
on you like this. I let my work get to
me. I get very abusive. I have a lot of
serious issues to work through.

THORPE: Shame my brother's not here to help
you.

BISHOP: Damn shame. Now look, I've got a
couple of tickets to Comiskey tonight;
how about you and me shoot down
there and see the White Sox. Maybe
we'll see Bo rip a couple.

Thorpe eyes him cautiously, then nods his head.

THORPE: Sounds groovy. Bo knows baseball.

BISHOP: Bo does know baseball. But you know,
Bo got cut by the White Sox last year.
He's been playing for the Angels the
entire season, Pauly. Or is it Peter?

*Before Thorpe has a chance to react, Bishop headbutts him and covers his
face with a chloroformed handkerchief, then drags him off and stuffs him
in the trunk of his car.*

BISHOP: This is unconventional police
procedure, but, man, you put that fat
girl through hell.

Int.—The Anteroom at White Castle—Late at Night.

We see Thorpe, hands bound behind him, seated in a wooden chair. His chest is secured by thick ropes, pinioning him to the chair. He has a slight cut above the eyes where the headbutt occurred. As he comes to, we see:

Bishop, taking off his jacket and slicking back his hair. In his left hand is a thick roll of duct tape.

BISHOP: I ain't gonna bullshit you, pal, this ain't gonna be very pleasant. You can shout, you can scream; you can plead; you can beg; you can whine; you can do whatever you want—nobody's gonna hear you. Besides, I've heard it all before anyway.

THORPE: You can torture me all you want, man, but I'm not going to tell you what you want to hear.

BISHOP: Torture is a very good word.

Bishop goes behind Thorpe and in one rapid gesture covers his mouth with duct tape. Thorpe attempts to resist, but his struggling is futile. Once Thorpe has been gagged, Bishop walks across to a table where an old yellow radio sits amid a bunch of junk. Turning to his captive, he says:

BISHOP: (Cont.) You ever listen to KLB-70, the Sounds of the 1870s? It's my personal favorite.

He turns on the radio, and a raggedy version of an "Oh, Susanna" can be heard crackling through the speakers. Bishop now places his left foot on a chair, lifts his trouser cuff, and produces a straight razor.

BISHOP: You a movie buff?

Thorpe shrugs.

BISHOP: (Cont.) I just want to make sure you know where we're headed with this thing.

Bishop now begins a rather clumsy dance, which goes on for about forty seconds. The dance is completely inexplicable and preposterous: a series of jetés, pas de deux, and even a bit of the old soft-shoe. Then he strides directly over to the chair where Thorpe is seated, straddles the captive, and brings the blade down right next to his right ear. As he does, he tears off the duct tape.

BISHOP: (Cont.) Mr. Thorpe, is there anything at all that you would like to tell me?

Thorpe gasps for a second, looking up into Bishop's demonic face. He is terrified. It looks like curtains. But he does not crack. Instead, he speaks, purposefully, meticulously, choosing his words carefully.

THORPE: I'm just happy to be here.

Bishop stares at him, then draws away. He tosses the razor blade over his shoulder. Then he unties his captive.

BISHOP: You're a tough nut to crack, Mr. Thorpe.

THORPE: So are you, Lieutenant.

BISHOP: Look, Thorpe, I know why you did it. If it wasn't for your brother, I might let you walk on this thing.

THORPE: I don't know what you're talking about.

BISHOP: Jesus, Chief, this is where your brother bought the farm. Your own flesh and blood. I mean, right upstairs. You don't even want to check out the spot where your brother spent his last few seconds on earth? For old-time's sake?

THORPE: You want me to walk up there so you can hang me by my toenails till I confess? Is that how you guys do it out in L.A.?

Flashback: Ext.—A Dark Alley—Night.

146

We see a mariachi musician dressed in a sombrero and serape leaning against a wall, playing a doleful song. At his feet is a hat with a sign reading: WON'T YOU PLEASE HELP A RECOVERING PEYOTE ADDICT? *Suddenly Thorpe leaps out of his car, kickboxes the musician into a coma, and smashes his guitar to pieces.*

Int.—The Anteroom at White Castle—Night

BISHOP: I just want you to see what he could see when he was on his way down. Then I'm through with you.

THORPE: Is that a promise?

BISHOP: Scout's honor.

THORPE: Whatever makes you happy makes me happy.

Thorpe rises from the chair, tears off the ropes, and follows Bishop up the stairs to the castle ramparts.

Ext.—Castle Ramparts—Night.

It is a dark night, and there is very little light on the ramparts. Thorpe and Bishop stand facing each other on the parapet where Thorpe's brother was murdered a few days earlier.

THORPE: You still haven't explained to me how I could have lured my brother down here, conned him into wearing my clothes, killed him, scrawled that message, and then driven seventy-five miles to Dutchman's Prairie all in one hour.

BISHOP: Your brother was already here. You'd invited him down for a little get-together. Maybe it was a Judy Collins concert or a Greenpeace fund-raiser where they like you to dress kind of formal. So you gave him some of your fancy duds.

THORPE:	He would have had to call in sick.
BISHOP:	He was a pussy. He was afraid of losing his job. He never would have made that call. So you said you'd make it for him. But you never did. You just showed up at his job that night.
THORPE:	But Miguel says he saw me there all evening, except for one hour.
BISHOP:	Miguel says he *heard* you there. What he actually heard was a tape recording of a man drying dishes for two hours behind a neatly stacked pile of pots and pans that he described, in his colorful language, as being as high as the hills of his rolling country. Miguel is an idiot.
THORPE:	Suppose the chef or one of the waitresses came in? Don't you think they would have noticed if I was missing?
BISHOP:	They would have thought you were in the shithouse for one very long dump. Besides, that was a risk you were willing to take.
THORPE:	It's an interesting theory. But I don't think it'll hold up in court.
BISHOP:	You got me there.

Suddenly a shadowy figure appears. The figure is cloaked and hooded, like the Grim Reaper.

GRIM REAPER:	We know not the day nor the hour.

Bishop seems startled, but Thorpe remains cool as a cucumber. The shadow is Sister W.

THORPE:	Friend of yours? Pulling out all the stops, huh, Lieutenant?

BISHOP: Can't blame a guy for trying.

THORPE: Yeah, well I think I'll be going now.

Thorpe descends from the ramparts and walks toward the exit, then freezes. From below can be heard the sound of voices, mounting the staircase from within. Thorpe is completely still, then slowly begins backing up. We see a wraithlike figure appear in the doorway, arms outstretched, inching forward, zombielike. It is Joey Bellini.

BELLINI: I'm not a bad person getting worse. I'm a sick person getting better.

As he moves ineluctably toward Thorpe, another figure appears in the doorway. It is Sherman Krebs.

KREBS: Today is the first day of the rest of your life.

Thorpe now edges backward as another figure appears. And another. Thorpe now begins to back up the steps to the ramparts, as two dozen zombielike figures close in on him.

DYSFUNCTIONAL
PERSON NO. 1:   I'm willing to see the glass as half full, rather than half empty.

DYSFUNCTIONAL
PERSON NO. 2:   Don't cower; empower.

DYSFUNCTIONAL
PERSON NO. 3:   Eating is defeating.

DYSFUNCTIONAL
PERSON NO. 4:   I abase myself before my weakness and accept that I am powerless to control it.

DYSFUNCTIONAL
PERSON NO. 5:   Acceptance fosters growth.

DYSFUNCTIONAL
PERSON NO. 6:   I don't have to be all better tomorrow.

DYSFUNCTIONAL
PERSON NO. 7:   I am powerless before my mint-flavored Higher Power.

DYSFUNCTIONAL PERSON NO. 8:	Don't enable your enabler.
DYSFUNCTIONAL PERSON NO. 9:	Eliminate car clutter.
BRITTANY THORPE:	Monte Carlo is divine at this time of year.

The figures, who now number two dozen, slowly begin to climb the stairs as Thorpe retreats to the very edge of the castle walls. When there is nowhere else to go, he turns to face Bishop.

BISHOP:	Writing that "Doce Pas" stuff in Spanish was a nice touch, Thorpe. You really had me going there for a while.

Thorpe gives him a long, hard stare.

THORPE:	You've got some serious issues to resolve, Lieutenant.

Thorpe now leaps from the ramparts, screaming. Sister W. lets out a strangled cry, then begins mumbling in Latin.

SISTER W.:	In nomine patris et filium et spiritu sanctus.

The rest of the group say nothing. They merely stare down into the courtyard at the broken body of Peter Thorpe. Bishop studies the body from afar, then lights a cigarette. He looks down at Thorpe's assembled patients without registering any expression whatsoever.

BISHOP:	Anybody else want to jump?

CUT TO BLACK.

THE END

five

I'll Play the Part, and I Won't Need Rehearsing

It is always a mistake to discuss a work-in-progress with fellow writers. They will invariably say something brutally condescending like, "It'll be funnier when you put the jokes in," or resort to the all-purpose put-down, "It's been done." Whatever words they use, the net effect will be to make you feel bad about your work. This is what other writers are here for—to inflict pain.

One day, a journalist friend called up and asked how the screenplay was going. I told her it was going fine. She asked how many pages I'd written that day. I said twelve. She asked what the pages were about. I told her they were about Amber Duggan, a calorically intolerant, spatially challenged woman who was the prime suspect in her shrink's brutal murder because the cops found sixteen Devil Dog wrappers with her fingerprints on them at the scene of the crime. My friend laughed—fairly hard, in fact. She asked me to read her some of Amber's lines. I refused. She insisted. I still refused. She started to get on my case. I still refused. Then she started wheedling. I have a low wheedling threshold, so I caved in and read her the opening exchange between Amber and Thorpe, where he informs her that she's nothing more than a self-indulgent pig. My friend laughed even harder. Then I said I had to get back to work.

Ten minutes later, the phone rang. It was my friend again.

"I don't want you to get upset with me, but there's something I have to tell you about your screenplay," she said. "Promise that you won't get mad."

"I can't make that promise," I said. "When people make you promise not to be mad, it's usually because they want to say something offensive, like 'Is that your *whole* penis?' "

"But I feel that I have to tell you this," she said.

"So tell me."

She hesitated. "I don't think you should include that scene about the fat woman in the film."

"She's one of the central characters in the story, and the screenplay's already half written," I replied. "But thanks for the suggestion."

"I still don't think you should include her. People will find it offensive. It'll make people think it's okay to make fun of fat people."

"It *is* okay to make fun of fat people."

She wasn't expecting that. So now she appealed to my sense of fair play. "These kinds of things contribute to large women's low self-esteem."

"Seven-thousand-dollar movies that make fun of fat people contribute to fat women's low self-esteem? Seven-thousand-dollar movies that no one is ever going to see contribute to fat people's low self-esteem? If seven-thousand-dollar movies that no one's ever going to see contribute to fat women's self-esteem, fat women have more problems than I thought."

"I just don't think you should ruin your screenplay by gratuitously including offensive material about fat people."

"It's not gratuitous. I really don't like fat people. They take up too much room on the subway."

"You're not serious about that."

"Okay, I'm not being serious. Some of my best friends are fat. But all of my fat friends are males, and none of them would agree to play the fat role in the movie, not even when I said we could describe them as *chronically large* instead of *fat*. The only reason Amber Duggan is a female is because I found a woman who was willing to play the part of an obscenely fat woman. It's nothing personal. There's no gender bias here."

"I still think it's offensive."

"Would it be less offensive if the character was a man?" I asked.

She thought about it for a moment. "Yes. But only slightly. No. No, it's just as bad either way."

"Thanks for your input," I said. "And now, good-bye."

AFTER THAT, I never talked about the screenplay with anyone. If people asked what the movie was about, I would explain the general premise of the movie, but I would never go into details. I maintained this policy all the way up until the filming of the movie. I deliberately kept the people who would be acting in the movie in the dark about where the screenplay was headed because I now had reason to believe that they, too, would find certain elements in the plot deeply offensive. When we shot the film, the only people appearing in the movie who had seen the complete screenplay were the man playing Tom Stoddard, Bishop's oafish sidekick, and the man playing the two Thorpes. Everybody else got their lines on a need-to-know basis only. They got their lines and that was it.

I started writing the screenplay to *Twelve Steps to Death* on July 10, 1994, and finished exactly three weeks later. Five minutes after I finished, I made a copy and sent it to Deborah Newmyer at Amblin. The previous month, she had sent me a short note asking where the script was. Gosh, I thought, maybe Spielberg really does need tight new scripts. I couldn't wait to hear her reaction. And his.

While writing the screenplay, I took pains to make sure that any scene could easily be shot in Tarrytown. Ironically, the local government had officially banned commercial filming without the village limits the day before Janet Maslin's article about the film ran in *The New York Times*, but there was no way that this stricture applied to me. My wife was active in the community. She did work with the elderly. She was involved with the PTA. 'Nuff said.

Whenever I would write a scene, I would check with neighbors or local businesses to make sure we could shoot in their houses, garages, back-yards, diners. That's why Thorpe's murder takes place in a castle, because some people we know in Tarrytown just happen to own a castle, a gor-geous folly built between 1897 and 1911 by some people who made their fortune in the macadam business. Hey, it's that kind of town. Writing the screenplay was the easiest work I ever did in my life, far easier than writ-ing magazine articles or book reviews because I never had to do any re-search and because screenplays are nothing but dialogue. Any idiot could write a screenplay. Idiots write them all the time.

In the sixteen months that I had been working on *Twelve Steps to Death,* I had been making mental notes of the people I wanted to be in the movie. All through the spring and early summer, as I learned how to direct and write a screenplay, I would jot down the names of neighbors who would fit various roles. The first person I decided to cast was Keith Jenkins, a very good friend who works as a physicist for a famous com-puter manufacturer. Keith is a quiet, retiring sort, and I thought he would be perfect for the part of Sherman Krebs, the chronic gambler. Early in June, before I'd even written the screenplay, I told him I'd like him to be in my movie. His initial reaction was surprise, followed by a twinge of ner-vousness. He reminded me that he didn't know how to act. I said I did-n't care; we'd use cue cards. I could see that he was amused by the idea of being in a film. Several years earlier, half in jest, Keith had suggested that a bunch of us launch a community theater in Tarrytown, where we would put on an annual murder mystery or something incredibly hokey like *The Bad Seed.* Either that or start a bridge club. I hadn't responded to Keith's overture at the time, not being particularly keen on theater in general. But now I reminded him of our conversation.

"You wanted to get involved in community theater," I said. "So now you can get involved in community film."

Keith still seemed sort of nervous about my proposal, but eventually he agreed. He asked when he could see the script. I told him he could see it when I'd written it. This was a bald-faced lie. Even though I hadn't yet written the screenplay, I already knew that it was going to be unbelievably offensive and politically incorrect. Keith, like all of my neighbors, had voted for Carter and Mondale and that Greek dwarf, so I knew that he would be somewhat put off by the tidal wave of abuse being directed at the recovery movement, which is basically a touchy-feely PBS/NPR/NEA/ACLU innovation. So I never, ever let him see the entire screenplay. I only let him see his lines. Mind you, his lines gave him a pretty good idea of how rude *Twelve Steps to Death* figured to be, but he never had a complete picture of how offensive it was until the night of its premiere in February 1995. By that point, he, like everybody else in the movie, was so excited about being a movie star that he didn't care about the film's content anymore.

After casting Keith, I next approached another good friend named Tom Staudter about playing the lead role of Turk Bishop. Although Tom is a writer and English teacher, and therefore works in a profession filled with sensitive, thoughtful, caring people, he is a burly man who has worked during his checkered career as a bouncer, a high school hall monitor, and a process server. Tom, one of my favorite people in the whole world, is not someone you can fuck with. He is, not to put too fine a point on it, one tough hombre. He would make a fine cop. Tom was thrilled when I asked him to be in the movie, and volunteered to play any part that was offered to him. So I penciled him in as the deranged cop.

Step by step, I lined up all the other cast members. Basically, my philosophy was this: Any neighbor who approached me about being in the movie got to be in the movie. By this point, *Twelve Steps to Death* had become a *cause célèbre* in Tarrytown, so lots and lots of people were interested in appearing in small roles or having me shoot at their homes, garages, castles. Quietly, without too much fuss, I cast them for their parts. Tom Masciovecchio, a computer systems director at a New York publishing company, and a serious, intense sort, would be perfect as the guy with the credit card addiction. His wife, Beth Ann Lacy, an outgoing person with a sunny disposition, would do fine as the woman suffering from Attention Deficit Disorder. Thom Wolke, a concert promoter with an office across the hall from mine in a Tarrytown professional building, seemed perfect for the part of a recovering child molester. A photographer friend named Margaret Fox sometimes had a spacy demeanor; I envisioned her as Gerry the Bulimic, while her husband, Tim Grajek, an illustrator, would do yeoman service as the man rambling on about his "mint-flavored Higher Power." Gene Rivieccio, a mountain of a man who works as the cook in my favorite restaurant, Bellas, could play a recovering mule humper, while his wife, Debbie, played a car-clutter addict.

The remaining dysfunctional roles were distributed to Keith Jenkins's wife, Christina Blatt, who would play a lush; Debbie Fernandes, a waitress at Bellas, who would play a happy-faced bozo; Kevin Mack, a GM line worker, who would play a man suffering from Chronic Lateness Syndrome; Ellen Klein, a local teacher, who would play yet another woman struggling with an addiction to car clutter. And my other accomodating neighbors, John Petry, Maureen Petry, Arthur Brady, and Dorothy Sweet. One final role went to Kate Chamberlain, the sister of my friend Rob Chamberlain, with whom I play basketball every weekend. Kate had once been an actress and her husband currently worked as Jean-Claude Van Damme's voice coach. But that wasn't why I put her in the movie. I put her in the movie because she was pretty. In a low-budget movie, you could use all the pretty women you could get.

In big-budget movies, casting decisions frequently depend on the availability of players, meaning that directors do not always end up with the stars they had originally envisioned for the parts. The exact same thing happened during the casting process of *Twelve Steps to Death*. I had originally planned to cast Drew Fixell, an economist who works for the state government, in the part of Joey Bellini, because he is the best-looking man in my circle of friends, but Drew and his family were going to be away on vacation in early August when we planned to shoot the film, so I had to find somebody else. That somebody else turned out to be Mike Berman, John's balloonologist friend, who had volunteered to work as a gofer on the film. Mike was younger than Drew and also good-looking, and he was very excited about being in the movie. So he got the part.

By the end of July, most of the smaller roles were cast. My daughter Bridget, who had once played the Dew Fairy in the seminal 1992 Winfield L. Morse production of *Hansel and Gretel,* was psyched about playing Peter Thorpe's vixenish daughter Courtney. Somewhat less enthusiastic, but unwilling to be cut out of any public relations stunt his sister was involved in, was my seven-year-old son Gordon, who would play the terminally cute Butch Thorpe. My wife, Francesca, who is British and thus values her privacy, wanted no part of the project from the beginning.

In scheduling the actual filming of *Twelve Steps to Death,* I knew that we would have to shoot around people's work schedules, trying as hard as possible to arrange shoots on the two weekends when my neighbors would be free. For the scenes shot during the week, we needed to cast people who either were on vacation or who had very flexible schedules. Here John proved to be an immense help. A few years out of college and unemployed, John had lots of free time on his hands, but he also had a lot of friends who had free time on their hands. One of these people was Lara Stolman, his girlfriend, who wanted desperately to be in the movie. Blessed with an arctic WASPish demeanor that she could turn on and off, Lara would be just right for the part of Brittany Thorpe, Peter Thorpe's superbitch widow, who mourned his untimely demise by flying off on a shopping expedition to Monte Carlo.

Next, we cast a young woman named Hella Winston in the part of Veronica De Fonzini/Sister Wilhemina, the airheaded nun who had once been Turk Bishop's girlfriend. John had gone to high school at Andover with Hella, and one day in July he brought her up to my office. As soon as she walked through the door I knew she was perfect for the part. She was twenty-five, vivacious, cheerful, strikingly attractive, and extremely voluble. She also loved the idea of being in the movie, because it would provide a much-needed respite from her job as a researcher on a cable TV program, which, it soon became apparent, she hated. In addition to her looks, her enthusiasm, and her availability, Hella had one other selling point: her car. Hella's wheels could come in very handy during the shooting of the film when we needed someone to drive to the train station or go pick up some equipment or drive into the city to drop off our dailies. So she got the job.

That only left two major roles to cast: Amber Duggan and Turk Bishop. For some time, I'd had my eyes on Doug Colligan, yet another neighbor, for the part of the maniacal police lieutenant who functions as the emotional epicenter of the film. Though Doug now works a magazine editor in Westchester, he had previously worked for Bob Guccione at *Omni* for nine years. So he was used to working with dysfunctional people. Doug had also been in Vietnam, so I reckoned he had just the right edge to play the main role in the movie.

But one night, as I was putting the fine touches on the movie, John pointed out that Bishop had to deliver about 50 percent of the lines in the movie and that no untrained actor was going to be able to memorize that many lines. John noted that many of the scenes contained lengthy speeches and that several of the longer scenes had to be done in a single take. There was no way Doug was going to be able to learn that much dialogue. Yes, we could use cue cards, but the footage would look horrible because you could see him reading his lines. To John's way of thinking, only one person was going to be able to remember that many lines.

Me.

"But I wrote the Peter Thorpe part for myself," I protested. "The Peter Thorpe character *is* me."

"Sorry, man, you've got to play the cop."

"I don't want to play the cop. I want to play the psychiatrist. I was looking forward to sticking that knife between Joey Bellini's legs."

"We all have to make compromises," John said. "You've got to be the cop. You're the only one who can remember all those lines. Otherwise, every scene will need a million takes, and we'll never get the movie shot in nine days."

This information really pissed me off. Even though the character of Turk Bishop totally dominated the film, because the story basically dealt with his moral dilemma—whether to bring a criminal he admired to justice or not—I hadn't written very many good lines for his character. Most of the good lines went to the two Thorpes and all the dysfunctional twelve-step people. I'd been looking forward to delivering those lines. And I'd *really* been looking forward to plunging that Bowie knife between Joey Bellini's thighs.

But in the end, I realized that John was right. Asking Doug to memorize that many lines of dialogue on such short notice was ridiculous and unfair. Doug would play the two Thorpes. I would play the cop. The next time I saw Doug, I ran the idea past him. He was totally, totally into it.

In fact, he was totally, totally into the whole idea of making a movie.

"When I was in the seminary thirty years ago, I actually appeared in a short black-and-white *Batman* movie where I played Robin," he informed me.

"That's good, Doug," I said. "That's very, very good."

THAT LEFT US with only one role to cast, but it was the toughest one of all. Amber Duggan. Let me explain.

When I sat down to write the screenplay for *Twelve Steps to Death,* I deliberately left out anything that would be hard to reproduce in Tarry-town. On the thematic level, this meant no helicopter crashes, no car chases, no self-immolations, no butt-fucking by toothless mountain men. In the personnel department, it meant no midgets, no hunchbacks, no Siamese twins. The only role that made any special demands on the performer was the role of Amber Duggan, who had to be a woman so fat she literally could not squeeze through one of the doors at the castle. But when I first mapped out the screenplay, Amber Duggan was not a woman, but a man named Bart Hogan.

This was the first lesson I learned about the difference between making a movie in Hollywood for countless millions and making a movie in Tarrytown for countable thousands. In Hollywood, when you want a fat actor, you hire a fat actor. The actor doesn't mind having other people joke about how fat he is, because rotundness is one of his major selling points. Fat actors know they're fat, and don't mind having attention drawn to it. John Candy, I am told, may have been an exception, but generally this rule holds true. And if John Candy didn't know that he was fat before, he most certainly knows it now.

This rule does not hold true in real life. Not all fat people, even obscenely fat people, think of themselves as fat. They compare themselves to other obscenely fat people and decide in their own minds that they are merely full-figured. Many fat people think of themselves as thin people who are simply going through a chunky phase. They are not comfortable with their roly-polytude, and in their mind's eye do not see themselves as being specimens of that species known as the Perennially Fat, the Incontrovertibly Fat, the Eternally Fat, or the Truly Fat. And even fat people who do accept the fact that they are fat do not necessarily believe this is anything to be ashamed of. They anoint themselves with terms such as "Rubenesque," "portly," or "pleasingly plump," and take solace in the belief that in previous centuries their sheer amplitude would have exerted a profound aphrodisiacal effect on the beholder.

The most important point of all is this: Large but otherwise ordinary people are not chomping at the bit to be cast in a movie where they have to spend ninety-three minutes being heaped with abuse by all the other characters just because they're a bit on the tubby side. Ordinary people do not leap at the opportunity to be cast as chunksters so fat they cannot even fit through a door. Ordinary people do not leap at the opportunity to deliver lines like, "I know what I am, Lieutenant. I'm a pig. I'm a wild beast."

So when I put out feelers to a couple of very large friends that the role of Bart Hogan was open, the feelers came back unfelt. None of my fat friends was interested in being a target of remorseless verbal abuse in a $6,998 movie shot in nine days in Tarrytown, New York. Maybe it's true that everybody in the United States has a deep desire to be in pictures. But not necessarily *my* pictures.

John bailed me out of this situation by finding Susie Lipof. Susie was a likable, enthusiastic, twenty-one-year-old girl from Florida who had come to New York hoping to get a job on *Saturday Night Live*. John had met her at a softball game in Central Park, but didn't really know her all that well. She was the one person in the movie who had no natural allies. Susie was not a fat girl, but she was not precisely a thin girl, either, and she did have a rather plump face. Most important, she didn't mind taking nonstop verbal abuse for ninety-three minutes if it would give her a chance to be in a movie. Susie wanted to be in the movies in the worst way.

A workable solution quickly presented itself. I would rewrite the Bart Hogan role for a woman, and we would stuff Susie into a fat suit that would make her look two hundred pounds heavier. This would inflate the budget by another hundred bucks or so, but it would eliminate an enormous problem. A fat suit was a necessity because it would make *all* parts of the body look beastly. Stuffing Susie's dress with pillows would have made her seem obese in some places but merely pudgy in others. What's more, there was no way to ensure that the pillows would stay in place, or that the pillows would look the same in different scenes. We wanted Susie to look uniformly ridiculous throughout the entire movie.

She did.

BY THE TIME the screenplay was written at the end of July, John had bought or arranged the rental of all the props we would need (nun's costume, fat suit for Susie, plastic Bowie knife, fake cellular phone, fake gun and holster for Turk Bishop). John also had lined up the camera rental at Pro Camera and Lighting Rentals on West 33rd Street in Manhattan. We could rent a real, professional Arriflex camera with a complete camera kit plus lights and tripods, et cetera, around noon on Friday, August 12, for $1,500 and keep it until the morning of Monday, August 21. This would give us nine full days of shooting. We also had to fork over $475 to pay for insurance on the camera; even an ancient Arriflex is worth at least $20,000). And we would have to rent some decent sound equipment for around $450 at ASC Audio Service Company in midtown Manhattan.

By this point, I already knew that my dreams of making a $6,998 movie were over. Despite all that stuff I'd heard about finding mysterious outlets for stolen film or recanned film that could be bought for 30 cents on the dollar, there was no way I was going to start shooting a film without knowing that the film would turn out okay. If anything went wrong with the film, we would have to go back and reshoot all the lost footage. This would mean going back and renting the camera and the sound equipment all over again, and hoping that everyone was available to reshoot their scenes. This would double the cost of the movie and turn my life into even more of a living hell than it had already become. I was not going to take that kind of risk. So I made a critical decision. We would buy our film the same place everybody else bought their film. We would buy it at Kodak.

In a certain sense, learning that the legend of the $7,000 movie was a pure myth took a huge load off my shoulders. I now recognized that there were fixed costs associated with making a movie and that no one who wasn't already in the business could get around them. You could lie about getting around them, because that looked good in the papers, but you couldn't actually get around them. Even if we shot at a ratio of three to one, about the lowest ratio in history, the film alone was going to run $4,000. Renting the camera would cost $2,000. Developing the film would cost at least three grand. Once the movie was done, even the most primitive editing was going to run another $5,000, and that didn't even include the cost of mixing, adding a soundtrack, or, most important of all, paying for a final print (around $4,000). Even without breaking out all the numbers, I now realized that *Twelve Steps to Death* was going to put me at least $20,000 in the hole.

I wasn't pleased with this information. But at least I now had some kind of grip on all the numbers. If John and I could shoot the film at a super-low ratio, we still could get this thing done at a price that would not impoverish my children for generations to come. And at least I now knew the upper limit of the expenses I would incur while making this film. We had it all on paper.

No, we didn't. Exactly one week before we began shooting, John told me that it would be madness to shoot a film without having a technical crew to man the equipment. Yes, he'd been to film school, and yes, he'd done a lot of work with a videocam, but no, he really didn't know how to operate a camera very well, and, no, Mike Berman didn't really know much about operating sophisticated sound equipment. Sure, we could wing it, but the results would be pretty awful. If you wanted to make a halfway decent film, you needed to hire a real cameraman and a real sound person.

He had a real cameraman and a real sound person in mind.

JOHN MET TED Sappington and his wife Kenna Doeringer by accident. One day, while investigating the cost of renting an editing room at Sound One Studios in New York, John met Ted and Kenna's roommate, who worked there. The roommate gave John a business card containing her home phone number. One night, John called. Kenna answered. John asked if the roommate was home. She was not. John asked if Kenna knew anything about the movies. She did. Just twenty-three years old, she had started out as an animator, then gotten into postproduction sound editing, and had recently been working at Sound One. What's more, her husband was a gaffer and best boy on several feature films who dreamed of being a full-time cinematographer, having already worked as director of photography on a number of low-budget short films.

John told Kenna that he was helping to make a $7,000 movie not unlike Robert Rodriguez's intergalactically celebrated *El Mariachi*. Kenna kind of yawned. She told John that everyone was working on a $7,000 movie not unlike Robert Rodriguez's intergalactically celebrated *El Mariachi*. She asked if we had a script. We did not. She said to call back when we did. Three weeks later, John delivered the script. Ted and Kenna liked it. They thought it was weird. They thought it was rude. They thought it was politically incorrect. But they wanted to work on the film. At this point, I was still frantically trying to get all the acting parts cast for the film, so I did not actually meet Ted and Kenna in person until the day before the shoot. Throughout this period, John acted as my intermediary. He told me that Ted would work for ten days for $1,000 and that Kenna would do the sound for $750. Obviously, I would have to rent all the necessary equipment. Ted also wanted to bring along a production assistant named Adam Grabel, who would work for $100 a week. But Ted made it clear that the shoot had to finish by Sunday night, August 21, because he and Adam had a real shoot to start on the following day. These conditions were more than acceptable to me. I now had a cameraman who knew what the hell he was doing. I had a soundwoman who knew what the hell she was doing. I had an assistant cameraman who knew what the hell he was doing. At long last, I had all my ducks in a row.

I HAVE TO admit that the days leading up to the filming of *Twelve Steps to Death* were a bit frantic. In the best of all possible worlds, you don't meet the people who are going to be shooting your film the day before you start shooting it. And in the best of all possible worlds, you don't hold your first and last rehearsal for the movie two days before you start shooting it. But circumstances forced us into a very unconventional preproduction schedule. Although I was now devoting almost all of my energies to polishing up the script and getting ready to make my first movie, I still had bills to pay. *Huge* bills. The only way I could pay them was by banging out a raftload of magazine articles that would provide enough income to tide me over for the next few months while I shot and edited the film. So, in the week leading up to the making of *Twelve Steps to Death,* I was locked twelve hours a day in my office writing articles for *GQ, Barron's, British Esquire,* and *Movieline.* This is not the way Oliver Stone gets ready to make a movie.

It's terribly embarrassing to admit this, but I didn't even *meet* some of the principal players until the night of that first and only rehearsal two days before we began shooting. John had assured me that his girlfriend would be perfect for the part of Peter Thorpe's widow, and he had assured me that Susie Lipof would be perfect for the part of Amber Duggan. Up until this point, John had always come through for me, so I had no reason to distrust him now. And, as things turned out, Lara Stolman and Susie Lipof were perfect for the parts they were supposed to play. Lara had an icy seriousness and a faint touch of haughtiness that made her ideal for the role of Peter Thorpe's WASPy widow, and Susie had just the right mixture of bounciness and toughness to play Amber Duggan. She also looked terrific in the fat suit we had rented. When we did the run-through on Thursday, August 10, everybody did their lines as well as could be expected. Yes, they were nervous, but at this point they were still reading their lines off the script, so there were no blatant screw-ups. I also assured them that there would be plenty of cue cards around if they had trouble with the lengthier speeches. The thing I liked the most was that everybody who was in the movie acted like they *wanted* to be in the movie, with the possible exception of Keith Jenkins, my physicist friend, whom I'd cast as the chronic gambler Sherman Krebs. Keith still acted like he was doing me a favor to be in my movie. I would deal with him later.

As for Ted and Kenna, what can I say? I shouldn't have waited until the very day we went to pick up the camera in Manhattan before meeting them; a real director would have been discussing shots and shooting locations weeks and even months in advance. But I was not a real director. My wife and I drove into Manhattan on Friday, August 11, and paid $2,894.61 for twenty cans of film at a Kodak retailer called The Film Center right across from Grand Central Station on 42nd Street. This was enough to finish the film if we shot *Twelve Steps to Death* at a two-to-one ratio, half the amount of film that Rodriguez used in *El Mariachi,* and in fact the lowest ratio in the history of motion pictures. I had a feeling we'd be coming back for more.

Next, we picked up Ted and Kenna at their Tenth Avenue apartment around 11 A.M. on Friday, August 11. We introduced ourselves, had a bit of a chit-chat, then went to gather all the equipment. First I shelled out $1,500 for the camera at Pro Camera and Lighting Services on West 33rd Street. Then I wrote a check for $475 in camera insurance. Then I forked over $423.04 for Kenna's sound equipment (DAT recorder, microphone, boom, batteries, blank tape) at ASC Audio Services Company on West 48th Street. The equipment took up the entire back section of my Toyota Previa van. Then we drove to Tarrytown. We unloaded most of the equipment in my living room, where it would take up half the available floor space for the next ten days, stuffing the less expensive equipment in the garage. We looked at a few of the shooting locales. We discussed the script. We decided which scenes we would shoot first. And we agreed to start shooting early the next morning as soon as the three crew members could get up on the commuter train from Manhattan ($135 for three weekly passes). Before we'd even begun shooting, *Twelve Steps to Death* had set me back $5,223 in equipment alone. That left me with a $1,775 cushion if I was going to beat Robert Rodriguez's record by $2. Unless I could figure out a way to get the film developed for nothing, I probably wasn't going to beat *El Mariachi*'s record.

How did Ted and Kenna react to me that day? I think they thought I was a very strange man. They'd been encouraged in this belief by John, who'd told them that I was a mysterious guy with a volcanic temper and that they'd be wise to keep their distance. That first day, they didn't didn't say a whole lot. They were polite but not especially friendly. On an encouraging note, it was apparent even at this juncture that they were piqued by the project we were about to embark on. They were fascinated by the concept. They were intrigued by the script. They were riveted by my braggadocio. More than anything, they seemed to be a young couple having a serious cash-flow problem who were really glad to get the work.

six

The First Cut
Is the Deepest

Movies are shot entirely out of sequence, the filming schedule being determined by weather, the availability of actors, and the availability of shooting locales. When you are making a low-budget movie in
Tarrytown, New York, using friends' homes, offices,
driveways, backyards, and, where possible, castles as
sets, you cannot always shoot when you want to
shoot; you can only shoot when the homeowners are
around to make sure that nothing gets broken and
that the extras don't steal the family heirlooms.

This hamstrung us from the very start. Ideally, we
would have liked to shoot the most visually arresting
scenes—Thorpe's murder, Thorpe's suicide, the
send-up of the *Reservoir Dogs* torture scene, all of
which take place at Axe Castle—on the first two days
and then film the less important scenes during the
week. Production-values–wise, these scenes were

about all that *Twelve Steps to Death* had to offer. But the Walders, who own the castle, were away on vacation the weekend we began shooting and would be gone until the middle of late the following weekend. They did not want complete strangers—nor, for that matter, me—wandering around their newly purchased neo-medieval edifice. This meant we had to delay shooting the all-important castle scenes until the second Saturday, Day 8, by which time we would all be completely burned out and probably running way behind schedule. But there was nothing we could do about it.

These were not our only scheduling problems. When I was writing the script, I consciously tried to set the action in locales that could be easily reproduced in Tarrytown. Any number of friends' homes could have been used for the psychiatrist's home, for his office, for Bishop's apartment, for Amber Duggan's pool. I also knew I would have no trouble shooting outdoor scenes behind the Tarrytown Reservoir and in a large field right behind my house because they are usually deserted in the morning, particularly on weekdays. Finally, I could shoot the funeral service in a friend's vast backyard, the confrontation between Bishop and Duggan at another friend's pool, and the scenes involving Thorpe's widow and children on the front lawn of my own house.

The only real problems were the scenes involving Sister Wilheminina/Veronica De Fonzini and Bishop. Originally, I planned to shoot these scenes inside a Baptist church whose pastor is a close friend of mine. But when I finally got around to telling my minister friend what the film was all about, he begged off, noting that his church actually sponsored a number of support groups (porkers, juicers, cardsharks—not his words) identical to the ones I was ridiculing in my movie. So he didn't think it would be such a good idea to get involved with the project.

Since I couldn't use the interior of his church as a set, and since I didn't know any other clergymen, I decided to shift the location of the nun's scenes, moving them from the inside of a real church to the inside of a fake convent. Convents, unlike churches, are easy to simulate because no one but nuns has ever been in them. So unless you're worried about a bunch of real nuns turning up at your premiere and complaining about continuity errors, you can make convents look any way you want.

In this sense, convents are a lot like Wisconsin: You can say and do what you please with them, because no one's going to go out and check.

To generate the starkness I had envisioned for Sister Wilhemina's cell, I decided to use a dismal, tiny, airless, lightless office in the same professional building where I currently work. The office has two minuscule rooms, a low ceiling, and three grimy windows that look out directly on a drab brick wall. The only light that ever comes into the room are one or two renegade sunbeams that get deflected off the brick wall into the cryptlike office every five years or so, where they die quick deaths in the funereal carpeting. This is what they mean by Depression Era architecture.

I felt confident that this dank, microscopic mousetrap would perfectly capture the claustrophobic, murderously depressing atmosphere of an authentic convent cell because for fourteen months this second-story abyss had been my workspace, in which I had written some of my most gloomy work ever. I'd moved into the office in March 1993 and lasted until May 1994, finally deciding to move out after reading a story in *The New York Times* about the psychologically ruinous effects of working in an office with no direct sunlight.

In May 1994, I'd moved upstairs when a larger, brighter suite became available. My landlord, Kabir Jafri, was having trouble renting my old office, in part because the real estate market in Westchester was so bad, in part because the room looked like a medieval nun's cell. So we both knew it would be empty in August when I shot my movie. Being a salt-of-the-earth type, Kabir graciously agreed to let me use it.

However, because the building also houses a law office, a psychiatrist's office, a data backup center, two concert booking agencies, an acupuncturist's clinic, and a graphic design firm, it would be possible for me to shoot only over the weekend, when all of these officers were closed. Even a low-budget movie requires lots of equipment, which would have blocked up the halls and turned the building into a madhouse. And if any of the other tenants had complained to the mayor's office in Tarrytown, where filming of movies is technically forbidden, it would have forced us to shoot elsewhere. Ideally, I would have preferred to shoot our first scenes outside, but since we only had two weekends, and since the second weekend of the schedule was already booked at Axe Castle, we had no choice but to spend the first Saturday shooting indoors at my old office.

As luck would have it, the first day of our shooting schedule was a bit overcast anyway, so it seemed like a good day to go inside. But there were other advantages to starting out by shooting the scenes involving Turk Bishop and Sister Wilhemina. In order to shoot a ninety-three-page script in nine days, we had to average more than ten pages a day. Although the scenes involving Sister Wilhemina were funny, they were also very long, and visually undemanding. For the most part, the three scenes that take place in her cell were extended monologues, only occasionally interrupted by her old boyfriend, Turk. They were easy to shoot, provided Hella and I didn't screw up our lines. If we could shoot all of these scenes in one day, we'd have fourteen pages of the script out of the way, and we would have polished off the least cinematographically appealing sections of the movie on the very first day. Since we were all just getting to know each other anyway, and since I had no real idea what the hell we were doing, it seemed like a good strategy to lock up these scenes early and get ahead of the game, so we would have extra time later in the week to set up more important shots.

We got started by moving all the equipment from my garage to my old office, which was completely empty. John pointed out that we really ought to have a crucifix on the bare white wall in back of Sister Wilhemina, so Mike Berman got cracking on a crucifix made out of two black balloons, which we then stuck on the wall. By noon, we were ready to start making motion picture history. Basically, we decided to shoot these scenes in lengthy single takes, using two shots (both actors in the frame at once), then double back and do a bit of coverage. (One actor reacts while the other one is speaking, one actor speaks while the other is silent.) The first shot, where Bishop comes to visit his old girlfriend in the convent, was 103 seconds long—a minute and three-quarters. This is an unbelievably long time for the camera to remain in one place; you would never see a sequence this monotonous in a commercial movie, except something like *Reservoir Dogs*, which is mostly shot in a single large room.

But in low-budget movies, you have to plan certain sequences where the camera doesn't move very much, or else you'll never get the movie shot. Every time you move the camera to shoot from another angle, another half hour of your shooting time is gone. The director of photography will always tell you that he can set up the shot in five minutes, but this is never true. There are always problems with the lights. There are always problems with shadows from the sound person's boom. The actors always have trouble fitting inside the camera frame. There is always a car antenna that needs to be adjusted, a window that needs to be closed, a rubbernecker who needs to be told to get the hell off the set. No matter what anyone says, a basic rule prevails on the sets of all movies, whether big or small: Every time you move the camera, another half hour of your shooting time is gone. And usually it's more like an hour.

So at all costs, we wanted the camera to move as little as possible. I knew this was a big risk. I knew that these scenes had the potential for disaster, because they were so static, so wearing on the viewer's eye. But it was a risk we had to take. We needed to get some points on the scoreboard right away. We had to hope that the nun's zany dialogue and Bishop's morose deadpanning would make people laugh, taking their minds off the fact that for long, long stretches, their eyes were locked in a single position.

Things got off to a shaky start because we had to send out for knee-high nylons for Hella ($2.20) and I screwed up my opening lines. When the nun asks Bishop if the person who killed his wife and kids was ever brought to justice, he replies: "Yeah, we found the driver. She was a schizoid, anorexic recovering alcoholic with Attention Deficit Disorder who was fleeing an abusive chocaholic husband who used to beat her whenever he had one too many of the nougat caramels."

That's a real mouthful, and I messed up the first take. The problem in shooting long takes is that if even a single line gets screwed up, the entire take has to be reshot. That's one reason why people don't usually do long takes.

Happily, the second take came off without a hitch. Hella knew her lines perfectly, and so did I. Two minutes later, we had a wrap. How was our acting? That was anybody's guess. But I didn't care one way or the other. The only thing I cared about was whether the lines were delivered in a lucid, intelligible manner, which, John and Ted assured me, they were. When you're making a low-budget movie, you don't go back and reshoot 103-second shots because you think the acting might improve in a fourth or fifth take. If you get the lines right the first or second time around, it's a wrap. Leave the fifth and sixth takes to the pros like Steven Seagal.

By the time we finished that first shot, I was starting to feel a bit cocky. We'd set up the camera around noon and within an hour we'd already shot one-sixtieth of the entire motion picture. At this pace, we could have this whole thing wrapped up by Monday. Piece of cake.

Then disaster struck. When we moved the camera around to set up the second scene involving the nun and her old boyfriend, Kenna noticed that we had no sound. The sprocket on her DAT machine—the one I'd rented the day before for $120 plus tax—wasn't turning. Shooting stopped as she yanked out her tool kit and tore the machine apart. Ten minutes later, she took out more equipment. Twenty minutes later, her worst suspicions were confirmed. The machine was busted.

Naturally, I was horrified to hear this. It was so unfair, so typical of the way the powers-that-be in the universe liked to gang up on the little guy. Nevertheless, Tarrytown is only a thirty-minute drive from Manhattan, so I figured the worst that was going to happen was that we'd lose two hours of shooting time while Hella and Kenna drove in and picked up a replacement DAT machine. After all, New York is a place where you can get loin of armadillo on seedless rye at midnight, or hire a girl dressed up like a squirrel to give you a blow job at three o'clock in the morning. New York is a municipality of seemingly infinite resources.

Seemingly infinite resources. But not infinite. No, even New York has its limits, as I now learned to my immense chagrin. New York, Kenna tersely explained, is not the sort of place where you can get a replacement DAT machine at one thirty-five on a Saturday afternoon. Maybe you could get one in L.A., but not in New York. The store that had rented us the DAT was closed until Monday. So were all the other stores that rented sound equipment.

Oliver Stone never has these kinds of problems.

I made a quick call to my friend Andy Aaron, who had worked on *Ishtar* and who owned his own sound equipment. Andy wasn't home. He was out on the easternmost tip of Long Island, 150 away, visiting his parents for the weekend. His equipment was back in Manhattan. Fast calls to a couple of musician friends were similarly futile. Time passed as Kenna desperately attempted to repair the machine. No dice. At two-thirty, she started making calls. One call. Two. Five. No luck. Finally, about three o'clock, Kenna tracked down a friend who had a small machine we could use as a substitute for the weekend. It wasn't a DAT, but it would do.

Kenna and I piled into Hella's car and madly dashed off to Manhattan ($6 for gas, $3 for bridge tolls). To salvage something from this disaster, Hella and I started rehearsing our next scene while careening down the Saw Mill River Parkway. The scene in question was the one where Sister Wilhemina confesses to Bishop that the woman who appeared to her on the laptop may not have been the Blessed Mother, because the apparition seemed to have a lot of freckles, and there was nothing in the Good Book about the Blessed Mother having freckles. Initially, the rehearsal went well. But then we hit the Cross Bronx Expressway, where traffic was pretty heavy, and Hella said we would have to suspend the rehearsal.

"This traffic is freaking me out, and I have to concentrate," she said. Seemingly, the combination of lunatic northern Bronx weekend drivers and all the confusing dialogue about the heavily freckled apparition at Lourdes was making it hard for her to keep her eyes on the road.

We continued our drive into the city, calculating what the odds were that a DAT machine would have broken down twenty minutes into a low-budget movie. Nothing like this had ever happened to her before, Kenna assured me.

"What would Martin Scorsese do if his DAT machine broke down?" I asked her.

"They'd have four spares on the set," she told me.

I might have guessed.

We picked up the loaner, though not before Kenna's friend extorted a promise that she would work, gratis, for several hours the next week on an editing job he needed done. Then we headed back to Tarrytown. By the time we hit the northern tip of the Bronx, Hella felt loose enough to rehearse the scene where the nun tells Bishop about the International

Association of Coagulative Calligraphers, an on-line bulletin board for experts in handwriting done in blood. I was highly impressed, almost stunned. She really knew her lines well. And she was a very competent driver.

We got back to Tarrytown at five and immediately got the cameras rolling, shooting another long scene involving Bishop and his old girlfriend. We did it in a couple of takes. So now we had seven pages of script out of the way. Remarkably, the distractions of the afternoon seemed to make it easier for me and Hella to act. Things went pretty smoothly except when we had to stop shooting for a few minutes to allow Hella to take her habit off. The nun's costume ($80, plus tax) was made of a cheap, synthetic fiber and it was giving her a horrible rash on the left side of her face.

"I'm Jewish," Hella noted, theorizing that the very fabric itself might be rebelling against her culturally dissonant impersonation of a nun. Or that her own bloodlines might be engaged in some sort of subconscious physiological insurgency against a costume so intimately associated with the oppression of the Jews down through the centuries.

We spent quite a bit of time hypothesizing about what was causing Hella's rash, all the while waiting for the redness to dissipate. We also talked about implausible elements in the story line. Adam, our assistant cameraman, observed that Hella, age twenty-five, but who looked twenty-one, did not really seem old enough to have attended an Ozzie Osbourne concert with the forty-three-year-old Bishop ten years earlier, since this would have meant she was dating a thirty-three-year-old man when she was only eleven. I said this was true, but pointed out that Clint Eastwood and Sondra Locke did this sort of thing all the time, as did many other celluloid couples. I also pointed out that comments such as Adam's were not helpful.

Eventually, Hella's rash went away and we resumed. We moved all the equipment into the window frame to shoot the scene where the nun and Bishop chat while sitting on this weird sort of catwalk outside her cell. While she was climbing out the window, Hella bruised her shin bone. The bruise never healed; a week later she was still sore. With this much carnage on the first day, I was starting to wonder if Hella was physically strong enough to survive the strain of a nine-day shoot. Of course, we all felt sorry for the poor girl, but we also had the shooting schedule to consider. Would the shin injury affect Hella's ability to remember her lines? As the only member of the cast who seemed to know her lines by heart, we were really depending on her. As we sat there mulling over these issues, I made a mental note to cast tougher, more durable specimens if I ever made another movie.

With the rash subsiding and the pain from the bruise now a dull throb, Hella agreed to soldier on. But we had to give her some help. She was tired, she was banged up, and she was worried that the nun's habit made her look absurd. She was starting to lose her grip. She was also losing confidence. So even though she seemed to know her lines perfectly, she asked if she could have the script taped to the wall outside my office just in case. That way, she could appear to be gazing off into space while the camera did her close-ups, when in fact she would be reading her lines directly off the screenplay taped to the facing wall.

Sounded fine to me. If we could lock up this scene in the next hour or so, we would have fourteen pages of the script shot by dinnertime. We'd still have to work very late that evening, but at least we'd be on schedule. So we quickly rehearsed, then shot the lengthy scene where Sister Wilhemina informs Bishop that the Blessed Virgin Mary had recently made a totally unexpected appearance on her laptop computer while she was visiting Lourdes. Great: another four pages in the can. Now it was time to move the camera for the final shot of this sequence. If we could get this scene in the bag, we would be way ahead of schedule, despite all the sound problems we'd had to combat earlier in the day.

Just then, the thunder started. I couldn't hear it at first, but motion picture sound equipment is so sensitive that it can detect a substandard blow job or a delicately nuanced racial epithet at three hundred yards. And thunder, even distant thunder, could wreck the take. "Please tell me that's a truck backfiring," I said to Kenna. "Please say that it's the Druze militiamen making a surprise visit to the Lower Hudson Valley." No, she replied, it was thunder for sure. Worse still, it was soon followed by lightning.

And then the rains came.

The rains came, and they stayed. By the time they stopped, the area where we had been shooting outside my old office window was thoroughly drenched, meaning that we could not shoot any more outdoor footage today. We had to bag the remaining page and a half of Sister Wilhemi-nina's conversation with Bishop and pick it up sometime later in the week. This meant real scheduling problems, because I had already arranged for all the actors in the psychiatrist's opening scenes to show up at my house early the next day. We could not change their schedules because most of the actors had to work on Monday and didn't feel like wasting a vacation day on a low-budget movie. And we could not shoot in my office build-ing during the week because the other tenants would complain, particu-larly if we were shooting outside the ladies' room. And we could not shoot the following Saturday because we already had the castle booked. The only day we could handle this dilemma was to come back and finish this scene the following Sunday, the last day of the shoot. At this point, Sunday, Day IX, got designated as the catch-all day when we would go back and shoot everything we had not finished earlier in the week.

Provided it didn't rain.

Looking on the bright side of things, Saturday had not been a com-plete wipeout. Three of the four scenes involving Turk Bishop and Sis-ter Wilhemina took place inside her cell. Excluding the final shot that took place outdoors on the catwalk, we'd still managed to shoot twelve and a half pages of the script in one day. On the notion that we were going to shoot ten pages a day for nine days, this put us two and a half pages ahead of schedule, amazing considering the busted DAT machine and the bad weather. More encouraging still, we'd finished shooting by eight o'clock in the evening on the first day of the shoot, which enabled Ted, Adam, and Kenna to go back to the city and get a good night's sleep, then resurface around ten the following morning so we could get an early start.

On the other hand, what we'd got in the can today were far and away the least complex scenes in the entire movie. There were no other scenes in the rest of the movie that would be as easy to shoot as these. Once we started filming the other scenes, there had to be more camera movement, more cutting back and forth, more coverage. What's more, from this point on, most of the movie was going to be shot outdoors, which meant that if it rained, we were screwed.

Still no word from Amblin.

SHORTLY AFTER WE began filming late Sunday morning, bloodshed erupted on the set. Tension was now building between John (assistant director/line producer/propmaster) and my son Gordon (Butch Thorpe), because Gordon, age seven, kept stealing the gun and holster ($13.53) I wore in the role of Turk Bishop, and John, age twenty-five, kept taking them back, saying that we couldn't afford to have any of the props wrecked by marauding seven-year-olds. And tension was now building between John and me because I kept telling him that Gord was my well-beloved son, in whom I was well pleased, so stop fucking with him. Finally, tension was building between my wife Francesca and the entire cast and crew because no one would ever tell her when they were ready to eat, thus forcing her to reheat vast amounts of food constantly.

None of these imbroglios immediately culminated in violence; that would come later in the week. The bloodshed occurred on the set during the filming of the opening scenes involving Peter Thorpe, the apparent murder victim, and his four extremely dysfunctional patients. These scenes were shot on the north side of my living room, where all the furniture had been rearranged to resemble a wealthy psychiatrist's office. The other side of the room was filled to overflowing with cameras, lights, sound equipment, and the crew. For the remainder of the film, the living room and adjacent dining room would serve as a warehouse for all the rented equipment. The living room would also serve as Mike (Joey Bellini, The Man Who Loved Too Much) Berman's bedroom, while the family room would sometimes house John, other times Ted and Kenna. Finally, my daughter Bridget (Courtney Thorpe) would vacate her upstairs bedroom to accommodate Hella (Sister Wilhemina) and Susie (Amber Duggan), while she slept on the floor of the master bedroom.

All this would become a source of tension and lead to more unpleasantness later in the film when my wife and son decided that they wanted their house back. (Bridget, who had once played the coveted role of the

Dew Fairy in the seminal 1992 Winfield L. Morse primary school production of *Hansel and Gretel,* was really psyched about being in the
movie, so she didn't mind sleeping on the floor.)

The first scene we shot that morning involved Peter Thorpe, played by
my neighbor Doug Colligan, a senior editor at *Reader's Digest,* and his
chronic gambler patient Sherman Krebs, played by my neighbor Keith
Jenkins, a physicist at IBM. In the screenplay and in the movie, Sherman
was the second patient that the audience sees, but Keith had a social engagement that afternoon so we agreed to shoot his scene first, then go
back later and do the scene with Amber Duggan, the fat lady, who is actually the first patient to appear in the film. This is the way movies are
made.

Keith had no trouble with his lines; if he seemed incredibly nervous
while saying them, it didn't matter to me because his character was supposed to be an incredibly nervous type. Doug (Peter Thorpe) also knew
his lines pretty well, but since he had to interact with all four patients,
he had about nine pages of script to deal with. Which meant at least nine
hours on the set, and an awful lot of lines.

This was a lot of memory work, so just to be on the safe side, we hid
his script inside a copy of *Philadelphia* magazine. This was the first of
many blatant product plugs I would scatter throughout the movie. As
noted earlier, I had long since given up any hope of lining up *real* commercial sponsors for the film, but many of the magazines I worked for had
enthusiastically volunteered to have their products plugged in the movie
as long as they only had to supply magazines or T-shirts. In exchange, provided *Twelve Steps to Death* became a cult classic, I would be able to shake
them down for easy, good-paying writing assignments in the future. It was
an unwieldy system of retroactive barter that had very little potential to
benefit any of us financially, but it was the best I could do under the circumstances.

Philadelphia magazine was run by Eliot Kaplan, a talented young editor who had published the first pieces I ever wrote for *GQ* while he was
managing editor there. In gratitude for helping me to establish myself as
a writer, I had promised Eliot years ago that I would one day make it up
to him. I now made good on this promise by having one of the two main

characters in the movie read his lines from a script hidden inside a barely visible copy of *Philadelphia* magazine, never actually explaining why the residents of a godforsaken town in rural Wisconsin would be reading such a geographically and demographically incongruous publication. When I promised Eliot to one day repay him for his help in launching my career, I was dead serious. However, I'm not entirely sure that this was what he had in mind.

Doug's scene with Keith came off splendidly. Both of them were stiff and nervous during rehearsal, but I didn't care. "Get it done; don't get it right," I reminded them before we started rolling the camera, and they basically did as I asked. We polished off the entire two-minute sequence in a series of short takes, never doing more than two takes of any shot, in large part because Berman was standing just out of camera range with enormous cue cards in case Keith forgot his lines. The one time we had to reshoot a take, it was because Keith absentmindedly looked directly at the camera. As I would do with many other performers throughout the shooting of the film, I took Keith aside and told him that looking at the camera would force us to reshoot scenes, which would cost me money. I said that occasional flubs were entirely understandable, then politely told him not to look at the camera any more or I would break his legs. I'm a lot bigger than he is, so he stopped looking at the camera.

By this juncture, the beginning of the second day of the shoot, Ted was subtly wresting visual control of the film away from John. Ted, who actually worked in the movie business for a living, had gone along with doing all those drab one-takes the day before because he knew we couldn't afford to lose any time and had to make concessions because of the weather and the DAT machine breaking down. So the camera hadn't moved around a whole lot on Saturday.

But by Sunday morning, things had changed. This was Ted's first job as a Director of Photography on a full-length feature, and low-budget film or not, he wanted to make the most of the opportunity. Even if we were shooting four consecutive indoor shots with the characters in identical positions, Ted was going to try as hard as humanly possible to make the shots look visually compelling. All of the actors' speeches would be broken up into small segments, reaction shots would be taken, and even the backdrops would be changed from scene to scene to achieve greater optical variety. I had always been confident that if the actors did their lines correctly, we'd get plenty of laughs out of this movie. But if *Twelve Steps to Death* was going to have any visual appeal whatsoever, Ted, not John, and certainly not me, was going to be responsible for it. From this point on, the film was basically directed by committee: I told the actors how to act; Ted and John conferred on the best set-ups and camera angles. But usually it was Ted's set-ups that got shot with Ted's camera angles.

After we finished with Sherman Krebs, the addictive gambler, it was time for Doug's scene with Joey Bellini, the man who found women more addictive than Marlboros. Joey was played by our all-purpose gofer, Mike Berman, who was supposed to look and act like a complete schmuck. Mike performed the role admirably. As the sequence opened, he was seen lying on the couch, dressed in a dark blue, pin-striped suit and a blue and white pin-striped shirt that made him look like a gangster, with a blue, polka-dot Perry Ellis tie completing the *intimidatore di tutti intimidatori* look. All of the clothing had been taken directly from my wardrobe. It was a humbling experience for me to realize that anytime during the shooting of the film that we needed someone to look like a schmuck, a gangster, a pervert, a sex maniac, or an asshole we could immediately go straight to my bedroom closet and find exactly the right clothes. But there you have it. Maybe I wasn't as natty a dresser as I'd always thought. Maybe I wasn't so very, very *GQ*.

Mike was told to lie on the couch and do all of his lines while the camera was in one position. Then we'd do cutaways to Doug's reactions. While Joey Bellini was explaining his craven attitude toward women, Doug would be seen raising his pants leg to reveal a leather sheath strapped to his right shin, from which he would extract an extremely sharp, extremely scary-looking Bowie knife. Doug had been in Vietnam, and was thus equipped to supply us with all the weaponry we needed in this film: hunting knives, straight razors, sidearms, mortar launchers, etc.

While Mike stared up at the ceiling, rattling on about his sexual prowess, Doug was supposed to rise from his seat, raise the knife high above his patient's groin, and then plunge the blade forcefully into the aperture between Mike's legs, within striking distance of his nuts. When

Mike reacted with horror and disbelief, Doug would return to his seat and counsel his patient to bear this object lesson in mind the next time he thought about harpooning some perky jailbait waitress from the local Dairy Queen. The sequence would end with the camera riveted on Mike astonished face.

Mike *did* react with horror, disbelief, and astonishment when we filmed this scene, but not for the reasons we'd envisioned. A few days earlier, propmaster, line producer, and assistant director John Domesick had purchased a plastic Bowie knife ($10, plus tax) that was supposed to be used in this scene. The Bowie knife was a joke: too big and too chintzy-looking to be taken seriously. Nobody on the set liked it. The way we planned to get around this was for Doug to pull out the real knife, and for the camera to follow the knife's descent from high in the air—as in *Psycho*—but then to shift to the plastic knife for the shot where the blade disappears between Mike's thighs into a bunch of pillows we'd placed between his legs. We figured this approach would work because at the actual moment of impact, the audience's attention would be focused on Mike's face rather than on his thighs. Thus, in theory, no one would notice that the knife was metallic in one scene but plastic in the next.

Everything in the Thorpe-Bellini sequence went well until we got to the knife attack. The problem was, the plastic knife kept bending whenever Doug stabbed the pillows that had been planted between Mike's legs. This looked completely hokey. So, eventually, with Mike's wholehearted approval, we decided to insert a piece of wood between his legs and let ace stiletto artist Doug, who had been in Vietnam, plunge the real Bowie knife into the wooden slab instead. Mike's crotch was being shot from six feet away, which would narrow the angle considerably, making it look like the knife was coming a whole lot closer to his groin than it actually was. In fact, the gap was about five or six inches, and since the knife was being plunged from only about eighteen inches away, the risk of a mishap was small.

I was standing in the adjacent dining room eating a stale doughnut ($.40) when I heard Mike's scream. I know that real-live directors like Martin Scorsese never walk off the set in the middle of a shot, but we had already done the knife-in-the-crotch shot three times and this fourth attempt was simply to see if we could get Mike to give a slightly more horrified reaction to his psychiatrist's unconventional therapeutic technique. Boy, did we ever. You could have heard his scream three blocks away. I rushed back into the living room where everyone was giggling shamefacedly.

Everyone except Mike.

"What happened?" I demanded, noticing that Mike seemed to be clutching the meaty, inner portion of his upper thigh. There was a bit of a pause. Then Ted spoke up.

"Doug stabbed Mike."

"Jesus!" I said, studying Mike more closely. Yes, the part of his leg that he was now grasping was, in fact, that extremely sensitive area of the inner thigh located approximately three inches from the human cock. I could see that he was in pain. Real pain. Christ, he was bleeding. All over my $500 Burberry's suit.

But I could also see that he was not in any life-threatening danger, and that the knife had not rendered him permanently incapable of giving pleasure to a woman, or, for that matter, to himself. That's why I said what I said next.

"Did we get it on film?"

Ted nodded. Boy, was he a pro. Only twenty-three, but a real gamer. There was a merry twinkle in his eye. What we had just witnessed could have been a tragedy. It could have ruined the movie. It could have ruined Mike's sex life. But it hadn't. And we had every reason to believe that the shot would be perfect for the final edit because of the highly believable way Mike had reacted to Doug's peculiar behavior.

From that point on, nobody on the set fucked with Doug.

DOUG'S NEXT TWO segments moved along at a nice clip. I persuaded John (line producer, propmaster, and assistant director) to play Jim Franklin, the man who is suffering from bulimia envy. (He is so jealous of all the attention his bulimic girlfriend gets that he beats her, and this makes her puke, thus becoming even more bulimic.) John agreed, but said that he wanted to play the role with a southern accent, to give it a kind of gnarled, antebellum quality.

"No accents, John," I said. "I'm surprised I have to tell you this, but if there's one thing that I truly fear from actors, it's when they start doing accents. The way I see it, the only thing a director has to do on the set of a movie is to make sure that the actors don't use any accents. And that's what I'm doing right now."

I elaborated on my theory. Accents, even in the best of mouths, are inherently hideous. They have a more disruptive effect on a film than a Dweezil Zappa impersonator at a Rotary Club fund raiser. But I also had practical reasons for not wanting John or anyone else to use a southern accent in my film. Ostensibly, *Twelve Steps to Death* was set in rural Wisconsin, about which none of us knew anything. The only reason it was set in rural Wisconsin was because for the purposes of the plot one of the Thorpe brothers had to be a White Sox fan and the other had to be a Cubs fan, and they had to live close enough to Chicago to get there by car in a few hours, but still live in a part of the country sufficiently rural that a town like No Quarter, with no other psychiatrists within a seventy-five-mile radius, could exist.

This ruled out such authentically desolate, remote states as North Dakota and Wyoming, but it also ruled out downstate New York, eastern Pennsylvania, central New Jersey and southern Connecticut—all of which are within easy driving distance of Shea Stadium and Yankee Stadium in New York City—and the entire southern half of California, all of which is within easy driving distance of Dodger Stadium and Chavez Ravine (Angels Stadium) in Los Angeles. Everybody knows that California and New York are densely populated states teeming with well-heeled neurotics, where you couldn't possibly drive more than three miles without finding a shrink—and New Jersey, Connecticut, and the Keystone State aren't all that much better.

Wisconsin, on the other hand, is the Cheese State, so obscure and mysterious that you could say just about anything you wanted to say about it, and no one would be the wiser. It's got Milwaukee on the east coast and Madison up the pike a ways, but the rest of the state looks pretty rural and, therefore, could easily be a mite short on psychiatrists. This being the case, it was entirely possible, and even likely, that deserted burghs like No Quarter and Dutchman's Prairie and Harlot's Fork could be flourishing out there in the hinterland, rustic enough to be psychiatrically retrograde, but close enough to Chicago for fans to go see a game. Anyway, this was a low-budget movie.

Unfortunately, it was a low-budget movie being shot in the suburbs of New York, with actors who mostly had East Coast accents. And, in this case, the actor had a *pronounced* East Coast accent. John, who had grown up in the suburbs of Boston, was a graduate of Andover. As a result, he had a distinctive frat-house, preppy way of talking that sounded anything *but* Cheeseheadish. To my way of thinking, adding a rural southern accent to this preppy/Cheesehead mix was merely going to complicate things.

But John was adamant.

"I could say, 'I live in Wisconsin now but I spent my formative *ye-ars* in Alabama.' "

John genuinely believed that the way he said "ye-ars" as if it had two syllables, made him sound like a redneck. It did not. Anyone, I pointed out to him, can make the word "years" sound like it has two syllables. To sound like a redneck, you have to be able to make the word "I" sound like it has two syllables. What John actually sounded like was somebody who'd gone to Andover who was trying to make fun of somebody from Arkansas who hadn't. He sounded like Tom Hanks in *Forrest Gump*. And I didn't want any of that *Forrest Gump* crap in my movie.

Eventually, I talked John down.

"Do the lines like your father," I advised him.

"What do you mean?"

"Just talk the way your father would talk," I tell him. "Talk with a kind of patrician accent. If your father could afford to send you to Andover, he could afford to pay for a psychiatrist. Talk like a person who can afford to pay for a psychiatrist."

I'm not sure John could follow me there, but when we next rehearsed the scene he delivered his lines in a stately monotone, like an Upper-Middle-Class WASP. That was exactly what I wanted. I wanted him to deep-six that annoying frat-house accent. I wanted him to talk like an adult.

John's scene, in which he rattled on a bit about Bulimia Envy, ended with Doug jamming a custard pie directly into his face and then sneering, "Mr. Franklin, I don't think I can help you." The scene, which we did in a single take, was oddly prophetic of events that were to take place later in the week. When you're making a movie, whether it's a low-budget movie or a big-budget movie, there are certain things that always happen. You always run over budget. You always fall behind schedule. Someone in the film always gets a crush on someone else in the film. The producer always moans about cost overruns. It always rains. Animosities always arise. Rival camps always emerge. Implacable hostilities are always smoldering just beneath the surface, threatening to erupt into outright hostility at any moment.

From the time Doug jammed that custard pie (actually an aluminum tray filled with shaving cream) into John's face, I should have realized that something seismic was taking place on the set. Yes, we were all pleased that the scene went so well. And yes, we all laughed when John did not immediately react to the pie, instead freezing his face in a sort of death mask before saying "Cut." But what I didn't realize at the time, but would realize much later on, was that when Doug stuffed the pie into John's face, everybody on the set was enormously, enormously, enormously pleased.

But nobody was more pleased than Ted, Kenna, and Adam, the technical crew. At the time, I couldn't tell whether they were pleased that John got the pie stuffed in his face, or because John was serving as a surrogate for me. For whatever the reason, they were a whole lot more pleased with that scene than they had any right to be. Uh-oh, I thought, harking back to the words of Dan Rather.

Tension City.

IT WAS LATE in the afternoon, we were doing okay timewise, we hadn't had to use very much film, and things seemed to be clicking actingwise. Now it was time to shoot the very first scene in the movie, where Thorpe has his confrontation with Amber Duggan, the calorically intolerant, spatially challenged razorback who is the prime murder suspect in the film. This was probably the most important scene in the movie because it establishes that Thorpe is not a very nice man, that his patients loathe him, and that at least one of his patients would like to see him dead. But it was also important because Amber was the red herring in the movie, the false murder suspect who would divert attention away from the real killer until very late in the film. Finally, this scene was important because Thorpe had secretly videotaped this session and left the tape where he knew his horrid wife would find it and turn it over to Turk Bishop, who would play it on his VCR again and again throughout the rest of the movie in a blatant ripoff of *Blow-Up, Blowout,* and *The Conversation* until he finally unearthed the fatal, telltale clue that Thorpe had somehow overlooked in his bid to commit the perfect crime.

For public consumption, I have always expressed profuse gratitude to my friends and family members for agreeing to appear in my movie and for learning their lines as well as they did. But the truth of the matter is, I think they were lucky to have gotten into the goddamned movie in the first place. What were they doing that week that was so goddamned important that they couldn't take time out to learn a few lines of dialogue and get a shot at immortality? Knowing that they would at least get the movie shown at a private screening in Tarrytown, with possibilities of further screenings in New York, Los Angeles, France, etc., it wasn't like I was asking my friends to lend me vast amounts of money, or drive me to Toronto to visit a sick aunt in the middle of the night, or donate a kidney. If you want to know my honest opinion, I think a couple of them could have spent more time learning their lines and worn snappier clothes to the shoot and maybe showed a little more enthusiasm for the whole project. It wasn't like they were doing *me* a favor. Hey, *they* all got complimentary baseball caps and T-shirts.

Susie Lipof was the single exception to this rule. Most of the people in the cast did a good job, but other people could have done just as good a job. It wasn't like I was asking them to play Othello. But without Susie, we never would have had a movie. Susie had to be willing to spend nine days enduring all kinds of verbal abuse. If she wasn't up to the task, we were screwed.

From the time we started shooting on Sunday afternoon, we all knew Susie was going to be just perfect. Her opening scene with Doug came off perfectly, as both of them really seemed to get into their roles. Doug was exquisitely abusive in a low-key way, and Susie responded with just the right amount of indignation and recalcitrance. By the time she stalked out of Thorpe's office after threatening to kill him, we had clearly established in the audience's mind that Thorpe was a very unconventional psychotherapist and that Amber Duggan was a woman with a very serious weight problem.

Before we shot the scene, we had to get rid of all the Chicago Cubs regalia I had stacked up on a bookcase behind Doug's head. John had done a little research in the previous week and found out that if you wanted to use any major league baseball trademarks in a movie, even a low-budget movie, you had to pay a licensing fee and also show the licenser the script, so the licenser can see the context in which the product will appear. In the extremely unlikely event that Columbia or Amblin or United Artists bought *Twelve Steps to Death,* I would have problems further down the road if I did not have the written consent of the Chicago Cubs to use their official logos in my movie. This being the case, I jettisoned all the Chicago Cubs material. I think this incident demonstrates that even at this point in the proceedings, I was already fashioning wild dreams of fame and fortune, and was already well on my way to insanity.

We shot Susie's scene with no problem, then broke for dinner ($46.98). It was six o'clock on Sunday evening. We had shot eight pages of the script, and what we'd shot today was much more interesting visually than those long scenes we'd shot the day before. None of the equipment had broken, all of the actors had done their lines the way I wanted them to, we were still shooting at a ratio of two to one, and we were right on schedule. If there was a dark cloud on the horizon, it was that my wife was getting tired of having a house full of people, Gordon and John were still arguing over that holster set, Mike was still walking gimpily because of the stab wound, Hella's shin bruise was turning an ugly shade of purple, and when Doug stuffed that custard pie into John's face, the cast and crew seemed to respond with much more enthusiasm than seemed healthy. Especially Gordon.

We ate dinner, then decided to shoot a couple more pages to stay ahead of the game. The easiest scene to shoot was the one where Bishop is in his apartment talking about the case to his partner Tom Stoddard. As was true with many scenes in this dialogue-intensive screenplay, this scene was incredibly boring: one man talking to another man for almost three minutes.

Of course, there was another big problem. Tom Staudter, the friend who was supposed to play Tom Stoddard, was up in Vermont visiting his brother. He was supposed to be back by Sunday night, but there had been complications. Now he wouldn't be back until Monday, maybe Tuesday. But Ted and Kenna said there was an easy way around that: We could rewrite the scene and have Bishop talking on the phone to his partner. Then we could use "wild sound"—independently recorded dialogue—and dub in Stoddard's lines later.

But we still had a problem. I hadn't had any time to learn my lines. I'd been busy all day directing the actors in the four Thorpe office scenes, and there'd never been any spare time to learn my lines. Also, I was tired. John suggested cue cards, but cue cards suck because you can see that people are reading off them. Then Mike, still favoring his groin, had a great idea. He would use his videocamera to tape the three pages of dialogue, then feed the dialogue directly onto the television set. I could lie on the sofa in my family room, pretending to be watching TV, while I was actually reading my lines off the screen.

To make the scene more stimulating to the viewer, I decided to writhe around on the sofa a bit. I'd recently seen *Cape Fear* for the second time, and very much enjoyed the sequence where Robert De Niro talks to Juliet Lewis on the phone while hanging upside down from an exercise beam like a mobbed-up orangutan. I didn't have an exercise beam in my house, and we didn't have the time to go out and buy one and install it on such short notice. But we could improvise. I lay on the couch and the crew covered me with T-shirts and athletic equipment, which I gradually threw all around the room in the course of the scene. There was a basketball, a soccer ball, a baseball bat, and a bunch of other junk. All this equipment helped to establish that Bishop was a typical, macho jock cop, and also that he was a bit of a slob. The scene also established that he tended to let his laundry pile up because he no longer had a wife to either wash it or tell him to wash it. It reinforced the sense of emotional discord brought into his life when that schizoid anorexic recovering alcoholic with Attention Deficit Disorder slammed into the car, killed his wife and kids, and ruined his life forever.

Or so I hoped.

We finished the scene about 11 P.M. Then everybody packed up and went home. We'd run very late, and because Kenna, Ted, and Adam had to return to the city, it meant we would get a late start on Monday. But after two days, we had shot twenty-five pages of the script, more than one-quarter of the entire movie. That put us about three pages ahead of schedule. Not even Elvis could make movies this fast.

seven

Making
a Big Splash

Monday we got started late because Ted, Kenna, and Adam had to come up from the city. They'd gone home around midnight, and didn't get to bed until one, so by the time they arrived in Tarrytown it was already noon. I was now inching toward the fatal moment when I would tell Francesca that the cast and crew would have to start sleeping overnight at our once-happy home, where twelve of us would now be bunking down in a three-bedroom house. But I wanted to delay that moment as long as possible. We'd been married for seventeen years, and had been through many rough times. I wanted our marriage to last at least until Thursday.

Monday was a gorgeous day, so we shot outdoors until it got dark. We knocked off an easy scene around one where Bishop interrogates Peter Thorpe's two kids about their father's relationship with his twin brother Paul. My wife got half the kids in Tarrytown to show up on my front lawn for an impromptu party. The party, held just a few days after Thorpe's death, was supposed to show that neither Butch nor Courtney Thorpe were all that broken up about Pop's brutal murder. And the fact that Mrs. Thorpe was nowhere to be seen, having trundled off to Monte Carlo on a shopping spree, would strengthen Bishop's burgeoning suspicion that Thorpe had murdered his own brother and taken his job as a dish-dryer because he'd rather have a demeaning job as a menial in a greasy-spoon restaurant out in the middle of nowhere than continue counseling his horrid patients and living with his appalling wife and children.

Thorpe's appalling kids were played by my son Gordon, age seven, and my daughter Bridget, age ten. Bridget had been going to Broadway plays with me since she was six, and also had some acting experience, having appeared in the coveted role of the Dew Fairy in the seminal 1992 Winfield L. Morse Primary School's production of *Hansel and Gretel*. So she was psyched about being in the movie.

Gord could have cared less about the film. Gord only wanted to be in the movie because his sister was in the movie, and now, after three days of wrangling with John about whether or not he could play with my gun and holster, he didn't really want to be in the movie at all. Gordon only agreed to do his lines if I promised to let him play with the gun and holster later in the day and secretly gave him an unspecified amount of money without telling his mother. Which I did.

We broke up this scene into one long take and a bunch of close-ups. Bridget knew her lines perfectly. Gord didn't. Gord also has a bad temper, so whenever he stumbled over a line, he would storm off the set. We finally got him to calm down and do his lines by first having me read them off a cue card and then having him repeat them. He did an adequate job, then left to play Power Rangers. We screwed up one take when Hella wandered into the background, but otherwise things were A-okay.

In theory, Hella shouldn't have even been there that day. She didn't have any more scenes to shoot until late in the week, and she had a job as a researcher on a cable TV program that she was supposed to go to. But Hella claimed to be having so much fun making the film that she called in sick and hung around the entire week doing whatever needed to be done. She picked up people at the train station, ran out on errands, wrote cue cards, and wore tight, revealing cut-offs beneath her nun's habit. She was far and away the most popular person on the set.

"You must really like this movie if you'd risk losing your job to stay here," I said to her one afternoon.

"Well, I really hate my job," she replied.

The weather being so glorious, we now shot the scene where Bishop visits the porcine Amber Duggan at her backyard pool and confronts her with damning evidence of her putative malfeasance: the incriminating videotape where she threatens Peter Thorpe scant hours before he was murdered, and the sixteen Devil Dog wrappers with her fingerprints on them, which were found at the scene of the crime. This scene, shot at the home of Steffi Walder, who would play a Somber Mourner at Thorpe's funeral later in the week, only took up about four pages of the script, but it was one of three showcase scenes I needed for clips in case I ever got on TV. The camera had to move; the shots had to be interesting. The scene couldn't suck the way all that nun footage on Saturday did.

I'd explained to Ted early in the going that I didn't give a damn how most of the scenes were executed, but I wanted the parody of *Reservoir Dogs,* the twelve-step meeting, and the pool scene to look really nice so I could go on TV talk shows and show the clips and pretend that the rest of the movie looked as good as these scenes. That way I could sell the film and earn back some of the money I was sinking into this forlorn project. The pool scene had to be a pip.

The key visual element in this sequence was Amber's porking out on a couple of bags of marshmallows planted on a table poised between her and Bishop. The camera was supposed to focus on this odious blimp's pitiful expression while she jammed one marshmallow after another down her bottomless gullet. After she's gobbled up a dozen marshmallows, Bishop was supposed to grab the bag and toss it into the swimming pool, then watch in disbelief as she plunged in after it.

This seemed like a simple set-up at the time I wrote the script, but when we got around to shooting the scene we realized that it wouldn't work. Susie couldn't dive into the swimming pool because the water would wreck the fat suit we'd rented and I'd have to pay to replace it. Fat suits cost $125 to rent for a week. Plus tax, of course. Pin money for Oliver Stone, but not for me. To get over this hurdle, we had to fake the splash by having Susie hustle out of the frame and seem to dive into the pool in pursuit of the marshmallows, when in fact it was Mike tossing a bucket of water into my face to simulate her desperate plunge.

This solution didn't work. The splash looked too fake. We tried a second approach, with Mike cannonballing off the side of the pool into the water just as Susie moved outside the frame. But Mike weighs only around 140 pounds, so the splash was too puny. We didn't get it right until the fourth take, when John and Mike simultaneously cannonballed into the water and drenched me with water. That did the trick.

We now decided to shoot a couple of obligatory but uninteresting scenes that had to be filmed outdoors. These included the scene where Bishop is first introduced, aiming his gun at the audience like the deranged sociopath he is, then talking on his cellular phone. The scene was a lay-up, and we were finished by 8 P.M. We wanted to knock off early today because the rest of the week figured to be backbreaking, and the crew needed some sleep. Ted, Kenna, and Adam went back to the city in Hella's car; John also drove in with them to drop off the first four cans of film at Du Art Film Laboratories on West 55th Street in Manhattan and pick up six more cans of film ($917.05), all on Hella's credit card. There would be no time to see what we had shot until after the movie was finished; I simply had to hope that everything would turn out fine. We were now thirty-two pages into the script, still slightly ahead of schedule. To date, the movie had set me back $6,767, not counting tips and incidentals.

Still no word from Amblin.

BY TUESDAY MORNING, my friend Tom Staudter had returned from his mysterious, very possibly unnecessary, trip to Vermont. Now we could shoot the numerous cop scenes. Originally, Bishop and his partner Tom Stoddard were supposed to have a series of indoor scenes where Stoddard tells his partner about the incriminating Devil Dog wrappers, the twelve-step program, the existence of Thorpe's twin brother. But it was much easier, and much more pleasing to the eye, to shoot these scenes outdoors. So I borrowed some golf clubs from Steve Mignogna, whose wife Regina would play Sister Damian Barabbas later in the film, and we headed over to a large, empty field down the street from my house that is vast enough to pass for the kind of public golf course that two deranged cops such as this pair would frequent. Stoddard and Bishop—that is, Tom and I—would have one of their long, meandering conversations while chipping and putting. And, in case either of us was nervous about our lines, Berman stuck a bunch of cue cards inside an ice cooler that Tom kept moving from place to place.

I was very happy to see Tom turn up that morning. Tom is six foot three and goes around 240 in a good year, and thus was perfect for the part of the cop's sidekick. Although he has a master's degree in creative writing from Johns Hopkins University and presently works as a college professor, he has also worked as a repo man, a bartender, a high school attendance counselor, a restaurant manager, and a process server for a local law firm co-owned by Artie Brady, who would play one of the dysfunctional townspeople at the twelve-step meeting to be filmed on Wednesday night. People don't screw around with Tom. I liked the idea of having my own little Mafia of large men on the set in case anybody in the cast started acting up. At all times, I wanted the cast to have a niggling fear that if things started to get out of hand, we would beat the shit out of them. I also wanted John to realize that if he didn't stop arguing with my son about that goddamned holster, we would beat the shit out of *him*.

Tom got through the first scene in fine form, expertly impersonating a somewhat dim rural policeman. Nevertheless, these outdoor scenes took much longer to film than they should have because of airplane noise. Tarrytown is about twelve miles from Westchester Airport, a busy little commuter airport, and we were directly under a flight pattern every single afternoon. Late in the day, planes went overhead every five minutes. Tarrytown is also close to West Point, and lots of military aircraft go overhead. On several occasions, we had shots wrecked by overhead noise. The crew began to suspect foul play. Ted had a theory that Robert Rodriguez had found out that I was trying to shoot a movie for $2 less than *El Mariachi* and had bribed a battalion of unemployed airplane pilots to buzz the set every afternoon to wreck our footage. But I refused to believe this.

Between Saturday evening and Tuesday morning, one noticeable development had occurred on the set. John and Ted had been locked in a low-key struggle for cinematographic control of the movie, and Ted was now winning. What's more, everybody on the set knew it. Ted was very civil when he and John would go off into a corner to discuss the next couple of shots, but the good shots were invariably the ones that Ted suggested. He was only twenty-three, but he was a professional. John had lots of experience operating a videocam and had been to film school for one year, but he didn't really know much about directing and never had any part in actually directing the actors in the film, which was my job. And as the week progressed, Ted and Kenna showed much less patience in responding to his ideas about setting up shots.

Ted, it was now clear, could think in a way that neither John nor I could. I mostly thought of each scene in terms of a problem that we had to solve right then and there. So did John. But Ted could keep a running mental inventory of how the various scenes would follow each other in the film, and he knew that it was important to have lots of lush, green outdoor scenes to offset the drabness of the eighteen minutes that Bishop and Sister Wilhemina would spend inside her dark, oppressive cell. Ted knew how the film would look when it was assembled. Ted, to put it as bluntly as possible, knew what he was doing. And since this was his first job as a Director of Photography, he was determined to make this thing work.

So John now found himself in a difficult situation. He'd desperately wanted to help me make this movie, and up until a week before we started shooting, it looked like we would end up making the film together with him holding the camera and Mike holding the mike. But once John persuaded me to hire Ted and Kenna, the rules of the game changed completely. From the start, I had only one interest: getting my film made. For a long time, it looked like John would be my right-hand man in doing so. No longer. With Ted and Kenna on the scene, John was the odd man out. For months and months, we'd joked that eventually I'd have to fire him, just like they always did in Hollywood.

It might come to that yet.

• • •

AT THIS JUNCTURE, let me say a few words about directing. Before I started shooting *Twelve Steps to Death*, I really hadn't spent much time learning how to direct. Yes, I'd taken that $279 Hollywood Film Institute course down in a theater on the Lower East Side, but Dov Simens had discussed the actual art of directing for only about forty-five minutes. Directing in his view was sort of like manual labor; you could hire somebody to do that. Producing was where the money was. I'd also read David Mamet's book *On Directing Film*, which said to ignore everything about directing that you'd ever been told, and Roger Corman's autobiography, which also didn't have a whole lot to say about the actual physical art of directing, but was mostly about money. Corman did say a lot about cheapo special effects, but we didn't have any special effects in our movie, so on balance Roger wasn't much help to me.

The night before we started shooting *Twelve Steps to Death*, I'd glanced at a book called *The Grammar of the Film Language*, which had a lot of material about setting up shots. That was the long and short of my education as a director. The way I saw it, directing was a lot like swimming: If you had two arms and two legs you could do it. In fact, to be a director, you didn't even need the legs. I also reckoned that whatever I eventually needed to learn about directing I would learn by making my own low-budget movie. Provided there was somebody else on the set who could teach me.

Ted, for example.

Most of what I knew about directing before shooting *Twelve Steps* I'd learned by watching films and making diagrams of interesting shots I could then steal. Scorsese and the rest of those film-school guys call this *homage*, but I prefer the word *theft*. So my original plan for directing *Twelve Steps to Death* was to cut together a lengthy series of interesting shots that I'd stolen from famous directors.

Since you waste a half hour everytime you move the camera and we were working on a ten-page-a-day shooting schedule, with no provisions for reshoots, we couldn't afford to shoot any scenes that weren't absolutely necessary. This meant that by Tuesday afternoon, we had to start throwing small, insignificant scenes that we didn't really need overboard. Ideally, I would have liked to have had a shot of Sister Wilhemina washing a car just like Whoopie Goldberg did in *Sister Act*; a shot of the killer's feet descending from a car (a generic shot seen in every movie made in the past fifteen years); and a shot of somebody getting kicked in the nuts (a generic shot seen in every movie made in the last ten years). I would have also liked to include some artsy, I Am a Camera shots like the scene in *A Farewell to Arms* where the camera, substituting for Helen Hayes, descends on Gary Cooper's face from overhead. And I would have liked to have stolen the shot where the sinister Christopher Lloyd's profile is eerily silhouetted against a full moon when he is first seen in Nick Castle's watershed study of middle-class mores, *Dennis the Menace*.

But by Tuesday afternoon, it was evident that some of these shots would have to be jettisoned if we were going to get the movie made on time. None of these shots advanced the plot in any substantive sense—they were all just jokes—and most of them would have required long set-up times. Also, we didn't have a full moon to work with, and couldn't just go out and build one the way Renny Harlin could.

Most important, I was now coming to terms with the fact that making a low-budget movie was like seeing your house on fire and being forced to decide which precious items you had the time to save before the conflagration consumed all that you most valued on this planet. Right at the top of the list would go family heirlooms, Series E savings bonds, old monaural Rolling Stones LPs, children, etc.

A movie's the same way. When you get a third of the way into the picture and realize that you're just barely on schedule, you have to decide what to keep and what to toss overboard. It was time to make my inventory. There was no way I was parting with the headbutt, the message scrawled in blood, the body being thrown off the castle ramparts, or the *Reservoir Dogs* parody. But these scenes would eat up hours and hours of precious time later in the week. So I couldn't afford any frills. I didn't want to wind up hopelessly behind schedule on the final day of shooting because we'd wasted time on a bunch of superfluous scenes earlier in the week. This made it much easier to decide what had to go. The nun washing the car? Out. A pair of feet ominously descending from a car? Out. A kick in the balls? Out.

"What about the flashback of Bishop beating up two recovering choc-aholics when he was still a cop out in L.A.?" John inquired.

"We don't need it," I replied. "We've already established that he's a psy-cho. And anyway, all the great screenplay writing books say that flash-backs are cheesy, intellectually bankrupt gimmicks used by hack direc-tors when they have their backs to the wall."

"So what?"

I took the next question.

"What about the flashback scene of Sister Wilhemina dressed as a French maid poised seductively on a motel bed years before she became a nun?" Hella asked.

"I don't want to rule that one out just yet," I told her. "Let's see how we manage our time the next few days."

TUESDAY, WE GOT terrific news. My friend Mary Ann Bohrer, far and away the finest publicist that the great city of Pittsburgh has ever pro-duced, the woman who had initially interested Don Imus in my book, had now arranged for a crew from Connie Chung's *Eye to Eye* to visit the set on Thursday. Now that was something to look forward to. If Connie Chung aired a segment about the making of *Twelve Steps to Death* on na-tional TV, I might be able to sell the film and become rich and famous. This, of course, would be an immense boon to the careers of Ted, Kenna, Adam, Susie, Mike, and John, who were all involved in the entertainment business in one way or another, but it would also be a boon to the career of my daughter Bridget, who had once played the coveted role of the Dew Fairy in the seminal 1992 Winfield L. Morse production of *Hansel and Gretel* and had already succumbed to the fatal allure of the flickering lights of Broadway. Hella, Doug, and Tom, of course, would probably have to keep their day jobs. As would my son Gordon.

Tuesday, we stayed right on schedule. We used cue cards for the scene where Stoddard and Bishop confer outside Amber Duggan's home. The only problem was the scene where Bishop discovers that Peter Thorpe's brother is a twin. Originally, this scene was to be shot with Stoddard and Bishop conferring in Bishop's car. But we ditched that idea because the scene would have been too static and too long, and because Tom had trouble remembering his lines. Kenna came up with a great solution. We would shoot the conversation between the two cops while Stoddard lay under his car repairing his muffler. That way, his torso would be visible but he wouldn't actually be speaking his lines at the time; we would record those lines separately in wild sound. He could record the lines at his leisure.

That solved half the problem. But Tom still had to rattle off an interminable list of Thorpe's patients, a feat that sorely tested his powers of memory. Tom devised a clever solution: He would read them off a notebook he would carry around for the rest of the movie. This would make him seem thorough, meticulous, and professional, yet somehow dumb, which was precisely the effect he was supposed to convey. Just before we shot the scene, Kenna noticed that his car had New York license plates, a continuity problem in a film set in rural Wisconsin. We covered the plates with a towel, atop which we positioned his tool chest. Then we shot the scene. It took less than two hours.

The last scene we shot that day took place at twilight. Stoddard and Bishop were aging jocks, so we decided to have them conduct their third conversation while playing a game of one-on-one basketball. Again, Tom was having trouble with his lines, so we pasted the script to my chest and then shot the scene with the camera looking over my shoulder. This didn't work so well, though, because I couldn't really move much, and it forced Tom to guard me in a rather awkward fashion, staring directly at my chest. We decided to bag this idea and simply give Tom plenty of time to memorize his lines. We cut a bit here and there to give the scene more flow, then shot it in two takes.

In this scene, I make five consecutive baskets from a variety of angles. This was an impressive display of shooting. However, I should point out that Tom, who weighs 240 pounds, never once put the body on me during the scene, and Tom, who stands three inches taller than me, never once tried to block my shot. In real life, this has never happened. One final thing: The basketball court is located in the backyard of the Dobson family, congenial neighbors who appear earlier in the film as happy townspeople. The backboard in their yard was actually planted in their lawn several decades ago, but over the years it has gradually sunk into the earth. Today, the basket stands about eight feet off the ground instead of the statutory ten.

My seven-year-old kid could have made those five shots.

THERE WAS ONE scene written entirely as a joke that I was not going to leave out of the movie, no matter what. That was the longest, continuous product plug in motion picture history, which we shot on Wednesday morning. Throughout the movie I had plugged *Movieline, GQ, The American Spectator, Allure, Philadelphia,* and my own book, *If You're Talking to Me, Your Career Must Be in Trouble,* which appears in many, many shots. Basically I had included these product plugs not because I thought they would help to sell products, but because movies that do not have blatant product plugs seem cheesy, downscale, and un-American, unless they are set in biblical times or in another solar system, where there are no products to plug. The plangent use of contextually incongruous, intrusive product plugs transmits a subliminal message of psychic reassurance to the viewer, assuring him that he is actually watching a real, live movie with an actual budget, and not some hokey piece of flotsam and jetsam that trickled in from the cultural culvert of some dipshit film school. Product plugs are not in any sense tasteful, but they are vaguely classy. They give even the lowest-budget film an aura of *gravitas*.

What I had in mind for the longest, continuous product plug in history was for me and Hella to kneel with our backs to the camera discussing the Thorpe case for three entire minutes so that the audience would have to stare directly at the brightly written word "FRED" emblazoned on the back of my white T-shirt. The Fred in question was Don Imus's brother, who runs a car repair shop in El Paso that has become famous because of his early-morning chats with his famous deejay brother during which Fred himself plugs a wide range of stellar merchandise, including these sturdy T-shirts, which can be obtained by calling: 1-800-272-1957. Don Imus had played a very important role in my career because in January 1994, when my book *If You're Talking to Me, Your Career Must Be in Trouble* (Hyperion, $22.95 hardback, $12.95 paperback) was published, he began reading excerpts from it on the air, browbeating listeners into buying it. Which they did. He'd also had me on as a guest many times since then and was constantly plugging the movie. So I owed him.

My way of repaying the debt was to film a 181-second scene where the camera never budges from the back of the T-shirt as a blatant plug for his brother's line of fine menswear. So Imus gave me hossanas, generous praise, hours of free air time, and a certain measure of radio celebrity. I gave his brother a three-minute plug in a scene in a low-budget movie that in all likelihood no one would ever see where a young woman playing Sister Wilhemina des Portes de St. Denis (née Veronica De Fonzini) discusses what she has learned by networking with the International Association of Coagulative Calligraphers, a group of computer nerds who happen to be experts in handwriting done in blood.

Are we square now, Don?

EVEN WHEN YOU'RE making a low-budget movie, you have to be very careful not to offend the artistic sensibilities of the technical people who are working with you. Although you, as the producer and director, have the power to force the cameraman to film a scene he dislikes, you would prefer not to do this. You, an amateur, want to keep the cameraman, a professional, happy and not compel him to film scenes he will be ashamed of. Otherwise, he might go into the tank and your entire film could end up looking sucky.

Ted didn't like this Fred Imus product-plug shot one bit. Even when I explained the logic of the shot, he still hated it. My spiel ran like this:

"There are some things that are bad for the film but good for the film's mythology, and there are some things that are good for the movie and bad for the mythology. It's bad for the movie that the DAT machine broke on the first day, but it's good for the myth because it's an unexpected development that demonstrates how hard it is to make a low-budget movie. And it provides me with another interesting anecdote that I can use to hype the movie once it's done. This Fred Imus product plug scene is one of those things that's bad for the movie, but good for the myth."

Ted understood this. He'd already heard me expound this theory about three hundred times. Everytime a plane went overhead and wrecked a shot, he'd heard me rationalize that it was bad for the movie but good for the myth. But he wasn't in the myth business. He was in the movie business. And no matter how well the product plug joke worked as an anecdote, he still wanted to make the scene redeemable in some cinematic sense. He needed a context to put this in.

Eventually, he hit on one.

"It's a little bit like Warhol," he said.

"Now you're talking," I beamed.

"But it would be funnier if Hella had her laptop," he said. "That way she could be kneeling in front of a crucifix worshipping while still screwing around with her laptop."

"It would also be funnier if instead of a crucifix we had a peace symbol," Hella volunteered. I agreed. "We'll get Mike working on a balloon right away," I said.

Ted had other ideas.

"I think we need a flickering light, to give it a mysterious look."

"One flickering light coming up," I responded. "Give it that Georges de la Tour feel." Folks nodded. They were used to extraneous comments like this by now.

So we shot it. Because Hella and I both had our backs to the camera, we could read all our lines off the laptop. I must admit, even while we were shooting this scene, we ourselves could sense what a long, long, *long* scene it was, and how boring it might appear to the viewer. But I didn't care. I wanted to get into the *Guinness Book of World Records* for having filmed the longest continuous product plug in the history of motion pictures, and by the time the camera had stopped running 181 seconds later, I had.

WE WERE MAKING good time. At lunchtime ($42.25), my publicist friend Mary Ann Bohrer called to say that the Connie Chung crew was definitely coming on Thursday. Fantastic. But there was more good news. Ted had a friend named David Shaw who owned his own Steadicam, an elaborate contraption that enables a filmmaker to shoot scenes of people walking toward the camera without having to use a dolly or resort to a jerky hand-held camera. And Shaw was willing to slash his going rate ($600 a day) to a mere trifle and come up and shoot a scene on Thursday. Terrific. This meant that we could shoot a scene with the Steadicam while the Connie Chungsters were filming us filming the scene with the Steadicam, while Margaret Fox, the official *Twelve Steps to Death* photographer, was shoot-ing black-and-white stills of the Connie Chungsters filming David the Steadicam Man while he filmed us walking away from the Steadicam. All of which would create the indelible impression that everything truly was up to date in Kansas City.

Buoyed by all this good news, we banged out the scene where Bishop asks the nun to go on-line with a bunch of electronic bulletin boards that might help him solve the crime. Hella read all her lines off the laptop. The scene was an easy set-up and we did it in two takes. Now we were rolling.

The only other scene scheduled for the afternoon was the mandatory Cops in the Shithouse scene. I'd written the Cops in the Shithouse scene because all cop flicks have the Cops in the Shithouse scene. *Witness* has a Cops in the Shithouse scene. *The French Connection* has a Cops in the Shithouse Scene. *The Naked Gun* has a Cops in the Shithouse scene. *The Professional* has a Cops in the Shithouse scene. Even *Mad Dog & Glory* has a Cops in the Shithouse scene.

It wasn't a particularly interesting scene; the information transmitted in this segment wasn't even that important. But it was an easy scene to shoot because while I stood at the urinal pretending to be pissing while reading my lines off the wall, Tom stood in the adjacent stall, pretending to do the same, while reading his lines off the inside wall of the crapper. We did it with a hand-held camera in the men's room on the third floor of my office building after all the other tenants had closed up shop for the day; it took two takes because I screwed up one of my lines. Forty-five minutes, all told, and we were out of there. Cops in the Shithouse. Nothing fancy. Nothing spectacular. Nothing flashy. Just Cops in the Shithouse.

Still no word from Amblin.

eight

The Kid
Doesn't Stay
in the Picture

On Wednesday night, August 17, 1994, on the fifth night of shooting, a catastrophe of Krakatoan dimensions occurs. Despite my herculean efforts to prevent it, despite my warnings, my admonitions, my exhortations, my veiled threats, the cast—or at least a faction of the cast—had finally erupted in outright mutiny. Halfway through the making of *Twelve Steps to Death,* the very worst thing imaginable had taken place: Acting had finally broken out on the set.

From the inception of this project, acting was the thing I most feared—more than inclement weather, defective equipment, massive cost overruns. When I'd cast *Twelve Steps,* I had deliberately snubbed all the people I knew with acting experience because I dreaded the havoc they would wreak on the movie once their emotional, facial, and gesticulative predilections swung into high gear.

First, they would demand that we shoot take after take until we got things right. Joe's life savings, exit stage left. Second, even though their achievements in the thespianic arena would invariably be of the Greater Elmsford Supper Club Presents *Joseph and the Amazing Technicolor Dreamcoat* variety, the very fact that they possessed any acting ability whatsoever—the arched eyebrow, the flailing palms, the riveting glare, the knowing stroke of the chin—would bring into bold relief the fact that no one else in the film could act at all. What I was looking for in *Twelve Steps to Death* was a seamless tapestry of functional, subdued, inobtrusive, no-body-here-but-us-chickens nonacting. In short, the kind of acting I'd been practicing since last Saturday. What I would get from experienced, semiprofessional actors would be a heinous collage of tics, schtick, gasps, attitude, and general hamminess. And they'd need four takes to get the job done.

In a sense, I should have been gratified that overt acting had not erupted earlier. After all, we'd already shot fifty pages of the script, yet to date we had managed to severely minimize the excrescences of actual thespianic activity. The only exceptions were a few hackneyed facial expressions from Susie, which I tolerated because Susie had come to New York to become an actress and deserved to have an occasional bone thrown her way, plus some petulant glares from my daughter Bridget, who, of course, had once performed the coveted role of the Dew Fairy in the seminal 1992 Winfield L. Morse primary school production of *Hansel and Gretel* and thus was prone to overdoing things. But other than that, none of the major characters had done any acting per se—not Tom, not Hella, not Doug, and certainly not me. If anyone else had even tried acting in my presence, I would have nipped that sucker in the bud. No, as far as I could tell, everyone in the production had been religiously faithful to my edict: "Don't get it right; get it done."

Lamentably, while I had worked closely with the major characters in the movie to ensure that they did not fall prey to the overpowering temptation to stroll the boards, I had not spent much time preparing the bit players. I had simply given them their lines about a week before we began shooting, figuring this would minimize the damage they could possibly inflict on the film. I'd given them their lines on such short notice because

I figured that seven days was just enough time for them to get over their initial nervousness and memorize their lines, but not enough time to dream up ingenious ways to rethink their characters' motivations and sabotage the entire scene. Here I was sadly mistaken.

There was one mistake I hadn't made, however, and for this I am justifiably proud. Not one of the bit players had seen the entire script. Though all of them had a general idea of what the movie was about, I had deliberately avoided giving them entire scripts. I did this for several reasons. One, most of my neighbors in Tarrytown are sensitive, caring people who buy Anna Quindlen books, so if any of them had ever seen my entire script, brimming as it was with vicious, unwarranted, totally uncalled for attacks on the recovery movement, they might very well have refused to appear in the movie.

Second, I feared that if the bit players did get a chance to read the entire script, they might start lobbying for more or better lines, or even ask for other roles. It was doubtless disconcerting to many of my neighbors that I had written roles for bulimics, sex maniacs, credit card addicts, and mule humpers and then gone to them and said, "I think you would be perfect for this part." But if they had been given a chance to read the entire script, the woman playing the bulimic might have asked for the more palatable role of the Margarita addict, while the guy playing the recovering mule humper might have asked for the more glamorous role of the person suffering from Chronic Lateness Syndrome. Though, now that I think of it, the man who played the recovering mule humper had *specifically* requested the role of the recovering mule humper. More unnerving still, the man who played the recovering mule humper was also the film's official caterer.

I still don't know what *that* was all about.

There was a third, even more compelling reason why I did not give all forty-eight characters in the film complete scripts: It cost about $5 a pop to run off a copy of each screenplay, so if I only made ten of them, I could hold down Xeroxing costs to about $50 for the entire cast.

The scene we were shooting on Wednesday night was one of the two most important scenes in the movie: the one-size-fits-all twelve-step meeting attended by all the dysfunctional residents of No Quarter, Wisconsin. This was a showcase set piece filled with lots of good jokes, and we had budgeted plenty of extra film for this scene so that we could cut back and forth between the various characters, and make at least one sequence in the movie look like a real film.

"I want to get on Leno and Letterman and to do that I need at least one good clip," I'd told Ted earlier that day when we'd banged out some short, easy sequences. "I don't care what the rest of the stuff looks like today, but this scene has to come out perfectly."

Ted assured me that it would.

Unlike our gabby nun scenes, which usually consisted of two or three long shots that could be polished off in no time at all, the twelve-step meeting contained thirty-six different shots. This meant that we could shoot all the crowd scenes early in the evening and let the bit players go home, then shoot the closeups of the main characters: Sherman Krebs, Joey Bellini, Amber Duggan, Tom Stoddard, and Turk Bishop. This also meant that the principal characters only had to do a few lines of dialogue at any one time, so if they screwed up their lines, we wouldn't have wasted much film. The scene took up six pages of the script, and it took us six hours—from eight at night until two in the morning—to shoot it.

The shooting of this scene reaffirmed why I was not Robert Rodriguez, much less Oliver Stone. When Rodriguez shot *El Mariachi,* he did it in Mexico with a bunch of his carefree, young friends. The advantage of being a young filmmaker is that you have a lot of carefree, young friends, and carefree, young people are usually free to shoot low-budget movies in the evening, because they don't have babies, and even if they did, baby-sitting rates are pretty cheap south of the border down Mexico way.

In Tarrytown, things were entirely different. Because I am in my late thirties or early forties, and because all my friends are in their late thirties or early forties, and because *Twelve Steps to Death* deals with a bunch of people in their late thirties or early forties who are weighed down by a long history of substance abuse or psychological trauma, just about all of the Tarrytowners I recruited to play the obnoxious characters at the twelve-step meeting were people in their late thirties or early forties. Why was that a problem? Because most of them had children.

Having children wouldn't have been a problem if I had only recruited one adult "actor" from each family. But this would not have been possible. Virtually everyone who wanted to be in the movie had a spouse who also wanted to be in the movie. The result? I had to pay for baby-sitters all over Tarrytown the night we shot this scene. Also, you can't live and prosper in a small, closely knit community like Tarrytown if you go around telling your friends, "I want you to be in my movie, but leave your husband at home." Consequently, we had massive baby-sitting problems. Keith Jenkins, who played the chronic gambler Sherman Krebs, was at the meeting that evening, but so was his wife, Christina C. Blatt, who played a gin monkey. Chris had also designed her husband's DON'T DISS THE DYSFUNCTIONAL T-shirt ($7.99 for the T-shirt, $11.94 for the T-shirt letters). So I had to pay for their baby-sitter. Tom Masciovecchio, who played a credit card addict, was there, but so was his wife, Beth, who played a person suffering from Attention Deficit Disorder. So I had to pay for their baby-sitter. Margaret Fox, who played a haughty bulimic, was there, but so was her husband, Tim Grajek, who played a man addicted to mint-flavored liqueurs. So I had to pay for their baby-sitter. Last but not least, my wife, Francesca, was also in the crowd scene, so I had to pay for a baby-sitter for my own kids. My wife was there for the same reason that my agent was there: I needed as many warm bodies as I could get.

The bill for baby-sitting that night came to $67, and this immediately put me in a foul mood because it was a totally unexpected expense. It really pissed me off to think that if we ended up making a low-budget movie for $7,001, and thus finished second to Robert Rodriguez in the quest to make the cheapest film in motion picture history, I would go to my grave knowing that the straw that broke the camel's back budgetwise would turn out to be the baby-sitting fees. I mentioned this concern to John. He graciously hinted that the final budget for *Twelve Steps to Death* would probably run well past $7,000 and that the baby-sitting expenses would ultimately be a mere burst of spume in a sea of red ink. These were not his exact words.

The evening started off inauspiciously. As soon as the cast was gathered together in my spacious office, which had been reconfigured to look like a town hall in a tiny hamlet out in the middle of nowhere, I explained what the movie was about. The cast included sixteen people with speaking parts, plus a couple of extras my wife had recruited to take up space and make the room look crowded. As soon as everyone had settled down, I launched into my spiel.

"*Twelve Steps to Death* deals with an abusive psychiatrist living in the wilds of rural Wisconsin whose patients are all in twelve-step programs. One day, he is found brutally murdered, so the cops have to figure out whether the murderer is the chocaholic, the credit card addict, the man who loves too much, the mule humper, the guy suffering from bulimia envy, the person suffering from Chronic Lateness Syndrome, and so on and so forth. The plot is additionally complicated by the fact that the cop investigating the murder is a man who got thrown off the L.A.P.D. for beating up a couple of recovering chocaholics after his wife and two kids were killed in a car accident by a schizoid, anorexic recovering alcoholic with Attention Deficit Disorder who was fleeing an abusive chocaholic husband who used to beat her up whenever he had one too many of the nougat caramels."

Instantly a very thin woman my wife had recruited as an extra got up and walked out. Another woman said she would appear in the movie only if she could hide behind somebody's head and didn't have to say any swear words. And a third said she would remain in the film only if she was never seen in closeup and didn't have any speaking lines.

I could see that the crowd was really pumped.

I now explained to the various cast members what I expected from them.

"The lines are funny, so if you just read them the way they're written, you'll get a laugh. Remember, you're supposed to be dysfunctional townspeople in a small town out in the middle of nowhere. So just be yourselves."

One by one, we now rehearsed them. Beth Lacy (the Attention Deficit Disorder person) got up and did her lines about not knowing who she was or where she was or why she was there. She didn't do the lines the way I hoped she would. She did them like Ophelia just before she takes the pipe. Yes, she was acting. But I didn't lose my cool, I didn't let on that I was displeased with her performance. When she was finished, I nodded graciously.

"Fine, fine," I said. "We'll get back to you."

Christina C. Blatt (Chronic Juicer) now got up and did her lines about wanting to have a fistful of Margaritas. I'd known Chris for eleven years, and was well aware that she was an artist who had attended the Rhode Island School of Design in the late 1970s, where her classmates included David Byrne of Talking Heads. So, right from Jump Street, I had my reservations about her. My apprehensions were justified. Oh, Chris did her lines okay, never stumbling or stuttering once. But, just like John on Sunday afternoon, she did them with a pronounced southern accent.

"No southern accents," I reminded her. "You're a person living in New York who's pretending to be a person living in rural Wisconsin. You can be northern white trash, but you can't be a redneck. You've got to walk that thin line."

Thom Wolke, a local concert promoter who worked out of an office downstairs from mine, now got up and did his line.

"I ain't looked up a little girl's dress since Ju-ly," he declared, with pride and passion. He pronounced the word "July" as "Jew-lie," and yes, his accent came straight from the heart of Dixie. He sounded like Gomer Pyle, U.S.M.C., or a zonked-out roadie for Lynyrd Skynyrd.

"No southern accents," I reminded him. "You're a person living in New York who's pretending to be a person living in rural Wisconsin. You can be northern white trash, but you can't be a redneck. You've got to walk that thin line."

Now Tim Grajek got up and did his line: "I am powerless before my mint-flavored higher power." Frankly, I'd been worried about Tim for days. A talented graphic designer and one-time rock 'n' roll performer, Tim had accosted me on the street the week before and told me, "I'm thinking of doing my line by whirling around to face the camera and staring at it like a zombie the way that guy does in that Calvin Klein Obsession commercial."

"I haven't seen that commercial, Tim," I replied, as a the cold hand of doom ran its glacial fingers around my heart. "But it's a thought."

The night of the shoot, Tim not only did his best Calvin Klein number, but also threw in a Boris Karloff–meets–Peter Lorre–by–way– of–Bela Lugosi Eastern European accent. Now I was starting to get nervous. *Real* nervous. Folks were acting up a storm here. The accents were totally out of control. I could feel my movie crashing down all around me in a sea of campiness.

Things only got worse as the impromptu rehearsal proceeded. Margaret Fox (Gerry the Bulimic) acted. Deb Fernandes ("Can't you see? The glass is half full, not half empty") acted. And Ellen Klein (the Car Clutter lady) not only acted, but because she is a native of Louisiana, she did her line with a pronounced southern accent that happens to be completely authentic.

Things were coming apart at the seams.

And then the heavens opened. Perhaps because of all those novenas I'd said as a child, perhaps because of all those years of getting up at five o'clock in the morning to trudge off to be an altar boy at daybreak mass, perhaps because of all those years I'd sent my mother monthly checks to cover her trips to Atlantic City, God finally took pity on me. Showering me with the bounteous fruits from His Cornucopia of Infinite Largess, God now delivered into my hands a single cast member who in no way, shape, or form attempted any thespianic, emotional, or linguistic innovation whatsoever. Divine mercy manifested itself in the person of Tom Masciovecchio, whom I'd cast as a credit card addict. When Tom was called upon to recite his lines, he rose from his chair, stared straight ahead, and said:

Hi, I'm Chuck and I drove thirty-three miles here tonight with a credit card addiction like you wouldn't believe. I charged two shotguns, a Glock 9mm, and a bow and arrow. And I don't even hunt. It's just that the gun shop was the only place that was still open.

I cannot begin to describe the exhilaration I felt as Tom delivered these lines without an ounce of passion, nuance, humor, or subtlety. He simply stood there and delivered the lines in a total and utter and complete monotone, staring directly ahead, emotionless, like the straight-arrow dysfunctional cheesehead he was supposed to be portraying.

"DO YOU SEE THAT?" I shrieked at the crowd. "DO YOU SEE WHAT TOM
JUST DID? THAT'S WHAT I WANT YOU ALL TO DO. THAT'S PERFECT. THAT'S
SUBLIME. THAT'S IT. JUST DO WHAT TOM DID. REMEMBER: DON'T GET IT
RIGHT—GET IT DONE."

From that moment on, the dark clouds of Sarah Bernhardtian artifice
cleared and we could shoot our movie in peace. The next time we rehearsed the lines, 90 percent of the accents had vanished. Oh, Thom
("I Ain't Looked Up a Little Girl's Dress Since Ju-ly") Wolke still had a
Dixieish lilt to his delivery, but because he looked so downhome with
his long hair and beard and gimme cap I decided to let it go, figuring he
could pass for a generic midwestern shitskull who'd listened to one too
many Dwight Yoakam records. But the rest of the cast soft-pedaled it.
They got up, they did their lines, they sat down. Not much emotion. No
body language. No hyperventilating. Were they happy with this? I doubt
it. But it was my movie. If they wanted to act up a storm, they should
sign up for the Sleepy Hollow Strolling Players' 1995 production of *Pal
Joey*.

The only remaining holdout was Tim Grajek. All the way across the
room, you could see that Tim just wasn't going to let go of that Transyl-
vania-on-the-Hudson accent. The accent had a stranglehold on him. But
mercifully, he did dispense with that Calvin Klein Obsession stuff. So I
let it ride. Hey, places like Wisconsin and Minnesota are loaded with
transplanted, dysfunctional Eastern Europeans, so I decided we could survive with one Vlad the Impaler accent.

By nine, we had the cameras rolling. It was boiling hot in my office that
night, so we had to keep turning on the air conditioner between takes.
Then we had to turn it off. You can't have an air conditioner running while
you're filming a movie because the hypersensitive audio equipment would
pick up the whirr. So, yes, people were uncomfortable. They were boiling. But they were troupers, and the shoot went perfectly. People knew
their lines and they delivered them properly. Those who had trouble used
the cue cards that Hella held up a few feet behind the camera. By 11 P.M.,
we were done with the crowd scenes, and by midnight we'd shot all the
closeups. Then we sent the bulk of the cast home.

That left an hour to shoot Sherman Krebs's lines, all filmed in an otherwise empty room. Keith Jenkins was a stalwart performer, perfectly convincing as a chronic gambler with a whiny, New Age side to him. Most of his lines were shot in one take. It had definitely been worth paying for that baby-sitter.

We packed up and got out of there by 2 A.M. I was pleased. We had survived the heat, the noise from the street, the nervousness of the cast, and the pressure to complete the shooting in a timely fashion so that the baby-sitting expenses wouldn't rip a hole in our puny budget. Most impressive of all, we had successfully squelched a grass-roots effort to undermine the dramatic continuity of our film by injecting an overtly theatrical element. This was the last time during the making of *Twelve Steps to Death* that anyone would make a serious attempt to act.

Victory was within our grasp.

VICTORY WAS SNATCHED away the following morning. All week long, the latent air of homicide that hovered over the film had threatened to erupt in a cloudburst of violence. Now it finally did. By the end of the day, one of the cast members would have quit the film, an unbridgeable chasm of rancor would have widened between John and me, and we would have lost an entire night's shooting because of an inconceivably idiotic oversight. By the end of the day, for the first time, we would have fallen behind schedule.

The morning didn't start out all that badly. At ten o'clock, Gene Rivieccio, the cook at my local diner who had also played the man who had not humped a mule in thirteen days—and was damned proud of it—turned up at my house with enough food to feed an army. Shortly thereafter, Mary Anne Bohrer turned up with the Connie Chung crew, who immediately started interrogating everyone on the set. No one seemed to mind being interrogated. Shortly after that, my agent, Joe Vallely, turned up, ready for action. I had a part lined up for him. It was the role of Father John De Fonzini—Sister Wilhemina's brother—the Catholic priest who had lost the ability to speak during a bicycling trip in Spain, and who conducted the funeral service for Peter Thorpe by using sign language. The last time my agent had opened his mouth, it was to get me the book

contract to write about the making of *Twelve Steps to Death,* a venture
that had now wrecked my marriage, ruined my relationship with my son,
and wiped out my bank account. So the decision to give him a non-
speaking part was by no means accidental.

While the Connie Chung crew wandered about with their microphones
and videocameras, Joe, John, Ted, and I discussed the set-up for the funeral scene. When I'd written the screenplay, I'd specified that Father
John De Fonzini would speak in Spanish sign language that his sister
Veronica would then translate for the assembled mourners. At the time,
I did not know whether sign language was a universal medium of exchange
that could be understood in any country, or whether it varied from one
nation to the next. I figured I'd find out later. I never did find out. I was
a terrible researcher. So here we were, the day of the shoot, and Joe
wanted to know what kind of signing he should do.

At that moment, I had the very last good idea I would have throughout
the making of the film. Wouldn't it be funny if, instead of using conventional sign language, Joe used National Football League penalty signals
to deliver the eulogy? That way, he could give the signal for illegal forward pass or backfield in motion and Hella could translate it as: "Take
an omer full of manna therein, and lay it up before the Lord, to be kept
for your generations." Surely, someone would laugh at that, just as they
would laugh at Hella when she translated the signal for "The field goal is
good" as "Eli, eli, lama sabachtani?" Surely they would laugh. Surely. And,
if and when they laughed, it would vindicate my basic philosophy of
moviemaking: that if you could just come up with one good idea a day,
in a matter of days, you'd have yourself a movie. Of course, movies shot
in nine days only have nine good ideas.

We were at this point in our deliberations when David Shaw, the
Steadicam Man, showed up. Steadicams provide movies with professional-
looking shots that make the films seem less amateurish and low-budget.
Normally, a Steadicam operator like David would earn between $600 and
$1,200 a day for his work, but because he was Ted's friend he agreed to
work for just $200. On the other hand, he only agreed to do one scene.

One scene was fine with me, if only because it so impressed the Connie Chungsters. When Mike Silberman, the segment producer, and his

crew had turned up that morning, they were doubtless expecting a bunch of halfwits wandering around like idiots with cameras they couldn't focus and cheapo, hand-held mikes stuck just outside the picture frame for the actors to shout into. Yet, thanks to Ted, here we were with our very own Steadicam operator, all set to shoot a highly professional-looking sequence. The Connie Chung crew was very impressed. So was I. Everything that Ted did on the film impressed me. His acumen reminded me that there were two things for which I would be eternally grateful to John Domesick. One was introducing me to Ted so that I wouldn't have to make a movie with John. The other was introducing me to Kenna so that I wouldn't have to edit a movie with John. Yes, by this point, Kenna had made it known that she was deeply interested in editing *Twelve Steps to Death* once we'd finished shooting it, and I'd made it known that I was deeply interested in having her do so.

The Steadicam notwithstanding, the scene we were shooting Thursday morning kind of sucked. It was a scene where Bishop walks around the town reservoir with Sister Wilhemina, discussing the case. Bishop had just gone through that whole castle door scene with Amber Duggan and now realized that she couldn't have possibly murdered Peter Thorpe because she was too fat to get through the door. The scene was about four minutes long, and felt like it.

Then Hella suggested a way to pep things up. She had a pair of black-and-purple Rollerblades in the trunk of her car. Maybe she could be a Rollerblading nun.

"I could Rollerblade all around you the way Sarah Jessica Parker does to Steve Martin in *L.A. Story*," she suggested. It sounded fine to me. That way, when the movie came out, film critics would recognize the allusion and think that we were paying tribute to whomever directed *L.A. Story*, the way Woody Allen is always paying homage to Jean Vigo and Ingmar Bergman. Visual quotations of this sort were an important part of contemporary moviemaking, an art form based almost entirely on plagiarism masquerading as homage.

Unless you're making a movie with a lot of car chases and decapitations, four pages of script will usually contain an immense amount of dialogue. That was certainly the case here. So we decided to break up the scene into three shots: two from the front, one from the rear. David strapped on the Steadicam and slowly walked away from us—backward—while Kenna strolled beside us with the boom. The Connie Chungsters walked behind all of us, filming the ridiculous sequence, while Hella and I tried to remember our lines. Which we pretty much did.

The sequence went fairly smoothly, though. The first take of the shot from the front had to be done over again because some teenagers who were fishing in the reservoir made faces at the camera. Fucking creeps. But the second take went fine. So did the remainder of the shoot, except for the time Hella nearly fell over. But even that worked in the context of the scene because it reinforced her stature as a pious ditz. I was tickled pink. We now we had at least three halfway decent clips that I could use in a trailer or on *Jay Leno:* the twelve-step town meeting, the scene where Amber dives into the pool in pursuit of the bag of marshmallows, and the Steadicam shot.

We didn't start falling behind schedule until lunchtime ($26.75). The Connie Chungsters were constantly asking me or Ted or John or my daughter to go off to the side for interviews, and all of us, except Ted and Kenna, were running at the mouth. This was not a complete waste of time because we really wanted the Connie Chungsters to get plenty of good material for their segment, and air it on national TV, and make us all rich and famous. But it still ate up valuable shooting time. So we didn't get started on the funeral scene until midway through the afternoon.

Even here, we endured needless delays. The day before, my wife had told a bunch of neighbors that we needed plenty of somberly clad mourners to turn up in the huge backyard of Regina Mignogna (Sister Damian Barabbas) for the funeral service. But only five appeared, so we had to go out and dragoon some more locals into participating in the film, including one man who didn't even know we were making a movie. He showed up in a blue sports coat, gray trousers, a dress shirt and a tie, but, enigmatically, completed the ensemble with a pair of tennis sneakers. This seemed a mite informal for such a gloomy occasion, but what the hell, the film was set in Wisconsin after all, and cheeseheads were famous for their eccentricity. So we got ready to shoot.

The scene where my agent delivered the eulogy in sign language came off quite well ($15, plus tax, for priest's collar and dickey). Everyone laughed at his bizarre gesticulations, even the women in attendance who had no idea that his strange gestures were actually studious reenactments of NFL penalty signals. You didn't have to know *why* it was stupid to know *that* it was stupid. Unfortunately, the funeral scene took about two hours to film, which was far more time than my son Gordon cared to devote to the endeavor. Gordon, like his mother, had never been especially enamored of this undertaking, and the idea of spending two hours in the hot sun, wearing a blue blazer that he absolutely despised, shooting one shot after another of the same scene, put him in a perfectly horrible mood. He wanted to be off somewhere playing with his friends, not standing out here making a dumb, low-budget movie. He was royally pissed off.

What finally did him in was the lying, the one thing psychologists say you should never do to a child. Beat them? Sure. Starve them? Fine. But never, ever, lie to them. Tragically, Gord's entire experience in the movie had been clouded by a miasma of deceit. It was like this: When I'd cajoled him into getting dressed up for the funeral scene, I'd told him that this was the only scene he had to shoot that afternoon. Technically speaking, this was true. But one scene usually consists of numerous shots, and each of these shots can consist of numerous takes. Even in a low-budget movie, a two-minute scene will usually consist of at least five shots, each of which requires between one and four takes. All told, it took us two hours to shoot the entire funeral scene, by which point Gord was in a murderous rage.

"Just one more shot," John told him.

"You said 'Just one more shot' an hour ago," Gord fired back.

"No, I said 'Just one more take,'" John replied. "But that was the last take of a different shot. This is the first take of the next shot."

Seven-year-olds don't go for this kind of crap, so eventually I had to intervene.

"You see, son, movies are divided into a large number of scenes, shots and takes."

"I don't want to be in your stupid movie."

"A scene consists of several shots, each of which can require several takes."

"I don't want to be in your stupid movie."

"If each individual take goes well, then the total number of shots and the total number of takes could be perfectly equal."

"I quit."

Gordon formally quit the movie as soon as the funeral scene was over. He was nice enough to finish out the scene, but the whole time he wore a vicious scowl on his face. This was not an inappropriate facial expression for a funeral ceremony at which his father was being interred in the cold, cold ground, so I didn't mind. But Gordon made it perfectly clear that his acting career, such as it was, was now at an end. Under no circumstances could he be persuaded to shoot his one remaining scene, where Bishop grills Thorpe's two children after the funeral ceremony. I tried to get his mother to reason with him, but no one can reason with Gord. He's a world-class ballbuster. So our shooting schedule for the afternoon had to be radically modified. Gord, who had already appeared in an earlier speaking role, would now have to be written out of the remainder of the movie.

I was really glad the Connie Chungsters were within earshot to capture all of this.

Later that night, when Gord went to bed, I would chat with him about the events that had transpired that afternoon. At the time, of course, I had considered breaking both of his legs or forcing him to eat a diet of tripe and Christmas puddings until he agreed to rejoin the cast. But now that a few hours had passed, I was no longer angry. The fact was, I admired Gordie for taking this courageous stance. Both he and his sister had been treated horribly all week. They had been forced out of their normal schedule, forced out of their beds, treated like subhumans. They had a right to be angry. But the single most important reason why I wasn't mad at Gord was that his acting really left a lot to be desired, his scenes needed to be trimmed anyway, and his attitude was poisonous, so he was no great loss to the picture.

• • •

Exit, Marlon Gordo.

THE DAY HAD started out well; then we'd hit a rough patch. Now things disintegrated completely. When we returned to my home at five o'clock to break for dinner ($38.97) and set up the last shot of the day, I spent about thirty minutes being interviewed by the Connie Chungsters. Three times John came out to tell me were falling behind schedule and to wrap up the interview. Three times I told him to take a hike. The fourth time he came out, I yanked off the CBS mike, stormed into the house, and screamed at him for five minutes, calling him every name in the book. I told him that the cast hated him, the crew hated him, my wife hated him, and my kids hated him. I also noted, parenthetically, that I wasn't all that fond of him myself.

John took all this in stride. From the moment we had begun discussing his participation in this project I had joked that at some point I would have to fire him, because that's what always happened in real movies. So I think he thought that when I was screaming at him now, I was just letting off steam. But I wasn't. I wanted him off the set. I wanted him out of the movie. I wanted to fire his ass.

But I couldn't fire him because his girlfriend, Lara, who played the part of Peter Thorpe's widow, Brittany Thorpe, was scheduled to shoot her big scene on Sunday, the last day of filming, and if I fired him now, she was certain to quit as well. This was the only reason I didn't give John his walking papers. The only reason. Absolutely, positively the only reason. Really. The only reason. So this is my advice to young filmmakers: If you're going to hire an assistant director that you may have to fire, don't cast his girlfriend in an important role because once she's shot her first few scenes in the movie, you're stuck with both of them for the duration. That's why the next time I make a movie, the assistant director will be a eunuch.

THE CONNIE CHUNGSTERS captured my explosion on tape; I think they were grateful for the material. The next thing I knew John was out on the front step being interviewed by Mike Silberman, who was asking what the fracas was about. I think the Chung crew may have felt that the explosion had been choreographed for their benefit, but it wasn't. By this point I really and truly hated John Domesick. If I had a gun, I would have shot him. If he'd had a gun, I'm sure he would have shot me. What was happening on the set of *Twelve Steps to Death* was exactly what I had always been told happened on the sets of real movies: Sooner or later, two of the men decided that it would be a good idea to kill each other.

If we could have salvaged something out of the day by shooting a usable scene that night, the day would not have been a complete catastrophe. Alas, the day was a complete catastrophe. The scene we were supposed to shoot that evening was the one late in the film where Amber Duggan is unable to squeeze through the narrow door at the top of White Castle, which had been built in the thirteenth century when there were no people as fat as Amber Duggan, and thus proves to Bishop's satisfaction that she could not have murdered Peter Thorpe. The door we intended to use was the trapdoor that leads to my attic. Obviously, the second-story landing in my generic, postwar suburban home does not look like a thirteenth-century Scottish castle. But we could work around that. We would make the second-story landing of my house seem more medieval by taping crepe paper and one of my daughter's tartan kilts onto the walls, and by shooting the scene in nearly total darkness with the camera gazing down at Amber from the top of the stairs.

The door in question was one of those hanging affairs with a folding ladder that dangles down from the attic. From a distance it seemed incredibly narrow. Even from up close it seemed incredibly narrow. At no time, and from no angle, did it look like a door that could possibly be wide enough to accommodate a Falstaffian lardbutt like Amber Duggan, busting out all over the place in that rented fat suit. So the shoot should have been a snap.

The shoot never got shot. Why? Faulty preproduction. In a real movie, someone would have measured the door weeks in advance to make sure that Amber could not possibly fit through it. But this was not a real movie, and it did not have adequate preproduction. Because of time and money pressures, we were always under the gun and a lot of little things didn't get done. One of the little things that didn't get done was measuring the door. As soon as Susie fatsuited up and began climbing the stairs toward the attic, it was apparent that she would have no trouble whatsoever fitting though the aperture. There was at least ten inches' clearance on each side. Goddamn it.

"Let's get some pillows," my daughter suggested. Well, we did. But even laden down with a half-dozen pillows, Susie was still far too thin to have any trouble whatsoever squeezing through the door. The pillows gave her a bigger gut, but they didn't make her significantly wider. She looked like a pig. What we needed was a blimp.

We tried more padding, but everyone already knew it was a lost cause.

"This is stupid," Susie finally declared, looking down dejectedly. Ted agreed. I agreed. Even Bridget agreed. Amber Duggan was supposed to be preposterously fat, but she was supposed to look fat-suit fat, not pillows-stuffed-in-the-pants fat. The pillows didn't sculpt her body the way the fat suit did; you could tell we'd stuffed padding under her dress. She didn't look like Amber Duggan; she looked like Clarabelle. What's more, she looked markedly different from the way she'd looked in previous scenes that we had already shot. By this point, Amber had already appeared in the movie four or five times, so the audience already knew how fat she was and how fat they should expect her to be in the next shot. Sure, she was fat. But she wasn't *that* fat.

So we ditched the idea of using my attic door and started frantically looking for another narrow aperture somewhere in my house. No luck. There were no suitable doors anywhere in my house and there were none at any of the neighbors we called. Let's face it: Americans are a large race of people, and American homes are designed with doors designed to accommodate large people. Nobody we knew had a door that was anywhere near narrow enough to prevent Susie from squeezing through it. In other words, we were screwed.

I decided to send everybody, including the Connie Chungsters, home for the night. The crew was exhausted. John and I could no longer stand one another. My son had quit the movie. This being the case, it seemed like a good idea to send John back to the city with his girlfriend, Lara, and have Mike and Hella go with them. That way, my family and I could get a break in the action before gearing up for the pure hell that the final three days of shooting promised to be. Everybody packed up and left.

That night, the house was ominously quiet. We were six days into the shoot and had finished just fifty-seven pages out of a ninety-three-page script. That left us five pages behind our shooting schedule with the most important scenes in the movie still waiting to be filmed. And we still needed to find a door too tiny for the porcine Amber Duggan to squeeze through. All of a sudden, I wasn't enjoying making movies any more.

nine

If You're Worried About Looking Ridiculous, You're in the Wrong Fucking Movie

It was Friday morning, Day 7, and for the first time, we had fallen behind schedule. Because of Thursday's reverses, we needed to shoot thirty-five pages of the script in just three days. This was an absurd amount of work, but if we couldn't make up a huge chunk of time today, there was no way we were going to finish the movie by Sunday night. With Ted and Adam slated to start work on another film Monday morning, and with the camera due back at the shop by noon on Monday, there was no possibility of extra shooting. Whatever we hadn't shot by Sunday night wasn't going to get shot, period. It was time to get some points on the scoreboard.

The first order of business was the narrow castle door through which Amber Duggan could not insert her girth and swarth. My wife had an ingenious solution. She pointed out that the garage adjoining our

house was made of charmless gray cinderblocks and had a vaguely medieval aura. True, the door leading from our hall vestibule down into the
garage was still too wide to obstruct Susie, but that could be solved by
constructing a second fake door and positioning it inside the real door.
It was a simple, elegant, and, in many ways, idiotic solution, but it was
fine with me. Hell, we were making a low-budget movie.

While the crew and cast were assembling at my house, trying to get back
on speaking terms, Francesca drove over to a local lumber store, picked
up a sheet of plywood ($14.86) that would just barely fit inside the door
leading to the garage, then raced off to visit Ellen Klein, the Cajun Car
Clutter lady who had the only authentic southern accent at Wednesday's
twelve-step meeting, and whose husband Larry is quite handy. Larry
dragged out his Black & Decker circular saw and sculpted an arched aperture in a vaguely feudal shape. Then my wife rushed home to paint it
Merovingian gray. By the time the rest of us had finished eating, the paint
was dry and the door-within-a-door was ready. We jammed it inside the
garage door, and it looked terrific. Unfortunately, there was no obvious
way to attach it to the stone walls. So we used strips of duct tape lining
the back.

To give the garage an even more medieval ambiance, my wife produced
a flag of Wales, sporting a fire-breathing dragon. It was a crappy-looking
thing that we'd bought for about a shilling (whatever that is) on a trip to
Cardiff many years ago, but my wife had long maintained that someday
that tatty old flag would come in handy. Today's events vindicated one of
the guiding principles of her life: Never throw out anything stupid, ugly,
or useless, because someday you might need it when you're making a low-
budget movie.

We unfurled the Welsh flag and hung it on the wall opposite the door,
so that when the camera peeked over my shoulder and past Amber's massive body, the effect would be decidedly Plantagenetian. By this point,
Susie had climbed into her fat suit and decked herself out in some garish clothing of a festively middle-of-the-nightish variety, since her character had just been summoned from her slumber to a mysterious assig-
nation at the castle. Now we ran into new problems. Originally, the script
called for Amber to vainly try squeezing through the door, thus estab-

lishing beyond the shadow of a doubt that she could not have passed through it to the castle ramparts and therefore could not be the murderer. In fact, the original script was so objectionable that it actually contained this passage:

Int.—White Castle—Late at Night.

We see AMBER DUGGAN *framed in the archway of the door leading to the ramparts of White Castle.*

DUGGAN: If I can't fit through, it means I'm home free?

BISHOP: Something like that. You could have still hired someone to push Thorpe, but then why leave all those Devil Dogs wrappers with your fingerprints? I mean, I'm giving you the benefit of the doubt and assuming you're not an idiot. No, if you can't get through that door, I think we can close the books on you.

DUGGAN: I'm a lunatic for doing this. If my lawyer finds out . . .

BISHOP: Walk up to that door and save yourself a lot of legal fees, Mrs. Duggan. Even from here, I can see the good money's on you.

DUGGAN frowns at this left-handed compliment. She takes a huge breath, puffs out her gargantuan form, and approaches the door.

BISHOP: No cheating, Mrs. Duggan.

DUGGAN stares at him coldly, then sucks in her jowls in an attempt to make herself thinner. This is not a pretty sight. She takes a last breath and approaches the door. She tries to walk straight through it. No good. Not even close. She tries again. Same result. Beaming, she tries to give STODDARD a high-five. He does not reciprocate.

BISHOP: Try it sidewise.

DUGGAN looks crestfallen but reluctantly complies. As mincingly as her porcine form will allow her, she tries to slide through the door sidewise. Alas, her gut is far too vast to allow passage.

BISHOP: Suck it in, Mrs. Duggan. And put some wiggle in your waddle.

DUGGAN now engages in a protracted attempt to squirm and jiggle her enormous carcass through the door, but meets with no success. Her face turns crimson from the effort as she huffs and puffs. But no matter how she contorts herself, she cannot get through the tiny aperture.

DUGGAN: Can we stop now? Have you made your point?

BISHOP approaches her, puts his arm on her shoulder, and begins to speak in a very soothing manner.

BISHOP: Mrs. Duggan, I want this to be over as much as you do. So let me ask you for one more favor. There's a female police officer downstairs with a bathing suit. I want you to put that on and try to squeeze through the door.

DUGGAN: If I had a rendezvous with my psychotherapist at dusk on the ramparts of a deserted old castle, don't you think he would have known something was up if I showed up in a bathing suit?

BISHOP: Mrs. Duggan, the criminal mind is inscrutable. It would really help us wrap this thing up if you'd just slip into a bathing suit.

DUGGAN: Well, if you're going to put me through the wringer like this, I might as well go whole hog.

Suddenly DUGGAN begins tearing off her clothes.

BISHOP: Jesus, give me a break.

STODDARD: Tommy, I don't think we should be here for this.

DUGGAN has now stripped down to a tight black corset and full slip, which amply reveal her mammoth proportions.

DUGGAN: Eat your hearts out, boys!!

DUGGAN resumes her assault on the doorway, squirming this way and that way, but does not even come close to crossing the threshold onto the ramparts.

> BISHOP: Tommy, grease her up with that margarine pail.

STODDARD *begins to slather the enormous woman with margarine, covering her thighs and buttocks with grease. She makes an herculean effort to squeeze through the aperture. But at no point does it ever appear likely that the woman could successfully negotiate passage through the door.*

> DUGGAN: If you could see me shimmy like my sister Kate . . .
>
> BISHOP: That's fine, Mrs. Duggan.
>
> DUGGAN: You gotta shake your moneymaker, shake your moneymaker . . .
>
> BISHOP: I think you've made your point, Mrs. Duggan.
>
> DUGGAN: Bend over, let me see you shake a tailfeather, bend over, let me see you shake a tailfeather . . .

The camera fades out as AMBER DUGGAN continues her joyous performance to the dismay of the attending police officers.

Admittedly, the scene was a bit gross. But that isn't the reason we didn't film it the way it was written. We didn't film it the way it was written because logistically we couldn't get it to work. As soon as Susie started wriggling around inside the plywood frame, the duct tape came loose and the flimsy structure tumbled out of the doorway. It was also clear that if Susie pushed too hard on the fake door, it might splinter in two. No matter what we tried, we could not keep the plywood frame from jiggling loose when Susie writhed around inside it. This made the scene look stupid: Medieval people, whatever their other failings, at least built things to last, so there was no way we could have a thirteenth-century Scottish castle door suddenly come loose off its moorings after seven centuries of durable service.

Oh, yes, while we were going through these procedures, the Connie Chung crew showed up and started videotaping our clownish efforts. This made us all feel very professional.

Eventually, it became evident that Susie could not shake her moneymaker, bend over to let us see her shake a tailfeather, shimmy like her Sister Kate, or any combination thereof if the door was going to stay in place.

We had to compromise. Susie would simply have to stand in front of the door, and her mere size would make it clear to the audience that she could not possibly have fit through it. We would shoot her from the front and back, with Bishop drawing a yardstick across her shoulders to illustrate how much wider they were than the narrow door. I wasn't happy with this solution, but time was running out and there was no other alternative.

"It looks completely fucking ridiculous," I told John, as Susie took her place in the doorway. We were now back on speaking terms. More or less.

"Hey, if you're worried about looking ridiculous, you're in the wrong fucking movie," he replied.

Good point. Emboldened by John's perspicacious insight, I said okay, let's shoot it. We did, polishing off the scene in about two and a half hours, which was good for Susie because the fat suit was literally making her sweat like a pig. First, we shot Bishop and Stoddard when they meet to discuss the width of the door. This was done in a single wide shot. Then Amber and Bishop had their exchange, which required three shots. The toughest part of this sequence was framing Amber in the doorway in such a fashion that the audience wouldn't see all the people who were standing right behind her: four members of Connie Chung's crew, Hella, Mike, Adam, Kenna, John, and Margaret Fox, a cast member (Gerry the Bulimic) and official film photographer who had come over to take some stills. By three in the afternoon, we were done. Susie could take off the fat suit forever.

She seemed quite relieved.

THE CONNIE CHUNGSTERS now had all the footage they needed, so they packed up and left. We did, too, loading all the equipment into the van and trundling off to the next location. The scenes on tape were the two meetings between Bishop and Thorpe, plus two brief encounters between Bishop and the inarticulate Mexican dishwasher Miguel Feneiro. I had originally set these scenes in a diner, after obtaining permission from Bellas, my beloved local diner, to shoot there. But when I wrote the screenplay, I didn't know anything about making movies. When I wrote the screenplay, I didn't know that it takes a minimum of one hour to shoot a page of script, meaning that Bellas would have to shut down for twelve hours while we shot the twelve pages of the script eaten up by these three confrontations.

This they were not able to do. They were running a business. The only option was to shoot the lengthy scenes after the restaurant closed at nine o'clock, but this would have meant shooting until five in the morning, which we could not do because we all needed to get up bright and early on Saturday morning to shoot the most important scenes in the entire movie, the ones that take place at the castle.

That wasn't the only problem with shooting at Bellas. The kitchen and washroom were far too small for the scene I had in mind; the shot would have been much too tight. These conversations were long, long scenes, and the only way to alleviate all that optical tedium was to have one of the characters do a lot of pacing back and forth. This would not have been possible at Bellas, so we had to look elsewhere. My wife approached one other Tarrytown restaurant to see if we could use their kitchen for a few hours of shooting, but they turned us down, partially because of insurance concerns, partially because I was not Woody Allen, who shot parts of *The Purple Rose of Cairo* in Tarrytown, and partially because they are emissaries of Satan. As late as Friday morning, we still didn't know where we would be shooting these scenes; as time started to run out, it actually looked like we might have to shoot the scenes in my own kitchen and pretend it was a greasy-spoon restaurant. This would make the movie look *really* hokey. Boy, was I glad the Connie Chungsters weren't around to see that.

Then, for the second time that day, my wife came through for us. Francesca had loathed this project from the very beginning; she'd grown to hate it more and more as the week dragged on and the tension between John and Gordon grew; she completely hated it after seven strangers pitched camp in our house and filled the living room to overflowing with filmmaking equipment; and she positively loathed it after the Connie Chungsters started sticking their videocam in her face and asking her what it was like to be married to someone like me. Francesca is English, and English people hate having their privacy invaded, especially by people with minicams. All things considered, she now recognized, it had definitely been a mistake to marry me.

But there is another side to the British personality. English people understand that just because you hate something doesn't mean you can't turn it into a positive experience. Take the Battle of Britain. Or the War of the Roses. So Francesca bailed us out by nipping down to the Neighborhood House, a community center for senior citizens in Tarrytown, and asking if we could shoot in their kitchen that evening. As one of the thousand points of light George Bush used to prattle on about, my wife had long been active in all sorts of community activities that self-infatuated people like me absolutely refused to have anything to do with. But this was the first time in memory that any of her nonrevenue-generating philanthropic activities were actually paying off. The director of the Neighborhood House not only said that we could use the facility, but that we could shoot there as late as we wanted, even if we went past midnight.

We went way past midnight.

THE FIRST THING we had to do that night was correct a glaring continuity error. Earlier in the film, Stoddard had distinctly told Bishop that the murdered psychiatrist's twin brother Paul worked as a dishwasher in a greasy-spoon restaurant seventy-five miles up the turnpike in Dutchman's Prairie. The Neighborhood House had two institutional kitchens on either side of the building, but neither one of them looked like a kitchen in a greasy-spoon restaurant. So how were we going to fix that, with no time left for reshoots?

Luckily, Tom himself wasn't around at the time, so we could fiddle around with his character. Here's why I use the word *lucky*. When I wrote the screenplay in July, I had deliberately crafted Stoddard's character as a bit of an idiot. Stoddard was always the butt of Bishop's wiseass, I-spent-eight-years-on-the-L.A.P.D. remarks. He was a lummox. But Tom, no idiot himself, hadn't played the character as an idiot. He'd somehow subverted the character into a stone-faced wise guy who gave as good as he got. Or so he thought.

I, unlike Tom, still regarded the Stoddard character as an idiot, an incompetent, a putz. This being the case, it would not be out of character for the bumbling police sergeant to have told Bishop that Paul Thorpe worked in a greasy-spoon restaurant upstate somewhere when in fact he actually worked in a retirement home. Stoddard was a fuckup; otherwise, what would he be doing on a police force in rural Wisconsin? So the first order of business was for me to get dressed up as Bishop and amble up the path to the Neighborhood House, then suddenly pull up short and exclaim: "Jesus, Stoddard said Thorpe worked in a diner. This looks like an old folks' home."

Admittedly, it was a cheesy solution to a continuity error, but Christ, we were making a low-budget movie.

ON TO RIO Caramba. We decided to cast Adam, the assistant cameraman, as Miguel, the terrified, dimwit Mexican dishwasher, because at the time Adam was sporting a mammoth Frito Bandito mustache and looked kind of Mexican, although he is actually Jewish. We also recruited Adam because the person who had originally been cast as Miguel backed out at the last minute because he thought the character was an ethnic stereotype. This was indubitably true, but consider the context. Every single character in the movie was a ditz, a schmuck, a psychopath, or an asshole, so why should we make fun of all these one-dimensional white people and then let Mexicans get off easy? This was the kind of crap you always encountered in Oliver Stone movies like *Natural Born Killers* and *The Doors,* where all of the white people were portrayed as fiendish sociopaths, but the Native Americans were always depicted as venerable repositories of timeless wisdom, sayers of sooth, if you will. Screw that, I decided. If we were having any Mexican dishwashers in this movie, by God, I was determined that they were going to be ethnically stereotypical Mexican dishwashers. How many Mexicans film critics were going to see this movie, anyway?

Viewed with the benefit of hindsight, maybe the ethnic stereotype didn't need to be quite as ethnically stereotypical as Adam made him. Yes, Adam did go a bit over the top, what with the pink-and-yellow straw sombrero that made him look like one of those statues WASPs always put on their front lawns, and a Juan Valdez–meets–José Jiminez accent he must have gotten from watching *I Love Lucy* one too many times. It was also his idea to repeatedly blurt "I am legal" in a state of near hysteria, and to pronounce the word *yes* with a pronounced "j." And at the crucial moment when Bishop (me) asked him how high the dirty moussaka dishes were piled the night Peter Thorpe was murdered, maybe Adam did go a little bit overboard with his magically stupid response:

"They were as high . . . they were as high . . . they were as high as the hills of my rolling country."

Needless to say, Adam's idiotic improvisation brought down the house.

I was pleased with the way the two scenes involving Bishop and Miguel turned out, because Adam did seem to be genuinely terrified of the cop who was interviewing him, and because Ted and John and Kenna assured me that I really did manage to deliver my lines with the sadistic air of menace that moviegoers would expect from a cop who had spent eight years on the L.A.P.D. Remember, the movie was being shot the same month that California governor Pete Wilson and billionaire businessman Michael Huffington were running for high public office on a vicious anti-Mexican platform, so it seemed entirely appropriate that an eight-year veteran of the L.A.P.D should deliver his lines like a wetback-hating psycho. Even if the movie was set in rural Wisconsin.

The only thing I didn't like about the scene was the woefully inadequate "mountain" of pots and pans that my wife had assembled. The premise of the sequence was that Peter Thorpe, after impersonating his dimwit dish-drying brother, could have snuck out of the old folks' home for two hours, hotfooted the seventy-five miles down to No Quarter, murdered his brother Paul, written the "DOCEPAS" message in Spanish, and then raced back to do his brother's job without anyone noticing that he was gone. How? By stacking up a nine-foot pile of pots and pans and dishes and then leaving a 120-minute tape-recording of himself drying dishes behind this Mount Everest of soiled kitchenware. I know this sounded absurd, but Christ, we were making a low-budget movie.

Unfortunately, my wife didn't assemble nearly enough pots and pans to construct a convincing, aerodynamically functional nine-foot-high pile. Yes, she drove all around Tarrytown gathering up every pot and pan she could lay her hands on, and we even pillaged the Neighborhood House itself in a desperate effort to make that pile look really impressive. But it never did. We just didn't have enough dishes. And no matter how we stacked them, they kept falling over, wrecking the takes. So, instead of erecting a pile of dishes so high the camera couldn't see over them, we had to settle for a rolling hill's worth of dishes, and then have Miguel say that on the night of Peter Thorpe's murder, the dishes were piled much higher than they were tonight, that they were piled so high no one could see over them, that they were, in fact, piled as high as the hills of his rolling country.

Next movie, I'll set aside more money for dishes.

THE WHOLE TIME we were shooting Miguel's scenes, my dear friend Doug Colligan (Peter and Paul Thorpe) sat over in a corner editing manuscripts he'd brought home from work. He actually sat there for about six hours, which is how long it took us to finish up. It was an unusual way for him to get into character, but like I said before, Doug had been in 'Nam. We ordered dinner at around nine ($48.75), then started shooting his scenes at 10 P.M.

As soon as Doug pulled on his inane white T-shirt, reading HAPPY TO BE HERE ($7.99) and turned his orange baseball cap around backward, and started saying things like "Far Out" and "Whatever Makes You Happy Makes Me Happy," I realized what a colossal mistake it would have been to cast myself as the Thorpe Twins. Sure, I could have handled the Peter Thorpe psychiatrist role with no problem because Peter Thorpe was a heartless, cynical dick, and so am I. But the Paul Thorpe character had to be a wifty, sappy, New Age airhead, and there was no way I could ever get loose enough to play that role. Doug, who'd been quite believable as a refined, affluent, successful psychiatrist, was even more credible as a zonked-out spacemuffin who'd taken way too much blue acid at Woodstock. Maybe this was his way of making up for all that time he'd spent in Vietnam when everybody else in the country was taking too much blue acid at Woodstock. For whatever the reason, he really did come across as a spacey, rustic burn-out. He was so, so loose.

The scenes pitting Bishop and Thorpe came off without a hitch. We got around all the nettlesome White Sox trademark infringement stuff by hanging a couple of white socks from a cabinet behind Doug and then having Bishop say, "White Sox fan, huh?" And that was that.

We had a good time shooting these scenes. For the first time all week we didn't have to worry about fading sunlight, or poor room ventilation, or not screwing up in front of the Connie Chung crew, or placating disgruntled wives or unhappy children. We could just shoot the scenes until we got them right. We could relax.

It helped that Doug knew his lines really well. We did trim a bit here and a bit there, but mostly these sequences were a snap. We shot about eight pages of script in four hours, and wrapped up around two in the morning. An hour of onerous loading, transporting, and unloading back up at the house and we were ready for bed. Oh, yes, everyone slept at my house that night. Now we were bedding down eleven people.

When I went to bed that night, I was relieved that we were back on schedule. We now had seventy pages of the script under our belts, right about the ten-pages-per-day we'd been trying to stick to. More important, the spirits of the entire crew had revived. John had taken a backseat now and was deferring to Ted's judgment on all the camera angles. A lot of the acrimony had subsided. We were within sight of our goal now, and tomorrow we had the whole day to shoot at the castle. At long last, we were going to have some fun.

If I could just keep Gordon away from John.

ALL OF SATURDAY'S shooting was scheduled to take place at Axe Castle, a massive Tarrytown folly built in various stages between 1897 and 1911 by a French family that had some money to spare. For many years, the castle had housed a brokerage firm; a few months earlier it had been purchased by an investment outfit headed by our dear friends Hanspeter and Steffi Walder, who also had some money to spare. They planned to turn it into an upscale hotel and restaurant. The castle was a mixture of various styles—French, Gothic, Romanesque—though sadly, not 13th-century Scottish. But since it was the only castle in Tarrytown, and absolutely the only castle that happened to be owned by any of our dear neighbors, we were glad to be able to shoot there.

Throughout the making of *Twelve Steps to Death,* I had held out the promise of the castle shoot as a big treat that the crew and cast could look forward to at the end of the week. Instead of shooting in deserted offices and bathrooms and neighbors' backyards, we would now be shooting in a real, live castle. It was, for all intents and purposes, the only genuine production value we had in the entire film.

When you're shooting a real movie, with a real budget, you always make sure to scout out the sets before you start filming there. Alas, in the case of Axe Castle, this was not possible. The Walders were away on vacation the week before we started shooting; otherwise we would not have waited until the next-to-last day to film the most important sequences in the film. More problematic still, Ted had never gotten a chance to survey the castle and think through interesting set-ups because by the time the Walders did return from their vacation, we were already busy making the film, working long into the evening every day. Ted did not get a chance to see the castle until Friday afternoon, and even then he'd gotten only a whirlwind tour because we had to rush back to the Neighborhood House to shoot the kitchen scenes. This is not the way you are supposed to make a movie. This is the way Ed Wood made movies.

Saturday morning, after breakfast, I broke the news to Francesca that she would have to play the town coroner. I'd originally written this part for my friend Andy Aaron, who had worked on *Ishtar,* and who'd leapt at the offer. But the day of the shoot, Andy had to go out of town or mend socks or watch his wife have a baby or attend a seder or something. Maybe he didn't really want to be in the movie after all.

Francesca didn't really want to be in the movie, either, but she did want to get the movie over with. So she agreed to play the part. There *was* the trifling matter of her lines. When we set up the shot, with her sitting beside Peter Thorpe's corpse (a stupid-looking dummy John had rented at a Greenwich Village gag shop for $85, plus tax, plus $14 for a wig, plus tax), clutching her laptop, she, like many other cast members with small parts, immediately tried to act. As always, I encouraged her not to do this.

"Just read your lines off the laptop," I told her. "Nobody expects a coroner to seem relaxed or natural. Especially not an English coroner. So just read your lines off the laptop, deadpan. Remember, you subscribe to Coroner/Net, the on-line, interactive database, so it's okay for you to read off the computer screen."

"But I feel so clumsy," she protested.

"Ces, remember: Don't get it right; get it done."

Alas, she was still nervous and uncomfortable. On the first take she got about halfway through her lines, then glanced away from the laptop at the stiff and lost her place in the script. We cut. I took her aside. I told her to simply read her lines. She tried again, with the same results. Then I used my ace in the hole. My wife is English, and English people are unbelievably cheap. I pounced.

"Ces," I explained, "Every take we mess up wastes money. *Our* money. Our children's money. If we can get this scene done in the next take, we'll still have money to send our kids to Oxford. If we keep messing up, they'll end up going to Central Connecticut State."

The next take was perfect.

BY TWO O'CLOCK in the afternoon, we had three scenes in the can. The coroner's scene required three takes. Then Tom and I did the sequence where we stand over the corpse and debate whether the message "DO-CEPAS" sounded Greek or not. This scene also required three takes because Tom improvised the lines, "Where's the ice truck? This guy's getting kind of ripe," and I could no longer keep a straight face. Three takes: More time, more money. Thanks a lot, Tommy.

Due to time pressures, we got rid of the scene where Seamus Fogarty, the White Castle groundskeeper, discovers Thorpe's battered corpse. This meant eliminating the scene where the camera lovingly follows a man's feet as he descends from a car, a film cliché I dearly would have loved to have in the movie. But you can't have everything. The message scrawled in blood was done with a hand-held camera following my fingers as I scrawled the letters "DOCEPAS" in corn starch mixed with food coloring, which we purchased at a Greenwich village gag shop called Abracadabra for $4.50 plus tax. Technically speaking, Doug should have been the one to scrawl the message because it was either Peter or Paul Thorpe's fingers that were writing the cryptic message, but Doug was out kayaking that day. Yes, he enjoyed being one of the stars of the movie, but not to the point where he would let that interfere with his weekend leisure activities. *Very professional.* Luckily, it didn't really matter whose fingers we used—you couldn't see the body that they were attached to—but the scene required two takes just the same.

Here's why. The first time I scrawled the message, I did it slowly, tortuously, the way a nearly dead person who had just been pushed off a castle turret would have. But after we shot it, Kenna reminded me that the person writing the message was not the dying Peter Thorpe but a very-much-alive Peter Thorpe, who had just murdered his brother. So why would the very-much-alive Peter Thorpe be scrawling a message like a dying man? He wouldn't. We got ready to shoot it again. But before we shot it, Ted noted that even though we knew that the person scrawling the message was the killer and not the victim, the audience wouldn't know this, and shouldn't know this. It would give away the film's ending.

So to trick the audience, I scrawled the message at a slow pace, sort of like a dying man, but also sort of like a perfectly healthy murderer who just happened to be a very careful speller. The Thorpes were both Catholic, so they would have been taught Palmer Penmanship at an early age, meaning that their handwriting would always be highly legible, even if they were writing in their own blood. Or their own brother's blood.

We broke for lunch, supplied by the Walders.

EVERY MOVIE, NO MATTER how bad, needs one great shot that can be used in stills to create the impression in the public's mind that the film is filled with innumerable other shots of similarly high quality. We got our one great shot in the Great Dining Hall of Axe Castle that afternoon. It was the parody of the *Reservoir Dogs* ear mutilation scene, where Ted took an overhead shot of Bishop entering the hall and approaching Thorpe, trussed in a chair, hands bound behind him, in the middle of the enormous room. The shot was taken from a kind of musician's balcony that hung above the banquet hall. Peeking down through the lens, you could see how the camera sucked up the blood-red color of the carpet, foreshadowing the blood that the audience now expected to be spilled by Bishop. We did it in two takes.

The rest of the sequence went very smoothly. The only problem was Bishop's stupid dance, the parody of Michael Madsen's sinister footwork in *Reservoir Dogs* just before he cuts off the cop's ear. I am a very bad dancer and do not like to dance in public, so I wanted this shot to be done in one take. I knew that the experience would be profoundly humiliating. Earlier that week I had read an excerpt from Burt Reynolds's autobiography *My Life* in which he talked about the butt-fucking scene in *Deliverance.* For reasons too obvious to mention, Ned Beatty, the buttfuck-ee, insisted that John Boorman shoot this scene in one take. That's the way I felt about this scene. Having my awkward, desperate, quintessentially Caucasoid hoofing captured on film for all time had to be a one-shot deal. No rehearsal. No reshoot.

There was another problem. When Michael Madsen turns on the radio to an oldies' station in *Reservoir Dogs,* he remarks that the station is exclusively devoted to hits of the 1970s. The radio thereupon begins playing the horrific Steelers Wheel hit "Stuck in the Middle With You," and his peculiar dance is synchronized with the song. But because we were shooting a low-budget movie, we did not have the money to use legitimate hits of the 1970s. So I told Doug that the radio station was KLB-70, which specialized in songs from the 1870s, because songs from that era would be in the public domain. The song I had in mind was either "The Camptown Races" or "Oh, Susanna!" which we would record at some later juncture. But we didn't actually have a song playing on the radio at the time that I did my stupid dance. So in addition to executing my clumsy dance, I also had to attempt to synchronize my movements with the beat and rhythm of a version of one of these songs that we had not yet recorded.

This is a lot to expect of a middle-age white man.

I managed. Completely shutting out the dozen or more people who were gathered in the room I steeled my nerves, wrapped my fingers around the straight-edge razor, and launched into the dance with an up-tempo version of "Oh, Susanna!" resonating in my ears. First, I did an awkward parody of Madsen's *Reservoir Dogs* number. Then I threw in some backward tippy-toe work. Then it was time for a couple of Fred Astaire *pas de deux* around the room. Finally, positioning myself directly in front of Doug, I finished off with a spiffy, Johnny Carson–like soft-shoe.

Then Doug went and ruined the entire shot by applauding with his feet.

Why was the shot ruined? Because it made me laugh, and I wasn't supposed to laugh. Not then, nor any other time in the movie. When Doug improvised his pedial applauding, I actually fell down laughing and the entire crew fell down with me. We stayed on the floor for about five minutes, yukking it up. Hardy-har-har. Chuckle-chuckle-chuckle. We definitely felt a sense of relief lying there on the floor, belly laughing. Previously you could have cut the tension in that room with a knife. Now you couldn't.

That didn't change the fact that the shot had been entirely ruined, forcing me to do my stupid dance a second time. This I did not care to do. I already felt like an idiot. And with Doug still bound in the chair, I seriously contemplated cutting out one of his eyeballs with the straight razor in my right hand just to make sure he did not mess up the second take. Goddamn kayaker.

Then Ted had a burst of inspiration. We could cut the scene just before I stood in front of Doug and did my soft-shoe, then cut to Doug's head rocking back and forth in time with the music, then cut back to me doing the soft-shoe, then cut back to Doug clapping with his feet. Then we could shoot the scene where I threaten to cut off his ear. All of which we did. At the conclusion of the scene, I ripped off Doug's black baseball cap and cut it to shreds with the straight razor. The camera caught me doing so. Doug hadn't been expecting me to do this; I think it was his favorite cap. But we were making a low-budget movie, and he'd nearly wrecked an entire take with his unscripted foot applause, and I was still pissed off at him for going kayaking that morning—would he have done that to Oliver Stone?—and, anyway, he was still tied to that chair, so the hell with him. It was very late in this endeavor to start cracking the whip on the cast, but better late than never.

• • •

SHOOTING OUR MOVIE that day would have been a whole lot easier if Axe Castle had an elevator. It didn't. This caused all kinds of problems when we got around to shooting the last three scenes—up on the tower, down in the driveway, back up on the tower—because Axe Castle is seven stories tall and we had to lug the equipment all the way up and all the way down twice.

By "we," I do not mean "me." Throughout the making of the film, I disappeared whenever equipment had to be moved. I could only be pushed so far. No, "we" meant Ted, Kenna, Adam, Mike, Hella, John, and whoever else happened to be around at the time. Carrying all that equipment up and own seven flights of stairs was murderous work, but having to do it twice was brutal. Too bad; it had to be done.

Here's why. The scene where Paul Thorpe is pushed off the castle ramparts by his brother had to take place at twilight. So we went up to the roof and shot it in a couple of takes. One hour down the drain. But the scene where the camera follows the flight of the rented dummy ($85, plus tax, plus $14 for a wig, plus tax) off the ramparts and down into the parking lot also had to take place at twilight—a few seconds after Thorpe is surprised atop the castle by his twin brother. In fact, the scene had to be shot *immediately* after the audience sees Thorpe being menaced by his brother. In a real movie we could have shot these scenes any day of the week. But this was a movie where we could only shoot in the castle for one day. We still had ten to twelve pages of the script to shoot on Sunday, with no margin for error because Ted and Adam were starting new jobs on Monday. There was no way we could come back on Sunday.

Oliver Stone can always come back on Sunday.

Unanticipated architectural nuances high atop Axe Castle created the most glaring continuity error in the entire movie. The ramparts of Axe Castle provide the highest unobstructed view in Westchester, including a really terrific view of the Hudson. Unfortunately, only one side of the tower was usable, the one with a makeshift wooden platform allowing people to look out on the majestic Hudson. The other three sides were sheer walls. So when we shot Doug as Paul Thorpe in his birdwatching mode, we had to shoot with the camera staring directly over his shoulder out onto the river. Directly over his shoulder, looking down the river, was the

New York City skyline. Directly over his shoulder, facing west, was the Tappan Zee Bridge, a four-mile structure filled to overflowing with Saturday night traffic. And the platform wasn't big enough to allow Ted to shoot over Doug's shoulder while pointing up the river.

Bear in mind that the castle, as depicted in the film, was a thirteenth-century Scottish edifice that had been transported to a small town in rural Wisconsin at enormous expense by a prosperous nineteenth-century cheese tycoon named Angus McDougal. Bear in mind that the hamlet of No Quarter, Wisconsin, had a population of just 350 souls, and was supposed to be miles and miles from the nearest town. Bear in mind that rural Wisconsin doesn't have any rivers as wide as the Hudson, nor any bridges as wide as the Tappan Zee. That night there must have been two thousand cars on the bridge when we shot the scene. That was twice the stated population of our fictitious, unbelievably dysfunctional town.

"It could be a bridge leading to the interstate," volunteered Doug.

"The bridge looks fucking ridiculous in the shot," I fired back.

"If you're worried about looking ridiculous, you're in the wrong fucking movie," John said for the second time that weekend.

In the end, we had no option but to shoot the scene with the bridge in the background. If we shot from the north, the Manhattan skyline would have been visible in the distance. And we couldn't shoot from south to north because the platform wasn't big enough to accommodate the crew, the camera, the lights, the boom, and Doug.

"Next movie, rent a helicopter," said Adam.

I marked that down.

We shot the ramparts scene, Tappan Zee Bridge and all. It was a continuity error, all right, but in our defense I dimly recalled that the first time Armand Assante spots the New York skyline in *The Mambo Kings*, the Twin Towers were clearly visible in the background. The scene was set in the early 1950s, two decades before the Twin Towers had been built. I mentioned this to the crew, but no one had seen *The Mambo Kings*. Anyway, the movie had been a bomb.

By now, it was starting to get dark. No time to shilly-shally; we had to run all the way downstairs with all the equipment and set up the shot of the dummy flying off the castle parapet. And we had to do it quick. Ted

got the camera focused, while all the way up on the ramparts Mike prepared to toss the dummy into the parking lot. This took about thirty-five
minutes. Remember: Everytime you move the camera, the next shot takes
at least a half hour to set up. More, if you have to run down seven flights
of stairs with a bunch of people who aren't in such a great mood. By the
time we were ready to shoot, it was nearly eight o'clock.

John hollered up to Mike, telling him to heave the dummy on the
count of three. He did. By this point, a vast and far-reaching multitude
had gathered in the parking lot. Virtually the entire cast was there. But
dozens of humble townspeople had also come by, some with their children. There were also a couple of guests who were visiting the Walders,
the owners of the castle. And there were even some people who had
drifted over from the adjoining apartment complex to see what the hell
was going on out here. At the time, the Walders were locked in negotiations with the village trustees to get the zoning for the castle changed so
that they could turn it into an upscale hotel/restaurant. The negotiations
had been hindered by fears among the castle's immediate neighbors that
the new establishment would generate immense amounts of traffic. So
here we were on a balmy August night with about seventy-five people gathered in the castle parking lot watching a dummy being thrown off the castle ramparts during the making of a low-budget movie.

It certainly gave the neighbors pause.

"Let 'er rip!" John cried and Mike heaved the dummy ($85, plus tax, plus
$14 for a wig, plus tax) overboard. As heaves go, it left something to be de-
sired. Although the dummy was freighted down by my $395 sports jacket
(ruined by the plummet, but I decided to treat this as an off-budget expense), a pair of trousers, a belt, and penny loafers, it didn't weigh more
than a few pounds. And, unfortunately for us, there was a bit of
a wind that evening. So when the dummy cleared the castle tower, it
didn't rocket out into the air and then tumble into the parking lot the way
we had expected. Instead, it dropped straight down three stories onto a roof
jutting out over the Banquet Hall of the castle. And it just kind of laid there.

Now we had a serious problem. Earlier in the day, we had shot the scene
where Bishop, Stoddard, and the coroner discuss Peter Thorpe's death.
Throughout this scene, the corpse was clearly positioned in the middle

of the castle parking lot, perhaps thirty yards from the walls. For continuity reasons, the dummy *had* to land in the parking lot. But here we'd filmed it falling onto a lower roof. Useless.

And now the light was fading.

Throughout the day, Steffi Walder (who had played one of the Somber Mourners at Thorpe's funeral, but who was also co-owner of Axe Castle) hadn't been very involved in the proceedings. She was busy entertaining guests and preparing food for the cast. Now, with the fate of the film hanging in the balance, she leapt into action. Thirty-five years earlier, she had escaped from East Germany fleeing the iron heel of Communism. Now her furtive skills were called upon once again. She ran upstairs, shimmied out onto the roof, and retrieved the dummy. Intrepid stuff. Now she carried it back up to the ramparts. By this point, the light was completely dissipating. We had time for one more shoot. And the dummy had to clear the walls and fall directly into the driveway. Otherwise, that earlier scene would make no sense at all.

At this point, for the second time during the making of the film, the hand of God intervened. Deep inside, I knew that no matter how hard Mike and Steffi heaved that dummy, it was not going to travel very far. At best it would clear the walls and tumble straight down into the bushes that ringed the castle. This would create mild continuity problems. But I could live with mild continuity problems. What I could not live with was a dummy tumbling onto that roof a second time. The dummy had to clear that lower roof.

With the light fading and the assembled multitude swelling to even greater numbers, I shouted up to Steffi and Mike to heave the dummy. John hollered "Action" and they tossed the dummy over the walls. First it went up. Then it came down. Even in that split second, you could see that the dummy was headed almost straight down, right back onto the lower roof.

Disaster.

Then, as I said, the hand of God intervened. The dummy hit the outer ledge of the roof, then caromed off into the distance. It *caromed*. The effect was hilarious. Magical. Macabre. There was something side-splitting about seeing a doomed man's body caroming off a wall. It was a million times funnier than a straight drop. Everyone waiting down in the drive-way exploded in paroxysms of laughter. Thunderous applause reverberated throughout the Hudson Valley, all the way up to Poughkeepsie. We had finally caught a break. If we had rehearsed that scene a thousand times we could not have captured a funnier shot. And if we had practiced that toss a thousand times we would have never gotten a better carom. For the first time since we had begun shooting this film, something wonderful had occurred. Stupid, but wonderful.

Cut, print.

THE REST OF the evening was a race against time. When I'd asked Hanspeter and Steffi if we could shoot some scenes at their castle, I'd assured them that we would be finished by ten o'clock, eleven o'clock tops. This was an outright lie. We were up on the castle roof until two in the morning, and by the time we finished packing up it was three. By the time we finished, some people had passed out drunk and some people had fallen asleep. Grown men were weeping. Policemen were turning in their badges. Kenna got so sick from lack of food and sleep and from the sheer physical exhaustion of supporting a boom for sixteen hours that we had to take her to an all-night diner at four in the morning and buy her a hamburger. It wasn't very tasty.

How did those final shots turn out? *Mezzo-mez.* The scene where the phalanx of twelve-step townspeople trudge up the stairs like zombies and corner Peter Thorpe worked to perfection because Ted could set up the camera on the far end of the wooden platform and shoot their approach from a long angle. But the final conversation between Thorpe and Bishop was less successful. Ideally, the scene would have been shot from over-head on a ladder or a helicopter. We didn't have a helicopter or a ladder. Poor planning. The shots were just too tight. There were also a million problems with lighting, because the reflection of the boom kept getting in the way. At one point, Kenna risked life and limb by climbing up on the highest point of the castle and thrusting the boom out overhead. If she'd fallen, we would have had senseless human tragedy, lawsuits of all descriptions, and a partially silent film. And Ted was also risking disaster all the time by positioning himself on the edge of the platform railing, which was a bit rickety.

There was one other dilemma. At the end of *Twelve Steps to Death*, Peter Thorpe is supposed to climb up on the castle walls and leap to his death. Obviously, this was not possible: Doug had to be at work on Monday. The best we could do was to have him duck down out of sight, and jerk the camera off into the darkness to suggest that he had leapt to his death. This was Ted's idea. As he explained:

"There was a movie called *Permanent Record* where the camera focuses on a guy standing on the edge of a bridge, then the camera pulls away, and when it comes back, he's gone. That lets the audience know that he's killed himself."

"Sounds fine to me," I said. "Wasn't Keanu Reeves in that movie?"

"Yes."

Eventually, we had ourselves a wrap. It wasn't, perhaps, the wrap we would have liked, but it was a wrap. If it hadn't been two o'clock in the morning, and if everyone, including Hanspeter Walder, hadn't been ready to pass out, I would have liked to stay there until we got every scene just right. But we didn't have the time. Besides, we had to be up by ten the following morning to finish all the remaining scenes we hadn't been able to shoot during the week. So, at two in the morning, we called it a day.

Saturday had been the most enjoyable day of the entire shoot. Filming at the castle exhilarated everyone. The Walders supplied plenty of food and booze. But the thing I remember most vividly about that evening was not the way the crew felt, or even the way I felt, but the way all the onlookers felt. During one of the breaks in filming, just before midnight, I looked out across the castle ramparts and took the whole scene in, not as a player or a director or even as a producer who was getting taken to the cleaners by making the most expensive $6,998 movie in history.

No, when I looked out on the vast assemblage I did it as an impartial observer, almost as a journalist, which is what I almost am. While the crew moved the equipment and the cast members rehearsed their lines, I gazed out at all my neighbors, and at their cute little kids, and at all the people who'd come by to help out or just to see what the hell was going on up here. And then and there, I waxed philosophical. There must have been fifty of us up on the castle ramparts for those last shots, and when the camera focused on Doug as he beat his desperate retreat up the steps and away from the twelve-step zombies, I studied the expressions on the faces of the crowd that had gathered.

Doug's wife, Louise, was there, and his thirteen-year-old daughter, Deirdre, and Hanspeter and Steffi, and people I play basketball with, and the wives of people I play basketball with, and the wives of people I don't play basketball with, and people I didn't even know. And as Doug beat his retreat from the engulfing army of dysfunctional fuck-knuckles, you could see that their faces were lit up like Christmas trees. Here we were, on a gorgeous August night, high atop a storybook castle in Tarrytown, and we were making our own movie. Neat-o. It was as if elves had visited Tarrytown and spread fairy dust among us, and even though the crew was physically worn out and ready to slit each other's throats, and even though the movie had wrecked my marriage and pillaged my bank account and shattered my nerves and ruined my relationship with my son and destroyed my friendship with John and forever wrecked any chance I had of coming back here to shoot another movie at Hanspeter's castle, it was all somehow worth it because never in my life had I seen so many people with such huge, radiant smiles on their faces, and, frankly, I don't ever expect to see that many again.

So, as I stood there that evening with the moon shining down upon us, I finally realized what this whole project was about. It wasn't about cinema, and it wasn't about epic pranks that got out of hand, and it wasn't about gathering good material for a book, and it wasn't about fulfilling childhood dreams. It was about friendship. When you got right down to it, the most positive element I was going to take away from ensnaring myself in this artistic and actuarial equivalent of the Bataan Death March was the goodwill of my fellow Tarrytowners. This is what I had learned from my weeklong adventure in the world of motion pictures: that making a low-budget movie in the small town where you live is basically a very expensive way to impress your neighbors.

Still no word from Amblin.

• • •

SUNDAY WAS SALVAGE Operation Day. We still had to shoot the meeting between Thorpe's widow and Bishop, which occurs one-quarter of the way through the film, plus the subsequent conversation between Bishop and Thorpe's vile daughter Courtney, but we also needed to shoot the scene where Bishop headbutts Peter Thorpe after he makes the fatal admission that he does not know which team Bo Jackson is playing for that year. This scene occurs three-quarters of the way through the movie. We also needed to finish the Sister Wilhemina–Turk Bishop outdoor scene that got wrecked on the first day because of rain, as well as the scene where Bishop asks Sister Damian Barabbas if Sister Wilhemina lives in the No Quarter convent. And we needed to reshoot the scene where Bishop first appears, aiming his gun off into the distance while chatting on his cellular phone with his sidekick Tom, who informs him that the station house has burned down after a couple of Yuppie cops making cappucino on a Bunsen burner have set the building on fire. Finally, Ted had to film Bishop watching a videotape of Amber Duggan threatening to kill Peter Thorpe, and then film a black-and-white videotape of the same scene, which Bishop could look at through the lens-finder of the videocam when he and Stoddard go out golfing together. The French maid flashback and any other flashbacks were out. Damnation.

This was an insane amount of work to do on a day when everyone had gone to bed at four o'clock in the morning and felt absolutely awful on rising the next morning even though Ted, Kenna, Adam, John, and his girlfriend, Lara, had stayed at the Ramada Inn at my expense ($175.23) because I didn't want to run the risk that Gordon would stab them all in their sleep. The one person who did wake up that morning feeling bright-eyed and bushy-tailed was me. This was, to coin a phrase, the first day in the rest of my life. By midnight, I was going to have my life back. By midnight, I would no longer have eleven people living in my house. By midnight, I would no longer have $50,000 worth of film equipment cluttering up my living room. Most important of all, by midnight, my wife and son would stop hating me. Well, start to stop hating me. So I was looking forward to Sunday's shoot like nothing I had ever looked forward to in my life.

Hella and I drove to the Ramada Inn to pick up the crew. We immediately found Ted, Kenna, and Adam, but John and Lara were hard to track down because they had registered under Lara's last name, and I didn't know what her last name was. Again: When Oliver Stone casts somebody named Juliet in a movie, he at least knows her last name. This was yet another example of the yawning chasm separating a master craftsman like Stone from a pathetic amateur like me.

To be perfectly honest, I did not initially believe Ted and Kenna when they said that John was nowhere to be found because he had registered under his girlfriend's name. I was sure they had murdered him in his sleep and dumped the body in one of those rented gondolas out back. The crew were no longer on intimate speaking terms with John; Mike was his only remaining ally, and even Mike, who liked everybody, was showing signs of wear and tear. Kenna had already informed me that when she started editing the movie ten days hence, under no circumstances would she allow John to come into the studio, not even to look at the footage. He could not be part of the editing process; he could not be part of the marketing process. As soon as we finished shooting today, John's participation in the movie was over. Otherwise, I'd have to find myself another editor.

I was saddened that things had come to such an dreary impasse. It would have been far, far easier on everyone if I had simply hired someone to abduct John earlier in the week or perhaps break his legs, making it impossible for him to show up on the set. But this was never a viable option. For one, I was still grateful to John for putting me in contact with Ted and Kenna and for recruiting Hella, Mike, Lara, and Susie to be in the film. He had done an exemplary job as a line producer, assembling props, organizing the cast, harassing me into getting the screenplay written.

But John did not know the first thing about directing a motion picture, and as the week rolled on Ted and Kenna, young, serious professionals, could no longer tolerate his interference in the film. By the second day of the shoot, the film was starting to slip out of his control, and by the third day of the shoot, the rest of us were letting him say "Action," "Roll sound," and "Cut" while directing the film around him. I would take the actors aside and told them how to do their lines, and I would also make suggestions about where we should shoot the scenes and what visual elements were important. Ted would set up the shots, patiently listening to John's suggestions, but then diplomatically ignoring them. Making this movie with all these separate camps was like making a movie in Eastern Europe with a Serb director, a Croat crew, and a bunch of Bosnians in the cast.

When I first started discussing *Twelve Steps to Death* with John, I had always joked that at some point in the film I would fire him, because that was what always happened in real-life movies. At the time we both thought this was quite amusing. But by the third day of the shoot I knew that I should have fired him, because the tensions on the set were never going to subside while he was around. John simply could not get along with anybody. I am not exaggerating when I say that my son's feelings toward John were naked hatred. Nor am I exaggerating when I say that those feelings were not confined to Gord alone. If John's dismembered corpse had been discovered halfway through the shooting of the film, every person on the set, with the possible exception of Mike, would have been a prime suspect. This really was just like Hollywood.

Why, then, didn't I fire him? Two reasons. Casey Stengel once said that the secret to managing a baseball team was to separate the players who knew that they hated you from the players who still weren't sure. In *Twelve Steps to Death,* John acted as a barrier between these two groups, serving as the lightning rod for all the animosity that normally would have been directed toward me. This was the one role he filled to perfection. At no point during the filming of the movie did anyone ever blame me for the long hours, the fucked-up shots, the general air of tension. They all blamed John. While they were all off hating John, huddling in tiny groups to discuss how much they despised John, I could wander off and rewrite him dialogue, or ask neighbors for permission to shoot in their backyards, or just plain think. John served as the most indispensable element in the movie: He was the whipping boy.

I was grateful to him for accepting the vital role of whipping boy. But that wasn't the reason I didn't fire him. The reason I didn't fire him was because his girlfriend, Lara, was perfectly cast for the part of Mrs. Thorpe, because she knew all her lines perfectly, because she was genuinely funny, because she brought a tremendous amount of enthusiasm to the project, and because we were shooting her big scene on the very last day of the film. If there had been any way on earth to shoot Lara's scenes earlier in the movie, I would have fired John five minutes after we had it in the can. But there wasn't—she had a job—so I didn't. We all hung together and put up with John's antisocial behavior because we needed to get the movie done, and there was no way we were going to get the movie done without Lara. Sometimes, you had to make compromises.

Sunday was the only day of the nine-day shoot that came off without a single hitch. This suggests that after nine days of working together, we were finally getting the hang of this thing. What was most amazing was that we got a very late start because everyone was still reeling from the effects of the past forty-eight hours. We didn't start shooting until one in the afternoon. But once we got in high gear, we stayed there. Lara did all of her scenes as Thorpe's bitchy WASP widow in one or two takes. She was fantastic. Then we filmed the scene where Bishop interviews Thorpe's bitch-goddess daughter Courtney. This scene had been cut down by about one-third after Gordon seceded from the film. Bridget took some of his lines; the rest we junked. Bridget knew all her lines and said them with just the right air of arctic Presbyterian nonchalance.

We now did the headbutt scene in the field behind my house. Ted decided to follow me and Doug around with the camera on his shoulder because that way we could knock off three pages of the script in one single shot and get a nice Woody Allen *Husbands & Wives* herky-jerky camera effect. The scene took two takes because the first time I tried it, I screwed up the headbutt. The second time around I snapped my my head forward in the general vicinity of Doug's forehead, then watched as he collapsed to the turf. To me, the headbutt felt awkward, stupid, and unpersuasive, but Ted and John both said that it worked fine. I took their word for it.

We quickly polished off the scene where Bishop is first introduced, pointing his gun directly at the camera like the psychopath he so obviously is. Then Ted and I jumped into the van for a fast spin around Tarrytown. We needed a series of shots of happy, thin people that could be used to open the movie, conveying the impression to the audience that No Quarter was a happy hamlet filled with healthy, physically fit people.

This would make Amber's abrupt appearance as a waddling piglet more shocking and establish how appalling Thorpe's clientele was, and why he would resort to such a desperate measure as jumellicide to escape them. It was a complete rip-off of Blue Velvet.

While the rest of us were out shooting the scenes in the field, Francesca called up all the thin people in our neighborhood and told them to stand outside their houses and wave at the camera when we drove by. Ted had the camera mounted on a tripod in the back of our van so we could gently sidle past neighbors' houses and capture them in typically seraphic, suburban poses. The only fly in the ointment occurred when Hanspeter Walder, proud owner of Axe Castle, drove past on his bicycle and very nearly fell off it. After all the trouble that I'd put him through, I felt bad that he had now almost broken his neck trying to help us finish the film. I felt even worse when I realized that Hanspeter was not thin enough to be used in this sequence, and that if he had fallen off his bike and broken his neck, it would have been a complete waste of time because there was no way we were ever going to use the footage.

The rest of the day was devoted to wrapping up odds and ends. We went back down to my office building to shoot the last part of that sequence where Bishop and Veronica first meet after so many years. No problems. Then we—actually, *they*—carried all the equipment up the hill to a nearby Baptist church where my friend Bruce Boria is the pastor. This was a scene where Bishop was supposed to talk with another nun—Sister Damian Barabbas—who would tell him that Veronica was inside. This was the set-up shot for all the other convent scenes, even though the convent scenes were actually shot in my old office. We did not obtain permission to shoot outside the church; I felt it was better if we shot the scene without obtaining Bruce's permission, because Bruce's church actually operated a number of twelve-step programs, and it would not look right if Bruce assisted me in the making of a film that suggested that people in twelve-step programs were basically a bunch of whining assholes.

We went back to my house around eight, broke for dinner ($42.85), then knocked off the shots where Bishop watches the videotape of Amber Duggan threatening Thorpe. We all felt a huge sense of relief at having finished the film, but I don't think anyone felt any exhilaration. It was like the Spanish Civil War: We were glad we had survived, but at what a cost in human lives! Because of the brutal schedule, we had not had any time to go into the city and look at the dailies. So we had no idea what the footage would look like. There was always the possibility that the film was defective, or that it had been lit improperly, or even that the film had been put into the camera incorrectly. We would not know any of this until the following night, when we convened at DuArt Labs in Manhattan and looked at the first six reels of film. So far, all we had done was to *shoot* a movie. Now we had to *make* a movie.

I had a sneaky feeling this was going to get expensive.

ten

Waiting Is
the Hardest Part

Because we shot *Twelve Steps to Death* in nine days, and because we were working fourteen-hour days while doing it, and because Tarrytown is twenty-five miles north of New York, and because we were only human, we never had any time to drive in to the lab and check our dailies. John had nipped in with Hella on Monday to drop off the first three days of footage ($6 for gas, $6 for tolls), but film takes several days to develop, so nothing was ready for viewing until the night after we finished shooting. This is a round-about way of saying that I spent the entire nine days of the shoot without any idea whatsoever what our footage would look like when it was done. Again, these are the kinds of problems that Oliver Stone never has to deal with.

Monday night, a large group of us descended on Du Art Film Laboratories on West 55th Street in

Manhattan to look at the first four days' footage ($1,434.24 to develop ten cans). The group included Doug, Hella, Mike, John, and Lara, as well as Mike Silberman and Margaret Bailey, producers from Connie Chung's *Eye to Eye*. We were ushered into a tiny screening room on the eighth floor and the film began to roll.

My immediate reaction was a mixture of exhilaration and relief, mingled with liberal sprinklings of despair. Bear in mind that the footage we were looking at consisted of every single take of every single shot of every single scene in every single sequence, presented in the order in which they were filmed, without any sound. Most of the time this meant that we were watching bad take/bad take/good take; or bad take/so-so take/bad take. Sometimes it meant adequate take/bad take/even-worse-take. Even more aggravating was the fact that the shots were being screened in the order that they were filmed, not in the order they would appear once the movie was edited. So the footage had a herky-jerky quality, and sometimes things got a bit boring.

Nevertheless, my overall reaction to what I saw up there on the screen was positive. Never having made a film before, and not being very handy with a camera, my greatest concern was that the film would come out poorly developed, like every photograph I had ever taken, or that everyone in the movie would have glaring red eyes. Also, somewhere in the back of my mind, I expected the footage to look like a porn flick. I expected it to be dark, grainy, shadowy, unbelievably cheesy. Secretly, in the darkest recesses of my subconscious, I expected the film to look like that mysterious, widely circulated porn flick where you can't tell whether it's that incredibly famous actress giving some guy a blow job, but it sure looks like it.

I was pleasantly surprised that the film did not look like this at all. The footage was just fine. The film did not look like a porn flick; many shots had interesting compositions; the lighting was good; the camera did not jerk all around the room; and the backdrops were visually appealing. It had definitely been worth paying Ted that $1,000 to work the camera, set up the shots, and for all intents and purposes make the movie. In gratitude, I paid him and Kenna an extra thousand.

The one thing I noticed immediately was that in no way, shape, or form did the movie look like it had been shot in the wilds of rural Wisconsin. Because we had filmed much of the movie outdoors in an affluent part of Westchester County, New York, the ostensibly dreary town of No Quarter, Wisconsin, looked quite charming. Far from being the "dump" Bishop had described it as at several junctures in the film, the town pictured in the footage looked absolutely beautiful. On one level, this presented us with a glaring continuity error: The town described in the script was semirural, downscale, ugly, flat, and drab, while the town actually pictured on the screen was suburban, prosperous, verdant, hilly, and lush. I didn't care. Better incongruous than boring, I rationalized. Besides, how was *Twelve Steps to Death* any different from all those recent movies that supposedly take place in Manhattan or Brooklyn but you can tell from the neat, clean streets and the poky little skyscrapers and the armies of bland white people that they were actually shot in Pittsburgh or Toronto or Vancouver or worse? Screw continuity; if the shots were watchable, that was good enough for me.

We spent all of that night and all of the next night watching the remaining footage ($1,703.93 for developing into a work print, including a 15 percent student discount when we identified Mike, who was enrolled at NYU's film school, as the executive producer). Every bit of film turned out splendidly, which was a huge relief. As for the actors on the screen, well, as the saying goes, the Lord giveth and the Lord taketh away. Even without sound, you could tell that the performances were of a less than uniformly high quality. From the very first time we screened the movie, it was obvious that Hella was reading some of her lines off the wall outside her cell in her first scene, that the cranial contusion I inflicted on Doug was the most pathetic headbutt in the history of motion pictures, and that nobody in the film could actually act, not even in the Lou Diamond Phillipian sense of the word. The moonlit shots at Axe Castle with the mammoth Tappan Zee Bridge clearly visible in the background were absurd, and all of the Sister Wilhemina–Turk Bishop scenes went on far too long. There were also a couple of scenes where the boom was visible at the top of the screen, and one or two scenes where we had stopped filming too soon or where the film had run out before the shot was over.

Nevertheless, I was far from unhappy with what I saw. Even without sound, you could tell that the showcase scenes—the *Reservoir Dogs* sendup, the mammoth twelve-step meeting, the poolside chat between Bishop and Amber Duggan—were very funny and had nice set-ups. Amber's preposterous fat suit always elicited chuckles from the audience, as did Sherman's DON'T DISS THE DYSFUNCTIONAL shirt. Most important of all, the movie did not look like something that old men would jerk off to in a darkened theater in Times Square. In this sense it had attained the loftiest plateau of cinematographic excellence that a low-budget movie shot in nine days could possibly hope to reach. Somewhere in all this footage was an actual movie that would make people laugh. Not that hard, and probably not that often. But from time to time they *would* laugh.

I WENT TO Canada for a ten-day vacation—a mistake, because there was absolutely no way I could relax with the project now in a state of limbo—and by the time I returned to New York, Kenna had begun editing the film. (John had taken a job as a producer on *The Rush Limbaugh Show* and had no further input into the movie.) The film was edited entirely at Sound One, the largest editing facility in New York, where films as varied as *Goodfellas, Sleepless in Seattle, Do the Right Thing,* and *Clerks* all have been edited. Kenna, who had previously worked at Sound One, arranged with the powers-that-be at the studio, Bill Nisselson and Stephanie Sacripante, to give us a break on our edit. The discount came to around 40 percent. I was really glad that John had introduced me to Kenna.

Editing goes like this. First, the film has to be cut into individual shots. Then the editor and director have to decide which shots work best and splice them together into a rough cut. On a real movie, like *Bonfire of the Vanities* or *Cabin Boy,* the editing process is a massive, time-consuming operation because there are often three or four usable takes and sometimes dozens of usable shots. (For genuine horror stories about the film editing process, read what Bob Evans has to say about splicing together

The Godfather in his book *The Kid Stays in the Picture.*) We didn't have that problem. Most of the time, our last take was the only good take, even if the take wasn't all that good.

Editing is essentially a salvage operation, where you take footage that isn't quite as good as you thought it was when you shot it and then try to make it better. Sometimes this can be done by cutting out extraneous shots. In other cases, a usable shot from a bad take can be spliced into the film to replace a bad shot from an otherwise good take. This is painstaking, laborious work, too painful to describe in detail. Suffice it to say that the best way to make a low-budget movie is to find a young person who really wants to become a full-time editor and then pay her to edit the film. I paid Kenna $325 a week for eight weeks to edit *Twelve Steps to Death* and paid her assistants Adam Grabel $800 and Josh Cramer $300 to do most of the grunt work over those two months. I also paid a dialogue editor named Jeff Kushner a flat $900 fee to clean up all the dialogue in the film—getting rid of all the bumps and hisses and creating a continuous background tone. Everyone involved in the project understood that the film had to be edited quickly, because the sooner we could get the editing process over with, the sooner I could stop paying $500 a month for the editing room, plus $700 a month for the editing equipment, plus $50 a month for the phones. Not counting charges for individual calls.

By the end of September, barely a month after we finished shooting, Kenna had a rough cut ready for screening. Rough cuts are extremely annoying to watch because they consist of all the shots that are going to be used, a number of shots that ultimately may be cut out, plus some overlapping materials between scenes that will be trimmed down at a later point. The shots do not mesh together smoothly. Also, the sound is rather poor, there is no music, and there's no real background noise. Rough cuts are choppy. Nevertheless, by the time you reach the rough-cut stage in the editing process, you have in your possession an object that will give the viewer a fairly clear sense of what the film will *look* like when it's done. If the audience can't follow the film in the rough-cut stage, it's not going to be able to follow the film, period.

To get some idea of how people were going to respond to the movie, I called up an old friend named Stephany Evans, who had once made a short film of her own, and invited her to the screening. I wanted to see if the film would make sense to someone who didn't already know the idiotic story. It did. She laughed straight through the screening. I also showed the film to my agent Joe Vallely, who had played the mute priest in the film, and to his wife, Janis, who knew very little about the plot. They laughed, too. While his wife was out of earshot, Joe told me that appearing in the film had been the most enjoyable experience of his entire life. I said that was very sad. As they were leaving, Joe asked me if the film was still under budget. I told him that I didn't want to talk about it.

Throughout September and October, I would come into the studio two or three times a week to consult with Kenna on the progress of the editing and to make decisions about various cuts. One problem was sheer length: In its rough-cut stage *Twelve Steps to Death* was 103 minutes long. Usually a page of a screenplay translates into a minute of film, but because *Twelve Steps to Death* has so little action and so much dialogue, we ran long. We really wanted the film to be no more than ninety minutes' running time, plus perhaps four to five minutes for the credits. Anything more than that would be pushing the audience's patience. So anything extraneous had to go.

We started trimming in early October. First, we saved two minutes by jettisoning the scene where John, playing a WASP stereotype suffering from bulimia envy, gets a custard pie squished into his face by Peter Thorpe. Kenna and I both felt that after Thorpe's initial meetings with Amber Duggan, Sherman Krebs, and Joey Bellini, the movie had already established what a bastard the psychiatrist was, so we didn't need to overdo it with this Dom DeLuise-ish touch. The film would work much better if we cut directly from the scene where Thorpe plunges the Bowie knife between Bellini's thighs to the scene where he goes birdwatching and gets pushed off the castle parapet by an unidentified assailant.

I also wanted this scene chopped out of the movie because John was supposed to be playing an uptight WASP, but in the confusion of the moment I had forgotten to tell him to shave. No uptight WASP suffering from bulimia envy would have turned up for his weekly therapy session dressed like he'd stepped out of the J. Crew catalog but sporting three days' growth of beard. WASPS aren't like that. They are nothing if not neat.

Kenna also suggested cutting out about five minutes from the Turk Bishop–Sister Wilhemina scenes, all of which went on far too long. There wasn't much we could do about the Steadicam Rollerblading scene because that consisted of three continuous shots filled with important expository material, and there was no natural place to trim. But we could get rid of the scene where she talks about the Blessed Mother having a lot of freckles because the only thing her dialogue did was to reaffirm that she was completely fried, a point that had already been firmly established in her previous scenes. "Kill your darlings," a famous writer—maybe Faulkner—once said in another context. I was sorry to see that freckle stuff go. It was some of my favorite material. But it had to go.

Certain problems in the movie could not be surgically repaired. The headbutt flat-out sucked. Hella's reading her lines off the wall could not be fixed. The Tappan Zee Bridge was in for the duration. The only way to mitigate the absurdity of these blatant screw-ups was to add diversionary music and sound effects later in the editing process. Or hope that people watching the film would give us the benefit of the doubt because this was, after all, a low-budget movie shot in nine days with a bunch of rank amateurs for actors.

By the middle of October, we had a final cut ready to be transferred to videotape. The videotape, though it lacked credits, music, voice-overs, and sound effects, was an actual film that could be shown as a work-in-progress at better film festivals everywhere. It was a complete film in a sense that *El Mariachi*, which had no synchronized dialogue, because it had been shot without sound when it was finished, was not. Thus, I now had in my possession a technically flawed, but entirely watchable, fully screenable film. The transfer to videotape, materials included, ran $1,063.56. It had now cost me $24,645 to make the film.

Unfortunately, I did not have a film that I actually could hope to sell to anyone. I did not have a film that could be shown in a commercial theater or on television. The film was now watchable in the same sense that student films are watchable: If you were willing to make allowances for its rough texture and poor sound, the way movie buffs often were, then you might enjoy the movie. But real audiences would not make those kinds of allowances. Real audiences would get pissed off at not being able to hear all the dialogue and at the absence of music and ambient sound. Real audiences would find the whole thing annoying.

At this point, I made a fateful decision, a decision every bit as fateful as Sherman Krebs's decision to bet his daughter Caitlin's $27,000 Harvard endowment fund on a basketball game pitting Kentucky against Georgetown. When I'd first gotten involved in this undertaking, my objective was simple: to see if it was possible for the man on the street to make a movie for $7,000, the way that *El Mariachi* guy said that he had. I had quickly determined that everyone involved in the hyping of *El Mariachi* was either an outright liar or completely full of shit. Unless you got the camera for nothing, the film for nothing, the developing for nothing, and the editing equipment for nothing, you could not make anything that could even vaguely be described as a movie for less than $20,000. But you *could* make a low-budget movie without a mix or sound effects or a decent soundtrack for $20,000 to $30,000, which was what the guys who made *Clerks* had done, and which I had just done. So technically speaking, my mission had been accomplished. I had tried, and I had failed. But in failing, I had performed a valuable public service, by warning aspiring moviemakers that Robert Rodriguez's $7,000 figure was a joke, that if you were going to try to make a movie at used-car prices, the used car was going to be a Jaguar, not a bombed-out Pinto.

The big problem was simple: I had now caught the moviemaking bug. Having trekked this far down the road to cinematic glory, I now wanted to go the whole nine yards. I wanted to make a real movie. Meaning: a movie with a professional mix, a Foley session, a soundtrack, and credits. Telling my friends that I'd made a movie and then asking them to come look at a product as rough and flawed and amateurish as the final cut of *Twelve Steps to Death* would be like telling my friends that I'd written a book and then asking them to read 256 typewritten pages all stapled together and bound inside a $1.49 colored folder with a drawing of an ax murderer on the cover. Well, yeah, it was a book. But it wasn't a *real* book. It wasn't a book you could buy—or sell—in a bookstore. It was a rough draft.

This is where the trap got sprung. This is where *hubris* took over. This is where I took leave of my senses. This is where I threw caution to the wind and cast my bread on the waters. Already $24,645 in the hole, I wasn't even vaguely content with what I had achieved. I wanted more out of life than to say that I'd made a glorified home movie. I wanted to make a real movie. I wanted people to talk about me in the same breath as D. W. Griffith, not Melanie Griffith.

Kenna helped me make this decision. Although Kenna had never deviated from her original position that *Twelve Steps to Death* was a hopelessly tasteless, politically incorrect diatribe where all of the protagonists were cartoon characters, she always thought it was a funny, salable project. Kenna firmly believed that if I opened up my bank account and spent some additional money to gussy up the edit, there was an outside chance that we could sell this thing. This would obviously benefit me; I'd get my investment back and perhaps become rich and famous. But it would also benefit her, because editors, not directors, are the people who make movies work, and she was the editor of this film. So she'd get lots of the credit.

I asked her how much money she was talking about. She handed me a budget. It made my hair turn white. Well, *whiter*. Whether we finished the film now or after we'd done some more postproduction work, there were certain fixed costs that simply could not be avoided. Getting the optical print was going to run another grand or so. Paying the negative cutter would be another $2,500 to $3,000. Then there was the $3,500-$4,000 needed to make at least one physical print of the film (something Rodriquez never had when he made *El Mariachi*), which would give me a print with a shelf life of roughly twelve screenings. There was also the little matter of credits, which were going to run about $1,000. These costs alone would inflate the budget well past the $30,000 level.

I was also going to have to set aside three grand for publicity, travel, and entering a couple of film festivals, not to mention about $2,500 to transfer the film to video and make one hundred videotapes of the final print as payment to people who'd worked on the movie. So, anyway you looked at it, I was going to have to shell out another $12,000 or so before the *Twelve Steps to Death* saga had run its course. That would bring the cost of the film up to $37,000.

Those costs were written in stone no matter what else I spent to improve the film. But the numbers Kenna started feeding me now were truly scary. To fix the numerous scenes in the film where actors had messed up their lines or where the DAT had picked up intrusive sound was going to run $250 an hour for ADR (Automated Dialogue Recording). Kenna reckoned we needed five hours of ADR studio time. Then there was the Foley session, where footsteps and slamming doors and people pissing into urinals were added, also at $250 an hour. And then there were sound effects, which were going to run me another three to four grand. I would also need music, which first had to be recorded and then spliced into the film. And after all that, we still had to do a mix, where all of these other elements were mixed together. That was going to run $175 an hour for a minimum of four days. What we were talking about here was going to nearly double the cost of the film.

Jesus wept.

The question was whether I was up for it. For some strange reason, I was. I wanted to make a film that looked and sounded like a real film, no matter how awful the acting was, no matter how ridiculous the story line seemed. I knew this was the only time in my life that I was ever going to make a film, and I wanted it to be a film I could be proud of. Well, *proudish*. Even before Kenna had finished running the numbers, I knew that I had crossed the Rubicon. I was going to break the bank and make a real movie.

My children would be feeling the financial reverberations of this decision for the rest of their lives.

AS SOON AS the final cut was ready, it was time for ADR (Automated Dialogue Recording) and the Foley mix. ADR is an opportunity for the actors to rerecord lines that they'd flubbed in the film, or to fill in dialogue that had come out jumbled or inaudible because of defective equipment, passing cars, bawling infants, rubbernecking onlookers, churlish bill collectors, helicopters passing overhead. But it is also an opportunity to use audial gimmicks to support or amplify the visual images: screams, gasps, background noises. A real movie would require forty to eighty hours of ADR (at $500 an hour) in which the actors would rerecord their lines until they got them just right. We planned on just three hours, at $250 an hour, a bargain rate. We actually did it in two and a half hours. That came to $625, but once you added in the cost of materials, the bill came to $873.58.

On consecutive nights in October, Tom, Hella, Doug, Kenna, our ADR engineer George Lara, and I convened at the studio to do the necessary patchwork. Hella and I had a bunch of lines that had gotten all screwed up because we were climbing out the window of her cell in an early sequence of the film and the mike couldn't pick up what we were saying. Tom had to redo all the lines where he's talking to me on the phone because they came out stilted and wooden and sounded like he was standing in a tunnel. Doug had to add a few screams for the two scenes where he is pushed off the castle ramparts as Paul Thorpe, then leaps to his death as Peter Thorpe. And we also needed someone to do the voice-over of the deejay speaking on KLB-70 during the *Reservoir Dogs* scene where Bishop threatens to cut off Thorpe's ear. Jeff Kushner, the film's dialogue editor, graciously offered to supply the deejay's comments.

The main reason we were spending all this money was to fix up the scenes involving Peter Thorpe's murder and suicide. As soon as we saw the dailies back in August, we all realized that the screenplay never actually explains to the audience what Peter Thorpe (actually Paul Thorpe) was doing up on the top of the castle eight or nine minutes into the film. In fact, we had never even mentioned that the building was a castle. The audience merely saw a five-second shot of a looming gray building, which actually looked more like an old church or a university library than a castle. It was kind of confusing.

To repair this, Doug did a voice-over of a phone conversation with his secretary, telling her, "No more appointments today, Mabel; I'm going up to White Castle to do some birdwatching." We then did a voice-over of the scene where the dummy is thrown off the top of the castle, with Doug hollering: "Shit," "Jesus Christ," and "Hey, what the hell are you doing?" We then played the tracks back to see which was most effective. "Shit," that old standby, worked best. As Kenna had predicted, when Doug's scream was heard while the dummy plummeted to its demise, the dummy seemed much less fake, much more human. And the "oof" Doug emitted when the dummy caromed off the wall was priceless.

The last fix we needed to make was Peter Thorpe's suicide at the end of the film. When we shot the scene back in August, it was impossible to have Thorpe leap off the castle walls because we had no stunt man and Doug had a good job as a magazine editor. So, after his final exchange with Bishop, he merely ducked out of sight. When we watched the dailies, this scene looked incredibly hokey. To be perfectly honest, it wasn't even clear from watching the images on the screen what actually was taking place up there on the castle parapet. To fix this, we needed Doug to scream something that would make it clear that he had just leaped to his death. We tried "Geronimo!" "Look out below!" "I'm just happy to be here!" "Cancel the rest of my appointments!" and the statutory "Oh, shit." I liked "Cancel the rest of my appointments," but Kenna thought it was too far over the top. So we settled on "Look out below!" That was it for ADR. The film had now passed the $25,000 mark.

TWO NIGHTS LATER, Kenna, George, and I convened at the studio for the Foley mix with Foley artist Brian Vancho. This is the session where a sound-effects specialist adds all the noises that a moviegoer's ears expect to hear: footsteps, running water, opening doors, rustling newspapers, collisions. He does all this in a room filled with bells, glass, gongs, sand, leaves, paper, clothing, furniture, everything under the sun. A real movie would be Foleyed throughout its entire length; every time a character breathed, some ambient noise would be added. (This would take three to four weeks at a cost of roughly $500 an hour.) But because we were making a low-budget movie, and because I am not rich, only the most important, obvious sound effects were added.

It was immediately apparent what an enormous difference these additions could make in a movie. The ominous sound of Doug unsheathing his Bowie knife before he jammed it between Joey Bellini's thighs now gave the scene a truly macabre feel. So did the sound of Thorpe's body impacting on the ground after he'd been pushed off the castle ramparts. The Foley artist also spruced up the sound of Amber Duggan plunging into the water in pursuit of her marshmallow cache and juiced up the scene where Stoddard offers Bishop a glass of O.J. while they're out on the golf course. Of course, the most important sound effect of all was the one where Bishop headbutts Thorpe toward the end of the film.

In some cases, the Foley artist himself performed a value-added function, inserting humor in a scene where none had previously existed. Take the Cops in the Shithouse scene. I'd originally written the Cops in the Shithouse Scene because all cop movies have the Cops in the Shithouse Scene. But there was nothing especially funny about this sequence; it was actually one of my least favorite parts of the movie. The only reason I didn't cut it out completely was because in the course of the scene Stoddard explains to Bishop that Paul Thorpe had made a 270-mile, round-trip junket to Chicago every day for the past two weeks to see the White Sox, which effectively established his *bona fides* as a diehard White Sox fan. And that information sets up the scene where Bishop tricks Thorpe into admitting that he doesn't know who Bo Jackson plays for. But the Cops in the Shithouse scene wasn't actually funny per se.

By the time the Foley artist finished up, it was. The scene, in which the two cops converse while taking a piss, lasts about ninety seconds. Halfway through, Bishop zips up his trousers and leans against the shithouse partition, talking to Stoddard, partially visible in the crapper. While his partner talks, Stoddard keeps on pissing. Fifteen seconds, thirty seconds. Sixty seconds. Ninety seconds.

This was one long whiz.

The pissing scene wasn't funny in and of itself. But once the Foley artist started pouring a steady stream of water into an enamel basin, the audience couldn't help but feel that they were witnessing one of the great feats of urination in the history of shithouse cinema. What made the scene even funnier was that Bishop never once reacts to his partner's epic urinary performance by getting out a stopwatch or doing a double-take. He just goes on doing what he's been doing the rest of the movie: ranting like a psychopath. Let's face it: He was a cop with a gun and an attitude. His obliviousness to the *Ripley's Believe It or Not* waterworks performance taking place just a few inches away reaffirmed his maniacal obsession with his work.

That was it for Foleys. The Foley mix took just four and a quarter hours at a rate of $250 an hour, for a cost of $1,062, plus $350 for materials. Another $1,412 down the drain. All the remaining sound effects—tweeting birds, lawnmowers whirring in the distance, backfiring car engines, ambient noise—would be supplied by Stuart Emanuel, the sound effects editor. Stuart and I had a deal whereby instead of paying him cash for the effects, I would buy him a disk drive. The disk drive cost me $3,053, but I had to throw in $60 for blank tape, plus $300 for something called a TASCAM transfer. To this day, I still do not know what a TASCAM transfer is. I simply wrote the check.

The movie had now cost me $33,876.23.

THE VERY LAST element that goes into the making of a film is the music. Like every other American male who grew up in the 1960s, I can play guitar badly, so when I first conceived of *Twelve Steps to Death,* I figured I would write and perform all the music myself. My daughter, who had been taking piano lessons for three years, had also volunteered to perform some public-domain classical repertory on her electric piano, which we could then record and add into the mix. I said I'd have to get back to her on that one.

Throughout the winter and spring of 1994, as I as preparing to make the film, I received a number of offers from professional musicians—people who actually made a living in the music business—who were willing to write an original score for the film. For various reasons, I turned them all down. For starters, I didn't want any professionals involved with the film because professionals would insist that the project meet certain aesthetic standards if they were going to have their names associated with it, and I could not guarantee that these or, for that matter, any aesthetic standards would be met.

Second, even if the professionals that I knew were willing to compose the music for free, they would insist that I hire real musicians to record the soundtrack and log expensive studio time to get it on tape. Frankly, I didn't feel like spending the kind of money that I was sure they would feel like spending.

Third, I had decided from the get-go that *Twelve Steps to Death* had to be a Walter Mitty operation, an easily reproducible exercise that ordinary people anywhere in the country could re-create for themselves in their hometowns.

Four, I really don't care for professional musicians.

After the film was cut, I momentarily wavered in this decision to freeze out the pros. Having watched the film dozens of times with Kenna, and having screened the rough cut for several friends whose opinions I respected, I fully understood that the movie dragged in the second half, where there were several lengthy scenes and far fewer jokes. This section of the film could really use a shot in the arm, and a bouncy soundtrack could supply it.

With this in mind, I tried to arrange a meeting of two musician friends and see if we could put our heads together and come up with some good ideas for the film. This was by far the worst decision I made during the entire two-year project. The musicians instantly took an intense dislike to each other. They hated each other's ideas. One of these friends, a very serious, very talented composer of classical music, failed to appreciate the spirit of festive camaraderie that had characterized the project up until now. Jockeying for artistic control of the soundtrack began immediately. Tempers flared. Nostrils snorted. Egos were bruised. Bad vibes vibrated. And yes, my classically trained friend did actually take me aside to say that he could not possibly lend his name to any project that did not achieve a certain level of artistic competence.

"Boy, have you got the wrong picture," I told him. I bought him a *caffe latte* and a croissant at a local bistro and said that I had errands to attend to. My dreams of forging a tenuous liaison between my various musician friends had now been smashed to smithereens.

But all was not lost. Eventually, a solution to my dilemma presented itself. Marilyn Jaye Lewis, a talented country and western singer whom I had known for ten years, was busy cutting a demo CD with a bunch of New York studio musicians. She generously offered to write a theme song for the movie. One day she sent me the CD, which contained four songs, including the proposed theme song "One Step Closer." I liked it. It had an upbeat sound. But I didn't like it nearly as much as "Something

Like the Railroad," a bouncy little C&W number, which, like all bouncy little C&W numbers, dealt with good love gone bad. Although there was absolutely nothing in *Twelve Steps to Death* about good love gone bad, I decided to use this song to open the movie. I liked the idea of kicking off the movie with numerous shots of thin, happy townspeople waving at the camera while Marilyn's perky little number rumbled along in the background. Then we would pull the rug out from under the audience by inserting an audially repugnant guitar chord to announce the arrival of Amber Duggan, the dysfunctional fat lady and prime murder suspect. That would still leave us with Marilyn's "One Step Closer" for the credit crawl at the end of the film.

That eliminated the first musical problem. I liked both songs; I particularly liked the jaunty bop of "Something Like the Railroad"; but most of all I liked the fact that Marilyn had already recorded the songs on compact disc so I wouldn't have to pay any money to use them.

The main portion of the soundtrack was recorded in one day at the apartment of my good friend John Lehmann-Haupt. John is a classically trained guitarist who had worked for twelve years at the posh restaurant Windows on the World, located at the very top of one of the Twin Towers in the World Trade Center. This meant that he had played "Malaguena" a minimum of 3,600 times over the years, this dark night of the soul culminating one afternoon when a bunch of Islamic fundamentalist terrorists blew up the building in early 1993 and put him out of a job. John was also a teacher at the American Institute of Guitar; that was how I'd met him. Three or four times in my life, I'd signed up for lessons in a determined effort to learn how to read music and play guitar properly. Each time I had failed miserably. But each time I had become fast friends with my teacher. John was no exception. After eighteen months of expensive lessons, I knew less about playing guitar than when I'd started. But I really like hanging out with John.

When I showed John the final cut of *Twelve Steps to Death* on videotape, he laughed at numerous junctures but said that he found the stuff about Amber Duggan/Mrs. Lardbutt a bit offensive. I chose to ignore this remark, figuring that people who spent one-third of their adult lives playing "Sheep May Safely Graze" and the other two-thirds playing "You've

Got a Friend" would naturally be imbued with a grace and sensitivity that people like me didn't have. I asked John if the indisputably offensive Amber Duggan material would prevent him from assisting me on the project. He said it would not, particularly if I paid him. I told him that there was $500 in it for him. He no longer found the Amber Duggan/Mrs. Lardbutt material unbelievably offensive.

John said that he had decent recording material in his apartment and could tape whatever I wanted on a DAT machine which could then be transferred to 16mm tape. He also had an electric guitar, a bass, some small percussion instruments, a piano, and a harmonica. He said that his apartment on the West Side of Manhattan was quiet, getting very little street noise, and that the only forseeable problem was a trumpet player who lived in the apartment directly overhead and who frequently practiced late in the day. But we could work our way around this by recording the soundtrack during the day, or by telling the budding Satchmo to knock it off for the afternoon. He suggested that we meet the following Thursday.

I arrived at 9 A.M. and explained the program.

"Being the consummate professional that you are, John, you have millions of ideas lodged in your head and fingers," I said. "I want to coax those ideas out of you. Basically, I want to rent your vast intellect for a day and ask you to play anything I want you to play. I hope that sounds fair."

"It does," he said.

We loaded the final cut of the film into his VCR and sat down to review it. We decided that the best approach was to watch the film straight through, then discuss what kind of music seemed appropriate for each scene, write down our decisions, and then record those pieces after lunch. John immediately intuited what I wanted: a mixture of sound effects, cheesy theme music for the major characters, and a lot of pompous, public-domain classical music that I wouldn't have to pay one red cent to use.

"First off, we need some insipid theme music for the cop and the nun," I explained. "Her scenes are all really long, and it would be great to have some incredibly sappy music playing in the background every time they meet."

John immediately began playing "The Water Is Wide," an old English folk tune that had been in the public domain for centuries. It started out very sweetly, then got a bit teary, and finally modulated into some astonishingly hokey chord changes. I loved it.

"I already have a recording of this on tape because I do it in concert, so we won't even have to record it again." John beamed.

"Great," I said. "The other thing I like is that Meryl Streep's new movie *The River Wild* closes with an up-tempo version of that song by the Cowboy Junkies. So we'll have a nice tie-in there, because every movie soundtrack made in this country rips off every other movie soundtrack: Coppola ends *Godfather III* with the same music that Scorsese starts *Raging Bull,* and John Williams has been recycling Gustav Holst for twenty years. And, believe me, I'm not knocking them; if I had any real money, I'd be using Aretha."

He nodded.

"Now," I said, "we need some stately, somber music for the funeral scene."

John played Handel's *Sarabande,* which, again, was absolutely perfect because that piece, Albinoni's *Adagio in G,* Samuel Barber's *Adagio for Strings,* and Carl Orff's *Carmina Burana* were used in every movie and just about every movie trailer made in the United States in the last ten years. I liked the idea of giving the film a big-budget, cookie-cutter, generic-classical sound. That spelled C-L-A-S-S. If the movie couldn't look like a real movie, it could at least sound like one.

John instinctively understood the kind of highfalutin ambience I was hoping to achieve, and his suggestions were superb. To confer an air of canned weirdness on the interminable, flickering-candle three-minute sequence where Sister Wilhemina and Turk Bishop chat with their backs to the camera, the one where the nun ends up talking about all those squirrels descending with a blinding light of love, John suggested the first movement of Bach's *Well-Tempered Clavier.* Again, a perfect fit. John also felt that Bach's uncharacteristically sunny *Wachtet Auf* could work well in the opening scenes of the movie should I decide to nix Marilyn's song and go with something a bit more upmarket.

We moved on.

"The first time the audience sees the cop, we need to have some of that

indy prod *High Plains Drifter*–meets–*Red Rock West*–via–*River's Edge*
twanging guitar in the background," I said. "Then we can use that as a
leitmotif throughout the rest of the movie. Leitmotifs are so professional."

John put down his classical instrument and picked up a solid-body electric guitar he'd built himself. He played a twangy E minor chord with an
upstroke, then resolved into an A minor, then back to E minor, then, for
variety, a C major. It was close, but not quite there.

"Less Duane Eddy, more Link Wray," I suggested, drawing on years of
playing in lethal high school bar mitzvah bands with names like The
Phase Shift Network and Baby's Death. "Make it sound more mysterious
and scary, like the Ventures on a bad day."

John got the tremolo bar working, and the next chords he played were
right on the money. And so it went. For the scene where Bishop confronts
the Mexican dishwasher, John played an uproariously festive rendition of
"Malaguena." Single bass notes were used to announce the arrival of
the murderer and to simulate Stoddard's hesitant, irregular thought pat-
terns as Bishop explains why Amber Duggan could not possibly have
committed the murder. For the scene where Bishop first discovers the
scrawled message "DOCEPAS" and the coroner says, "Sounds kind of
Greek, doesn't it?" John grabbed his steel-string guitar, on which he
played single notes, bazouki-style. Then, for the exchange where Bishop
berates his sidekick for his phenomenal ignorance of Greek culture, he
played clusters of single notes, Zorba style. It was hilariously stupid. John
was certainly a pro.

Things were really zipping along now. For the scenes involving Paul
Thorpe, the drug-crazed New Age twin who took too much blue acid at
Woodstock, John went to open G tuning on the steel string and finger-
picked some genuinely horrifying Ramblin' Man music that deftly captured the narcoleptic inanity of sixties' folk music.

"I call this Tom Rush open-tuning finger-picking," John explained.

"Give it a little more of a Richie Havens feel," I suggested. "I want it
to be totally obnoxious."

John complied, sprinkling in a heavy dose of "High Flyin' Bird Way up
in the Sky" blather.

"That's great." I smiled. "That sucks so bad."

Equally atrocious was the lame background music John supplied for the scene where Peter (actually Paul) Thorpe goes birdwatching on the castle ramparts just before his murder takes place.

"Try to convey that languid, late-afternoon Erik Satie feel," I suggested. "I want something really bland and noncommital. Something Impressionistic, Windham Hillish."

"C major seventh should do the trick," John decided, tenderly strumming one of those flatulent, meaningless chords that the Paul Winter Consort and Kenny G have built their entire careers around. "C major seventh resolving to F major seventh, then back to C major seventh."

"Really awful." I beamed. I was delighted by its poignant, Percy Faithian crappiness.

"At Matt Umanov's [a famous guitar store in Greenwich Village] they used to have a sign that read ABSOLUTELY NO MAJOR SEVENTH CHORDS IN THIS ESTABLISHMENT," John noted.

"Now I know why," I replied.

We broke for lunch at a local diner ($14.35), then John came back, tuned up, rehearsed for a few minutes, and started cranking out the material. By three, he had the Bach and Handel pieces recorded and edited, and by six we had all the other theme music and sound effects, including an all-purpose "Danny Boy" just in case we got stuck for some corny background music somewhere. That left the crown jewel: our duet. The *Reservoir Dogs* parody scene required some music coming out of the juke box to accompany Bishop's ridiculous hoofing. In *Reservoir Dogs,* before cutting off the cop's ear, light-footed psychopath Michael Madsen had asked his victim if he ever listened to an L.A. radio program that specialized in the Sounds of the Seventies. But *Twelve Steps to Death* didn't have a budget that would cover the use of authentic recordings from the 1970s, so instead John and I recorded Stephen Foster's classic "Oh, Susanna!" a nineteenth-century, public-domain number we had every reason to believe had been very popular in the 1870s. We did two takes. I played guitar and sang the melody; John played harmonica throughout the first verse, then sang harmony. We had a good time doing this; the result was quite fabulously down-home. It was the Grand Ole Opry at its worst. Truly awful. Puke-ophonic.

That was that. John transferred the reel-to-reel tapes to DAT, I gathered up my stuff, and was out of there by nine. If only the rest of the movie had gone as smoothly as this, we would have been done by Halloween.

A COUPLE OF days later, Kenna and I sat in the studio and transferred the music to tape. Mostly, the music slipped into the film the way I had imagined it on Thursday. But Kenna disagreed with a couple of my choices. She thought that Marilyn's songs were too bouncy for the beginning of the film, preferring something more low-key. So we went with the antiseptic "Sleepers, Awake," the kind of Renaissance Muzak you always hear in restaurants called La Trattoria. Kenna also felt that the insipid "Danny's Boy" worked much better in the scene with the Rollerblading nun because it heightened the sense of festering mawkishness that was the fulcrum of their relationship. Finally, Kenna felt that the bass notes plunked out while Bishop was explaining to Stoddard why Amber Duggan could not have fit through the door were too crisp. To underscore what a dimwit Stoddard was, she inserted strips of blank leader between each of the notes, creating a pause between each beat. This gave the bass notes an elephantine thuddishness, dragging them out over a span of several seconds, perfectly synchronized with Stoddard's lummoxian thought processes. Adding a soundtrack and transferring John's tapes to 16mm cost around $1,000. But we also had to rent the editing room with a phone for an extra week. The movie had now cost me $35,567.97.

By Thanksgiving weekend, the editing process was complete, and we only needed to get into the studio for a few days to mix the film. Originally, the mix was scheduled for the first week of December. Then misfortune struck. Everybody and his or her brother was down at Sound One frantically attempting to tart up their films in time for Robert Redford's enormously important Sundance Festival, the mav/indy Cannes. The mixing room would not be available until the first week of January. Even though the movie was just days away from completion, we now had to wait five weeks before we could add the finishing touches.

At this point, I'd like to step away from the editing process and give the prospective filmmaker an idea of what his daily life will be like if he ever decides to make a low-budget movie in a small town using his friends and neighbors as actors. Basically, his life will become an uninterrupted nightmare as soon as the film has been shot. Early in the morning, friends will start ringing up to find out when the movie is going to be ready for viewing, and why it wasn't ready sooner. Out on the street, the filmmaker will bump into friends who'll ask if the film is still under budget. Then his editor will call to say that the ADR session has been canceled. Then more friends will call to find out when the movie is going to be ready for viewing, and why it wasn't ready sooner. Then, at noon, he'll get a bill from the editing lab that will read:

2 MULTI CHANNEL TRANS RM F	$260.00
900 16MM FULLCOAT MAG RM F 3M	$49.50

He will not know what any of this means, so he'll call his editor to find out if the bills are legitimate and be told, yes, pay them. Then more friends will call up to ask if the film is still under budget. If it happens to be Christmastime, and friends call up to invite him out to go caroling, he will refrain from accepting their invitation because he knows that at some point between the singing of "Oh, Tannenbaum" and "We Three Kings of Orient Are," a half-dozen carolers are sure to ask when the film will be ready for viewing and why it wasn't ready sooner. Instead, he'll stay at home puzzling over the bill that reads

TRANSFER IN TRANS RM F "MONO"	$44.00
ADR IN STUDIO E	$625.00
1/4″ TAPE STUDIO E 2400 FT.	$30.00

He will sit there, in the funereal shadow of the Christmas tree, wondering whether there is any way to determine if he really did use 2,400 feet of quarter-inch tape in Studio E. But he will not turn on the Christmas lights, because if he does friends will know that he is home and will stop by to ask when the film will be ready for viewing and why it wasn't ready sooner.

Later in the day, he will consider visiting his bank to liquidate one of his IRAs or redeem one of his children's Series E Savings Bonds to pay for the ADR in Studio E or the TRANS in Studio Room F, but instead he will put off the transaction until tomorrow because if he ventures out into the street he is sure to bump into one of his neighbors who will ask if the film is still under budget. Inevitably, he will go to bed that night, like every other night, cursing the day he ever heard the words *El Mariachi.*

DECEMBER WAS AN absolutely ghastly month, with the bills piling up, pushing the film's budget well past the $40,000 mark. My daughter, who was born on December 25, 1983, did not seem all that overjoyed by the presents she got on Christmas Day, but I pointed out that she'd wanted to be in the movie, so she had to bite the bullet like the rest of us. Bridget, who had once played the Dew Fairy in the seminal 1992 Winfield L. Morse primary school production of *Hansel and Gretel,* sulked for a week. As the year drew to its insolvent conclusion, the bills continued to pour in, and my wife continued to pay them. For some strange reason, I forgot to check the mail on December 31, so when I opened my mailbox on January 1, I got to start the New Year with a bill for $974.25 from Sound One. Normally, at the beginning of a new year, I vow to lose twenty-five pounds, read Marcel Proust's *Remembrance of Things Past,* and start being nicer to my wife. But in 1995 my only New Year's resolution was never to make another low-budget movie.

Finally, January 3 rolled around and we could get into the studio for the mix. The mix is the absolute last phase of the editing process, a laborious procedure where the various tracks are mixed together and the sound level of each sequence is adjusted. The mix on a real movie would take around six weeks and would involve a whole passel of editors. Our mix took two editors and three and a half days.

Mixing is an incredibly boring procedure, with the editor constantly freezing the frame, then rewinding the film to adjust sound quality. At the mix, the sound levels are adjusted shot by shot, and the music and sound effects are mixed in. But the process does make a huge difference in the way you look at the movie, especially the sound effects. When you're watching a film, there's a part of you lodged somewhere between your ears and your eyes that really wants to hear the thud of the bottle, the slam of the door, the rustling of the newspaper, the scraping of the feet, little of which gets picked up by the mike when the film is actually being shot. The better the quality of the sound, the less boring the movie is. Tweeting birds, barking dogs, backfiring car engines, nattering lawnmowers, and ominous funeral chimes all make a huge difference, vastly augmenting the watchability quotient of a movie.

Every morning of the mix I came into New York on the train ($13.50 round-trip fare) and sat behind a console while David Novak, the rerecording editor, and Kenna mixed in the effects. My input was required only about once every two hours, when a decision had to be made as to which track fit best. Thus, I was the one who decided whether Doug should holler "Look out below!" when Thorpe leapt from the castle walls at the end of the film. Four days of lunches cost $102, with the mix itself running $4,725. There were also such incidentals as 35MM full C Mag 3M NVD, whatever that was ($1,150). And there was tax. Yes, one of the things that I learned while making *Twelve Steps to Death* is that whenever anybody in the film industry quotes you a price, they always forget to include the tax. The total mix cost ran $7,475 all by itself, but the tax added another $616.69 to the final budget. In fact, the tax alone on *Twelve Steps to Death* had now come to nearly $7,000. Luckily, it was all tax-deductible. All in all, the mix went very well, but the movie had now cost me $43,113.28. I was not yet a broken man, but I was getting there.

BY FRIDAY MORNING, the last day of the mix, the film was ready for a final screening before being sent to the negative cutter to prepare for the actual print. The negative cutter is the person who goes back to the film that was actually taken from the camera and makes sure that it matches up with all the editing changes that have been made on the print the director and editor have been working on for the past three months. (All the sound editing is done on a separate optical negative.) But before we sent the work print to the negative cutter, we scheduled a final screening. Anxious to see how the finished product would be received, I invited Hella, Tom, and several of the Connie Chungsters over to see what we had accomplished. I also invited Marty Beiser, managing editor of *GQ*, whom I had known for years. Marty doubtless thought that I wanted him to see the film because of our long friendship and because I could rely on his dispassionate objectivity. But I actually wanted him there because I wanted *GQ* to pay for a New York screening so that I could get some more publicity for the film and hopefully sell it to somebody like Miramax and get out from under this ponderous mountain of debt.

The screening was a huge success. Marty laughed a lot. Hella laughed a lot. Tom laughed a lot. The Connie Chungsters laughed a lot. Ted laughed a lot. Kenna, who had now seen the film several hundred times, laughed a lot.

Still no word from Amblin.

eleven

The Golden Headless Horseman

From the moment I began working on *Twelve Steps to Death,* people from all walks of life would bombard me with questions about my plans for the film once it was done. Would I try to get it shown at Robert Redford's Sundance Film Festival, and thus become rich and famous like the guy who made *El Mariachi*? First, let me finish *writing* the film, I'd say. Would I try to get my film shown at Cannes? First, let me finishing *shooting* the film, I'd respond. Had I considered entering my film into the highly prestigious Berlin Film Festival, a kind of Aryan Sundance held every February in that cheerful central European metropolis? First, let me finish *editing* the film, I'd tell my interrogators. Was I planning on going the film festival route, wending my way through the labyrinth of tiny film festivals that dot the planet, trekking from Charleston to Denver to San Sebastian to Gdansk in a desperate attempt to drum up interest in my film?

No, was my reply.

Almost from the beginning, for various reasons, I'd known that the big festivals were out of the question. For starters, due to assorted editing holdups, *Twelve Steps* wasn't even ready to be shown until the last week in February of 1995, too late for Sundance, too late for the Berlin Film Festival, and too late to be entered at Cannes. More to the point, the Cannes Film Festival doesn't usually present that many films shot in nine days in Tarrytown, New York. They've got Altman films to show. And Godards. For some reason, I had trouble getting this concept across to my friends.

My reasons for shunning the smaller film festivals were a mix of the strategic and the financial. Film festivals are a good way of attracting attention to your film if you have no other way of attracting attention to your film. But I didn't have that problem. Months earlier my friend Mary Ann Bohrer had volunteered to do publicity for the film, and she'd gotten me all kinds of media coverage. What's more, I had a book coming out explaining how I'd made the movie. So there really wasn't much point in entering the film in a film festival in Denver where a few hundred people might hear about it, when I could just as easily rely on Connie Chung or Don Imus to spread the word, such as it was, to countless millions.

I had another good reason for avoiding the smaller film festivals. Festivals do a whole lot more for the towns that hold them than they do for the filmmaker. Festivals, which are partially and in some cases primarily subsidized by the fees that the filmmakers themselves fork over to have their movies shown, are basically an inexpensive way for the local gentry to pretend for at least one weekend that their pitiful burgh is in fact a vibrant cultural hub. *We may not have a symphony orchestra, an art museum, a skyscraper or a halfway-decent newspaper, but we do have our own film festival.* It doesn't cost a whole lot of money to put on a film festival, and by charging desperate bohos from all over the world a couple hundred bucks to screen their lugubrious, black-and-white explorations of the doomed love affair between a Macedonian goatherd and a Senegalese Chiclet box designer, the locals get to feel important for around forty-eight hours. Well, screw that. Frankly, I'd rather be gnawed to death by famished marsupials than to fork over a couple hundred dollars of my hard-earned money as the entrance fee to some godforsaken film festival in some forlorn corner of the hinterland just so the leading lights of Palookaville could feel like they were trailblazing cultural avatars.

I had a third good reason for avoiding the film festival circuit. *Twelve Steps to Death* had started out as a prank, designed to answer one question and one question alone: Was it possible for the man in the street, with no previous experience in the film industry, to make a motion picture for $7,000? The answer was a resounding no: Everything I'd ever been told about making feature films for used-car prices was an out-and-out lie. But it *was* possible to make a movie for around $25,000; and for another $20,000 to $25,000 it was possible to make a real movie with a soundtrack and sound effects and Foleys and voice-overs and a professional mix, the kind of movie someone could watch and listen to without getting totally pissed off at the cruddy sound and the crummy lighting. This was the film that I had made. Or, at least, this was the film that I thought I had made.

With a sticker price fast approaching $45,000, *Twelve Steps to Death* now constituted a prank that had gotten woefully out of hand. Financially, I was in way over my head; unless I found someone willing to buy and distribute the film, I was out the $45,000 and my marriage, such as it was, was over. Obviously, once I decided to ante up all that additional money for a mix and a professional edit, I had at least subconsciously persuaded myself that I had a chance—however small—of selling the film to a distributor. But I didn't want to spend the next ten years of my life trying to peddle it the way some small filmmakers did: by following every lead, attending ever convention, entering every film festival. I had bills to pay, kids to raise, stories to write, a life to lead. Every day I spent trying to market *Twelve Steps to Death* was another day I could have spent writing magazine articles and earning real money. In short, I didn't want to throw good money after bad. What I wanted more than anything else was a quick verdict on the commercial viability of my film. I didn't want to spend five years and another $45,000 going all around the world to see if anyone was interested in buying my movie. I wanted an answer *now*.

There *was* one quick way to determine whether *Twelve Steps to Death* was a salable entity. That was through Connie Chung. If *Eye to Eye* pumped a segment about the movie into tens of millions of households, it was a certainty that plenty of people in the movie industry would end up seeing it. If anyone was interested in the film, they would call me. If they weren't, they wouldn't. *Eye to Eye* was the perfect litmus test. If Connie Chung aired a segment about my movie and nobody called up to ask if they could see it, buy it, distribute it, this would be a pretty good indication that *Twelve Steps to Death* was dead on arrival.

The Chungsters had spent two days on the set and three more days in the studio during the various stages of editing, so they had plenty of footage. Now, in order to finish their segment, they needed a grand finale. So they had a few questions. When *Twelve Steps to Death* was ready for its premiere, where would I hold the screening? Would it be at Axe Castle in Tarrytown where we'd shot it? Would it be at one of those glitzy screening rooms in New York? Or I would I hold the premiere in a screening room in L.A.?

The answer was none of the above. By the time the movie was ready to be shown, Axe Castle was undergoing renovations to transform it into an upscale restaurant and was closed to the public. Screening rooms like Robert De Niro's place in TriBeCa hold only less than 100 people, and I needed a room large enough to accommodate the entire cast and crew, plus scores of engrossed townspeople for whom the project had become a *cause célèbre*. And L.A. was just too obvious.

So, in the end, the choice came down to two venues: a theater in downtown Milwaukee or Sleepy Hollow High School in Tarrytown. Milwaukee was a viable candidate because for about eight months I had been doing five minutes of movie commentary every Wednesday morning on a popular drive-time radio program at WKTI-Milwaukee and had become a bit of a celebrity. The two deejays who hosted the show—Bob Reitman and Gene Mueller—loved my ranting and raving about space invaders like Melanie Griffith and Lou Diamond Phillips, and when they found out that the movie was set in rural Wisconsin, they generously offered to hold a screening at one of the older theaters in downtown Milwaukee.

I must admit that the idea of premiering the movie in the Town that

280

Made the Beer That Made Milwaukee Famous did have a certain myth-ical allure. But ultimately I decided that Milwaukee would have to settle for being host of the second showing of *Twelve Steps to Death,* not the intergalactic debut. I simply couldn't expect the entire population of Tar-rytown to jump on a plane and fly to Wisconsin just to see the gala pre-miere of a movie some of them hadn't been that enthusiastic about in the first place, even though they were starring in it. No, the first showing would be held right here in Tarrytown, where it could be seen by all of the people who had helped make it, by all of the townspeople who had fallen under the movie's spell, by all of the people like my wife, who had-n't, by all of my oldest and closest friends, and by the Connie Chungsters, who probably weren't interested in going all the way to Milwaukee just to film another one of my little gags anyway. Yes, the world premiere of *Twelve Steps to Death* would take place at the First Tarrytown Interna-tional Film Festival in the 600-seat auditorium of Sleepy Hollow High School on February 25, 1995 at 7:30 P.M. (Snow Date: February 26, 2:00 P.M.).

Holding my very own film festival had been in the back of my mind for at least a year. My logic was impeccable: The object of entering a film festival is to win a prize so that your work will get more attention. But if winning prizes is the main reason you're competing in a film festival, does-n't it make more sense to hold your own film festival with a jury stacked with your friends, relatives, and in-laws, thus guaranteeing that your film will win first prize?

Let's break down the numbers. Merely to enter a film festival, you have to shell out between $100 and $500 for an entrance fee, but then you also have to add in the cost of airfare, a couple of nights in a hotel, plus meals, tips, and bribes. Since most film festivals are held in dinky little towns out in the middle of nowhere, you're probably not going to be able to get a cheap flight. You're going to have to fly on an expensive regional airline. Or spend two days on Amtrak. So the whole deal is going to run you around $2,000, and you won't even be assured of winning a prize.

Conversely, holding a film festival in your own town is only going to set you back a few hundred bucks to rent the high school auditorium, an-other $100 to pay a couple of maintenance men to clean up afterward, and whatever you have to fork over to rent a projector. Even factoring in the expense of invitations, postage, a few refreshments, and a cheapo award you can give to yourself, the whole deal is probably going to run less than a grand.

Besides your own glitzy offering, how many other films should you show at your festival? My favorite number is none. Again, let's do the math. You enter a film festival because you want to win a prize, preferably first. So why not further narrow the odds against finishing second or ninth by holding a film festival that only shows one film? Sure, I originally considered the idea of holding a legitimate festival where anyone who so desired could enter their work into competition. But nobody in Tarrytown was going to show up to see *their* films, which would almost certainly be the usual *film noir* crap, so what was the point in paying all that money to rent the theater for a couple of days, and pay a projectionist and the maintenance man?

And what if somebody entered a film that *didn't* suck? Admittedly, this was a long shot, but what if some sincere, hardworking independent filmmaker turned up with a movie that was actually watchable? Even a heartless, amoral, calculating cynic like me would feel bad if I tricked some poor schmuck into entering a totally rigged film festival in Tarrytown, New York, where the superlative film that he'd poured his heart, his soul, and his life's savings into would get jobbed out of the prize or prizes it so richly deserved by a jury packed with my stooges. No, this was a hideous crime I could not afford to have on my conscience. The First International Tarrytown Festival would present but one film and award but one prize, and that prize would go to me.

Immediately I set about preparing the festival. First of all, I would need a truly international jury consisting of at least one French citizen. So I called Nicole Danquin, an old friend and sister-in-law who lives in the south of France, and asked her to fly over in February to head the jury. This she most graciously agreed to do. Next I called my two colleagues Virginia Campbell and Ed Margulies, the editors of *Movieline*, which had published some of my most pernicious essays in the previous five years, and asked them to fly east to be jurors on the take. Los Angelinos to a fault, they were most enthusiastic.

Then I called my friend Andy Aaron, a producer at the Television Food Network, and at one dark point in his career a writer and producer on *The Chevy Chase Show*, but best known for having worked on *Ishtar*. As soon as he picked up the phone, I browbeat him into keeping the night of February 25 free. Andy, it will be recalled, was supposed to play the town coroner in the movie, but he had backed out at the last minute, much to my wife's chagrin, so he kind of owed me. Andy had also been one of the first people to warn me that making a low-budget movie would wreak havoc on my finances, and now we were going to find out if this was true. Andy said he would be there.

Last but not least, I called my mom.

Mom wasn't as enthusiastic about being on the jury as the four other panelists. "That tendinitis in my knee is acting up," she told me when I asked her to take the train up from Philadelphia and chair the jury. She also rambled on about arthritis, rheumatism, emphysema, the usual laundry list of senior-citizen infirmities. I wasn't buying it. I thought Mom was goldbricking just because it was February and she didn't like visiting us during the winter because my wife, who is English, and thus incredibly cheap, always keeps the thermostat at 68 instead of the tropical 78 my mom is accustomed to. I also think that deep down inside, my mother would have preferred to go the casinos in Atlantic City for the weekend rather than participate in this garish Norman Rockwell–Meets–David Lynch extravaganza. I told my mother that I understood her reservations, but that I really expected her to be up in Tarrytown for the film festival.

"How many sons who write, direct, produce, and star in their own movies and then hold their own international film festivals do you have, anyway?" I asked her, trying desperately to appeal to her jaded sense of maternal pride. "Forget your tendinitis and arthritis; you get up here on the twenty-fifth or you're off the payroll."

Mom said she'd think about it.

AS SOON AS the First Tarrytown International Film Festival was scheduled, I made an important decision about how to position the film. In the past few months, whenever people asked if I'd managed to bring the film in under budget, I'd told them the God's honest truth: No. Without breaking out the specific numbers, I'd explained to them that the myth of the low-budget movie was just that—a myth—and frankly admitted that *Twelve Steps to Death* had turned into the most expensive $7,000 movie in history.

People didn't like it when I told them that. People need their myths, their dreams, their illusions. People needed to believe all that *El Mariachi/Clerks* maverick/indy hype. Deep down inside, everybody in the United States has a desperate need to believe that some day, if the breaks fall their way, they can quit their jobs as claims adjustors, legal secretaries, certified public accountants, or mobsters, and go out and make their own low-budget movie. Otherwise, the future is just too bleak.

It took me an incredibly long time to realize this. I'd gone into this project determined to make the cheapest movie in motion picture history. When it became apparent that I was not going to be able to do this, I consoled myself with the thought that I at least would be performing a public service as a journalist by exploding the myth of the low-budget movie. By hearing my tale of woe, John Q. Public would be spared my tortuous ordeal and would be saved from financial disaster. My experiences as a filmmaker would serve as a bright beacon of sanity in a sea of madness, warning aspiring filmmakers to swerve away from monetary shipwreck scant seconds before their dreams were sundered on the shoals of fiscal lunacy. For this, I was certain, the public would be everlastingly grateful.

I couldn't have been more wrong. When people found out that I hadn't actually made *Twelve Steps to Death* for $6,998, they were royally pissed off. "Liar, liar, pants on fire!" was their attitude. You *promised* us that you were going to make a movie for $6,998, and we all believed you, and then you went back on your word. Charlatan. Imposter. Fake.

This presented me with a huge problem. All things considered, I felt that *Twelve Steps to Death* was a pretty funny movie. Okay, the acting sucked, and the camera never moved, and the pacing was terrible, but the movie still made me laugh. It also made the handful of people who had actually seen it at one stage of development or another laugh. But it soon became apparent that their affection for the movie was largely contingent upon its having been made for $6,998. As $6,998 movies went, it was the cat's meow. But as soon as I hinted that the movie hadn't cost $6,998, or $16,998, or even $26,998, folks started to back off. Making a movie for $6,998 when you didn't know what they hell you were doing seemed like a miracle. But *anyone* could make a movie for $45,000. Like, big fucking deal.

Face to face with mass civic derision, I had no choice but to fudge the numbers. I know that this was an immoral, unethical thing to do, but re-member: I still wanted to sell this sucker. Judging from the reactions I'd elicited so far, the selling point of *Twelve Steps to Death* was not going to be that it was funny or clever or timely or rude, but that it had been made for next to nothing by a bunch of bozos out in the suburbs somewhere. So, at this point, I made a critical decision. I decided to lie. The next time somebody asked me how much it had cost to make *Twelve Steps to Death*, I'd give them a completely irresponsible, utterly ridiculous figure. $6,998? No. $5,998? No. $2,998? No. The figure I ultimately settled on would be $35. The way I looked at it, if you were going to tell a lie, you might as well tell a big lie. That's what Josef Stalin did, and look where it got him. So from that point onward, anyone posing the big question about the film's budget would be given the same bewildering figure, $35. And if any-one asked how it was possible to make a ninety-three minute film for just $35, I'd tell them a bunch of other lies.

What these other lies were, I hadn't yet decided.

THE WEEKS LEADING up to the world premiere of *Twelve Steps to Death* were as nerve-wracking as any other period in my pathetic life. First, I had to bust into my life's savings to pay the past two months' bills at Sound One. That came to $9,639.67. And, believe it or not, things got so des-perate that I had to put $7,000 of the bill on my credit card. Having set out to make a $7,000 movie and put it all on my credit card, I had now made a $45,000 movie and put $7,000 of it on my credit card. Ironies, ironies.

That wasn't the end of the bloodbath. Next, I had to pay the negative cutter to—what else?—cut the negative. Another $1,875 up in smoke.

Then I had to pay for the film credits. Another $1,000. Then I had to pay DuArt a king's ransom to actually make a print of the movie. Something the Mariachi man had never done. Bear in mind that when Robert Rodriguez finished shooting *El Mariachi,* the film didn't have any sound. The dialogue was recorded after the film was shot, on a Marantz tape recorder, with a Radio Shack mike. Then it was edited on video, with the dialogue vaguely synchronized with the images on the screen. The *El Mariachi* that was actually shown in movie theaters was a film that Columbia Pictures had spent a ton of money cleaning up. And a lot of that money went into fixing up sound. Can you imagine what kind of reception *Twelve Steps to Death* would have gotten if I'd invited six hundred people to a crowded auditorium in a high school in Tarrytown in the middle of February and then made them watch a movie with all the sound coming from a boom box? They would have cut my nuts off. Especially the ones who'd come all the way from Los Angeles. Or France.

The festival wasn't going to be as cheap as I'd hoped, either. Initially, I figured I could rent the room for a couple of hundred bucks, then pay some maintenance men a hundred or so to clean up afterward. Because the auditorium had its own screen, 16mm projector, and sound system, I reckoned the entire bill for the festival would come to no more than $750, including invitations, postage, and a few liters of rotgut. But when Kenna came up to Tarrytown to check out the equipment, she discovered that the equipment could not project the seventy-five feet from the projection room to the screen, that you needed two projectors anyway because you wouldn't want to have to stop the film to keep switching reels, and that the sound system was useless. My wife made a few calls and found out that we could rent the projectors and a mobile sound system for $811.88. Toss in the room rental, maintenance men, insurance, invitations and postage, and the cost of holding the festival came to $1,969.72. Maybe I should have to gone to the Gdansk Film Festival after all.

Looking on the bright side, first prize was in the bag. And I got a break on beverages and food because one of my neighbors, a lawyer named Bob Spencer, offered to hold a postfilm reception in his law offices across the street from where I worked, and because Gino Rivieccio, the man who had played the recovering mule humper in the movie, offered to cater it. I also saved about a hundred bucks on the Golden Headless Horseman Trophy when my agent offered to pay the art teacher at the local grammar school to sculpt or weld or whittle something suitably tasteful. But instead of using the high school teacher, I got my brother-in-law—an artist who had attended the Royal College of Art in London—to design a bunch of tacky awards. He bought a couple of X-men statuettes, lopped off their heads, jammed little daggers into their backs, and then spray-painted them both gold. Two years earlier, my agent had persuaded me that *Twelve Steps to Death,* which had now turned into the financial equivalent of Armageddon, would be, quote, unquote "good for my career." Now he acted like his picking up the tab for a couple of cheap statuettes was a gesture of Croesian munificence. Screw you, you bastard.

I SPENT THE two weeks leading up to the First Tarrytown International Film Festival in a state of pure dread. No, I was not worried about how the film would be received. The auditorium was going to be packed with my friends and neighbors, so if they didn't laugh I'd torch the place, and we'd all disappear in a Nibelungian maelstrom of suburban self-immolation. What worried me was the print. Would it be ready on time? DuArt had promised us that they'd have the film ready by Monday, February 20, five days before the screening, but people had been promising me things for months, yet deadlines kept getting missed. Here I was, with the room already rented, and hundreds of friends coming into town from Los Angeles, Washington, Maine, Boston, Chicago, and France, yet I couldn't be absolutely, positively sure that the print would be ready. Then I went and further complicated matters by appearing on Don Imus's morning radio program and giving out the number of the *Twelve Steps to Death* hot line, offering free tickets to the first one hundred callers. An hour after I got off the phone, I had thirty-eight callers, each demanding at least two tickets. By the end of the day, I had 131 callers. And that's not counting the dozen listeners who got my home phone number from Information and called my wife. If that print wasn't ready on time, I was going to be in big, big trouble.

In theory, the days immediately preceding the premiere of a director's debut film should be filled with terror as the filmmaker worries about how his film will be received by the public. But I can honestly say that I never experienced any trepidation of this sort. I didn't have time to experience trepidation of this sort . . . Every waking hour in the week before the First Tarrytown International Festival was consumed by a different sort of trepidation.

February 20 came and went.

The print still wasn't ready.

One of the basic truths about filmmaking that everyone who gets into the business has to learn is that film labs were put on this earth by satanic forces to drive mere mortals insane. Put it this way: *Those whom the gods would destroy they first turn into directors who honestly believe film labs when they say that they'll deliver the print in plenty of time.* In my case, my biggest mistake was being honest with the lab and telling them that the premiere of the film was February 25, 1995. It takes about a week to turn an optical and a negative into a print because first you have to get a person called a timer to make sure that all the coloring is coordinated to your specifications. So, just to make sure the lab had plenty of time, we handed in our raw materials on February 8. That gave DuArt seventeen days to get the job done. DuArt said they'd have the film by Thursday, the sixteenth. Well, they didn't. Then they said they'd have the film by Monday, the twentieth. They didn't. Nor did they have it by Tuesday, the twenty-first, by Wednesday, the twenty-second, or by Thursday, the twenty-third. Bear in mind that I had relatives from France scheduled to fly back home to Europe two days after the festival, that I had friends from Los Angeles who would be arriving in New York on Thursday, and a couple of hundred Don Imus listeners whom I'd already put on the guest list.

Throughout this ordeal, I would call Kenna five times a day to make sure that the print would be ready by Saturday. She would patiently repeat the same message: The lab had a rush job, we were lower on the totem pole than the big-time filmmakers—the regular customers—but don't worry, labs never miss a deadline. They go right up to the edge, but they make their deadlines.

Then I'd call Ted five times a day and ask him the same question. Ted would patiently repeat the same message: The lab had a rush job, we were lower on the totem pole than the big-time filmmakers—the regular customers—but don't worry, labs never miss a deadline. They go right up to the edge, but they make their deadlines.

Sure.

The week preceding the film festival, I slept perhaps four hours. That is, four hours the entire week. Every night, I would lie in bed, staring at the ceiling, wondering why this was happening to me. The ceiling would stare back and say: "Because you wanted to be a filmmaker." By Wednesday night, I was seriously considering calling off the festival. Then I found out that my friends from Los Angeles were already in New York. My wife also pointed out that if we rescheduled the film festival, we would have to make something like three hundred calls to guests telling them the bad news. And my brother-in-law and sister-in-law were going back to France the following Monday.

Throughout this nightmare, Kenna kept insisting that the print would be ready by Friday night. Meanwhile, I tried to look on the bright side of things: At least the editing process was over, so I was no longer getting horrifying bills from Sound One reading:

QUANTITY	DESCRIPTION	UNIT PRICE	AMOUNT
27	Mixing in Studio B NVD	$175.00	$4,725.00
4	8-Track Sonic NVD	$400.00	$1,600.00
11,500	35MM Full C MAG 3M NVD	$0.10	$1,150.00

But that wasn't much consolation.

Thursday night, still no print. That evening I screamed at my kids, rebuffed my brother and sister-in-law's condolences, and was unspeakably nasty to my wife. Finally, the dam broke. As I turned out the lights in our bedroom that evening, Francesca, who had been a pillar of strength throughout this entire ordeal, exploded.

"All you care about is yourself!" she shrieked. "You think you're the only person in the world who has problems! You think that nobody in the entire world has a bigger problem than you do."

I didn't say anything. There was nothing to say. I felt betrayed. I felt humiliated. I felt that our marriage was on the rocks. I stared at the ceiling for at least an hour. Maybe two. Then I spoke.

"But Ces, nobody in the world does have a bigger problem than me. I've invited 600 people, including 200 Don Imus listeners that I don't even know, to a film festival in the middle of February in the middle of nowhere, and I don't even have a print. If 600 people show up at Sleepy Hollow High School on Saturday night, and I don't have a movie to show them, they're probably going to lynch me. And five'll get you ten that they'll lynch you while they're at it."

But Francesca was already fast asleep.

FRIDAY AT NOON, Kenna called to say that the print would be ready by four that afternoon. No, it wasn't ready yet, but trust her, by four that afternoon the print would be ready for viewing. Labs didn't miss deadlines.

At four, I met Ted and Kenna at the lab. I forked over another $1,980.92 to go with the $1,610 I'd paid earlier in the month for the timer and the print. Then we were ushered into a screening room and the film was projected for us.

Not since my firstborn, breach-birth child's head was extracted from the loins of its mother by forceps had I felt such relief. The film looked great. The credits looked great. No, DuArt had not followed Ted's most important instructions—to change the lighting on the scene where Peter Thorpe is murdered so that it would look like twilight—but I didn't care. This was a usable print. This was a watchable print. This was a film that I could proudly display at the First Tarrytown International Film Festival.

I was not going to be lynched. And at this late date in the proceedings, that was all I really cared about.

AT A LITTLE after 6:30 P.M. on the night of February 25, 1995, hundreds of friends, neighbors, and Don Imus listeners began to gather in the hallway outside the Sleepy Hollow High School Auditorium in North Tarrytown, New York. The room could hold approximately 600 people; we had no idea how large the crowd could be. We had invited about 400 people, but another 150 Imus listeners had called to say they were on their way, most of them bringing guests. Also, Marshall Fine, film critic for *USA Today*, had written about the festival in Thursday's edition of the paper, as had the local Gannett paper. Although the local paper had indicated that all the seats for the festival were already taken, there was still a possibility that a few interested locals might straggle in. It was entirely possible that we would have to turn people away.

None of this made any difference to me whatsoever. When the Connie Chung crew began taping the proceedings, producer Margaret Bailey asked if I was nervous.

"No," I replied, with complete candor.

"Why not?" she asked.

"Because I have a print," I replied.

"But what if people don't laugh?" she asked.

"I don't care," I replied. "I have a print. You can ask people to come all the way from Los Angeles, Washington, Boston and the south of France to watch a bad movie, but you can't not have a print. My conscience is clear."

By seven o'clock, it was obvious that we were going to have a full house. Townspeople, decked out in their finest regalia, turned out in droves. There was the mayor. There was the ex-mayor. There were the village trustees. And the village librarians. And my children's schoolteachers.

Friends and colleagues from the media turned out in full force. There were dozens of people I'd worked with at *Barron's, Spy, GQ, Forbes, The Wall Street Journal.* My two best friends from Philadelphia had made the trip. Friends I hadn't seen in years popped up, including one who'd driven all the way from Maine. And, of course, there were at least two hundred people I didn't recognize. Imus fans.

Mom didn't make it.

Crowd control was a problem. For months, I'd been warning my friends that my wife would be checking off the names of all guests as they entered the auditorium, and that anyone who didn't show up would be purged from my Rolodex forever. So it took awhile to get people seated.

But making the appropriate check marks on that list was important. I didn't want this turning into one of those seminal events like the night Wilt Chamberlain scored 100 points and years later 500,000 people claimed that they'd been there at Convention Hall in Philadelphia or Madison Square Garden in New York the night he did it, even though he'd scored them in Hershey, Pennsylvania. I wanted irrefutable physical evidence of who had, and who had not, been there. That very afternoon I had changed the message on my answering machine, declaring "If you do not have a legitimate medical reason for not having attended my festival, don't even bother to leave a message. You're call will never be returned." It had taken me two years to make this goddamned movie. If I could make the effort, they could make the effort. Yes, Irish-Americans hold grudges.

It took more than an hour to get everybody seated. I tried to speed things up by wandering down the long line and pulling VIPs out of the crowd.

"Anyone who actually appeared in the film does not have to stand in line," I noted. "This is also true of composers, sound effects personnel, and editors."

By 7:45, we were ready to roll. All but ten seats in the rear of the auditorium were filled. This was the best of all possible worlds: We had, for all intents and purposes, a full house, but we weren't going to have to turn anyone away. At precisely 8 P.M., or thereabouts, I strolled to the podium and got the show rolling.

"*Bonjour, mesdames et messieurs,*" I began. "*Soyez les bienvenus au premier festival du film international de Tarrytown.*"

I looked up.

"I'm practicing for Cannes."

They got a good yuck out of that.

"Good evening, ladies and gentlemen, and welcome to the First Tarrytown International Film Festival. This is my festival—I paid for it, I named it, and I win it."

They laughed at that, too.

"To confer a patina of a veneer of a smidgen of a soupçon of legitimacy on this out-and-out travesty, I have convened a distinguished panel of international luminaries who at the conclusion of the screening will award me the coveted Golden Headless Horseman, known in French as *Le Chevalier Sans Tête en Or*. The jurors are Max Spinner, designer of the Golden Headless Horseman Award, and my brother-in-law; Virginia Campbell, coeditor of *Movieline* and a fine human being; Ed Margulies, also coeditor of *Movieline,* and a native of Hollywood; Andy Aaron, who worked on *Ishtar;* and Nicole Danquin, who is from France. Nicole is also my sister-in-law."

They laughed, laughed, and laughed. To my delight, they understood implicitly what was going on here. This was really going quite well.

"By cellular phone hookup," I continued, lying, "we have our foreman in absentia, Agnes Catherine McNulty, a retired Medicare claims specialist for Germantown Hospital in Philadelphia, and also my mother. The jurors have received no remuneration for appearing here tonight, nor have any travel considerations been paid for their expenses. However, several of them are staying at my house this evening, so any deviation from the agreed-upon procedure for the awards ceremony will be harshly dealt with."

Still laughing.

"*Twelve Steps to Death* was shot in nine days right here in Tarrytown last August and cost $35 to make. As will soon become obvious, no professional actors were used. Now some of you may say, why landsakes, Mr. Queenan, how on earth could you possibly make a movie for $35? The answer is multifaceted. First, of course, there was the love of a good woman. Second, my unshakable faith in Almighty God, which stood me in good stead during the dark night of the soul when we didn't know if we could get the print made in time for this festival. Third, we were able to shoot and edit the movie this cheaply because of an unprecedentedly large number of Double Coupon Days at Sound One Studios in New York, plus a Byzantine series of cost-cutting rebates at DuArt Labs, also in Manhattan. But the most important factor of all to bear in mind is that people literally paid me to be in this movie. By the time we finished this project, grown men were weeping. Policemen were turning in their badges. Certified public accountants were howling at the moon, begging please, please let us appear in your film."

The crowd was definitely into this.

"To those of you who say that $35 seems a bit on the low side, that something more in the range of, oh, say $49,960.39, seems more plausible, I can say only this: There may be some give in our figures. Even as we speak, a debate rages over whether Kevin Costner's new movie *Waterworld* actually cost $85 million—the studio's figure—or $165 million—*The Wall Street Journal*'s latest calculation. If Kevin Costner can be allowed $80 million worth of latitude, surely an intrepid filmmaker raised in the housing projects of North Philadelphia is entitled to a tiny bit of leeway. I should also point out that we ran our final numbers on one of those PCs equipped with a Pentium chip, so again, the figures could have some give."

The crowd was still with me.

"*Twelve Steps to Death* is ninety-three minutes long, and will be followed by a brief presentation ceremony at which I will be awarded the prize I so richly deserve since I paid for it. Well, actually, my agent paid for it, the first financially advantageous thing he's done for me in years. I hope you enjoy the film as much as we enjoyed making it. I really, really, really hope you like it. I welcome your chortles, your guffaws, your belly laughs, and your shrieks of absolute delight. But remember, whether you like this movie or not, I get the award at the end of the night. Because this is my film festival."

"Enjoy."

At long last, it was time to premiere the film.

ABOUT EIGHTEEN SECONDS into the screening of the film, I knew that this was going to be the happiest *night* in my life. (My kids were born in the wee, small hours of the *morning*.) The crowd started guffawing as soon as they saw the Iron Maiden typeface of the words *Twelve Steps to Death*. A very good sign. They laughed enthusiastically when the little dog started barking as the credits were rolling. Obviously, it didn't take much to keep this crowd amused.

Very early in the film, the crowd started laughing heartily. All of the seemingly can't-miss material turned out to be authentically can't-miss: the knife plunged between Joey Bellini's thighs, the cunnilingus joke, the

O.J. joke, the scene were Amber Duggan leaps into the water in pursuit of her marshmallows. People laughed hysterically when Miguel, the lawn jockey incarnate, appeared on the screen, and they thoroughly enjoyed the scene where Peter Thorpe's body caromed off the side of the castle into the parking lot. I'd always been concerned that the second half of the film seemed to drag, but the crowd didn't care. They found things to laugh at: the nun on Rollerblades, the Cops in the Shithouse, the *Reservoir Dogs* sendup, and finally, Turk Bishop's bitter final line: "Anybody else want to jump?"

As soon as the music came up at the end and the credits started rolling, the crowd rewarded me with the obligatory standing ovation. So thoughtful. I waited until the credits had faded out, then strolled up to the podium, thanked everyone for coming, and handed out all the awards. One went to Ted and Kenna for Best Cinematography, Sound, and Editing by a Single Family. One went to Susie, for Best Supporting Actress in a Thankless Task. Two went to my kids. The big ones went to me. The crowd rose to its feet as one.

The evening had been phenomenally successful. From start to finish the audience had laughed at the film. Sometimes they laughed at the jokes, sometimes at the horrible acting, sometimes at the sight of their neighbors up there making fools of themselves. I could not have asked for a better response. As I stood there, basking in my triumph, my thoughts flashed back to a small, doomed child growing up in a rat-infested, crime-ridden, disease-plagued housing project in North Philadelphia sneaking away on Saturday afternoon to the Alden Theater. Surely, tonight's events confirmed, nay examplified, the indestructible nurturing power of the American Dream.

Then I looked over at my children. It was wonderful that *Twelve Steps to Death* had elicited such an amazing response from the audience. But I was now $49,960.39 in the hole. And if I didn't find some way to sell this goddamned thing, there was every reason to believe that my beloved daughter Bridget would end up in a rat-infested, crime-ridden, disease-plagued housing project in North Philadelphia. As for Gordon, well, the little bastard had quit the movie halfway through the shoot, so he deserved whatever he got.

Twelve

Dissed
in Dallas

Within days of the First Tarrytown International
Film Festival, things started to percolate. Alonso Duralde, director of the USA Film Festival in Dallas,
called up and said he wanted me to present the film
late in April. Great. A few days later, Duralde called
back and said that he also wanted me to serve as a
juror in the short films category. Hotel, meals, air
fare, and a $500 honorarium. Boy, a couple hundred
more gigs like this and the film would have paid for
itself. Plus: a free trip to Dallas. Yippi-ti-yo-ti-yay! So
just forget everything negative I said about film festivals in the last chapter. *Most* film festivals were a
waste of time, a sham, a desperate attempt by the pathetic local bohos to pretend that they lived in a sophisticated, cutting-edge municipality. But not the
USA Film Festival in Dallas. In my book, the USA
Film Festival was A-Okay.

Especially if they gave me a prize.

That wasn't the only good news. Mike Maggiore, director of The Film Forum in Manhattan, a prestigious art house theater specializing in maverick/low-budget/indy-prod materials, had heard about the film through my friend Andy Aaron, and asked me to send him a tape. According to Maggiore, Andy had described it as the funniest film he had ever seen. Of course, Andy had worked on *Ishtar*, so everything he said had to be taken with a grain of salt.

There was more good news in the hype department. Don Imus let me rant about the movie for two hours on his morning radio program, and reiterated his pledge to have the New Line guys look at the film or else forgo any hope of getting tickets to the U.S. Open in September. And Andy Aaron also lined up a screening with Lewis and Jay Presson Allen, a pair of New York theatrical producers who happened to be his sister-in-law's parents. According to Andy, the Allens wanted me to come in and discuss the possibility of distributing the film through artsy-craftsy cinemas all across the country. Andy had told the Allens that *Twelve Steps to Death* was the funniest movie he had ever seen. Of course, Andy had worked on *Ishtar*, so everything he said had to be taken with a grain of salt.

Meanwhile, expenses were still mounting. I had to fork out another $1,700 to get the print transferred to videotape, then an extra $833.53 to make one hundred VHS cassettes, plus a couple of high-quality three-quarter-inch tapes. As soon as I received the tapes, I started stuffing them in envelopes and sending them out in the mail. One went to Dallas. Two went to Imus. One went to the Film Forum. One went to Virginia Campbell, co-editor of *Movieline*, who had a good friend at MGM/UA Home Video. Andy Aaron, who had worked on *Ishtar*, also needed a couple of copies to pass along to friends in the business. And naturally I sent one to Deborah Jelin Newmyer at Amblin.

Meanwhile, my agent was on the case, lining up a meeting with a film entertainment lawyer in New York. The *Washington Post* ran a swell article about the film festival in the "Outlook" section. The Associated Press also ran a flattering item about the event. Phone calls from listeners to Imus affiliates began to pour in. A radio station in Providence,

Rhode Island, wanted to sponsor a screening of the movie. So did a public library in Chappaqua, New York. But I had my sights set on much bigger, brighter venues: Los Angeles. Rome. Tokyo. Cannes.

Perhaps the most gratifying moment of all came on April 6, 1995, when I opened the latest issue of *Movieline* to find an absolutely breathless review of the film. Under the headline A STAR IS BORN, the distinguished critic Max Wadier had written the following kind words:

February 25, 1995, is a date that will forever be remembered as the saddest day in the history of this magazine. That was the day that Joe Queenan, who has written some of the most memorable articles in the history of American journalism, premiered his first film, *Twelve Steps to Death*. As a result of the lucrative offers he will now be deluged with as a director, screenwriter and, yes, even as an actor, it is unlikely that we will ever again see his byline gracing the pages of *Movieline*. Mr. Queenan is a very fine writer and an extraordinary human being. But he goes where the money is.

Twelve Steps to Death had its premiere, and won the coveted Golden Headless Horseman Award (Le Chevalier Sans Tête en Or) for best film, at the First Tarrytown International Film Festival, which, coincidentally, is located in the suburban New York town where Mr. Queenan lives. A black comedy rivaling the very best of Billy Wilder, *Twelve Steps to Death* stars Mr. Queenan, in an absolutely breathtaking acting debut, as Turk Bishop, a police detective who has been thrown off the Los Angeles Police Department.

Twelve Steps to Death was shot in just nine days in Tarrytown last August. Mr. Queenan, who wrote the screenplay in eight days, cast his film almost entirely with neighbors, seemingly using threats of physical violence if any of the performers messed up their lines. By limiting each shot to between one and three takes, Mr. Queenan was able to shoot the movie for just $35, making Twelve Steps to Death the most inexpensive film in motion picture history.

"If I hadn't sprung for lunch on the last day of shooting, we could have done the whole thing for nothing," Mr. Queenan told Movieline, explaining that he was able to hold down editing and post-production costs by capitalizing on "an unprecedentedly large number of Double Coupon Days at Sound One Studios in New York."

Moviegoers who do not share Mr. Queenan's abrasive sense of humor may be offended by the ferocity of his onslaught on the recovery movement. But no one watching this film for the first time can question his extraordinary talent as a writer, a director, and a performer. Combining the deft comic delivery of a Bill Murray with the razor-sharp wit of a Woody Allen, Joe Queenan has made the most impressive directing debut since Orson Welles made *Citizen Kane*. Aficionados of articles such as "Mickey Rourke for a Day" and "Young Guns" will be saddened to see Mr. Queenan depart our company for the gilded cage of movie stardom. But those of us who know him, love him, respect him, and envy him have known one thing all along: God only loans magazine editors a talent like this for a precious short time. On a frigid midwinter night in Tarrytown, N.Y., God called in the loan. Now God has dispatched his remarkable terrestrial emissary to Hollywood.

The silver screen will never be the same.

THE PUBLICATION OF the *Movieline* article was the highwater mark in the *Twelve Steps to Death* saga. To have my work honored in a periodical that truly knows no peer in the world of entertainment journalism should have been the highest honor I could achieve. But I could take no real pleasure from the almost fulsome homage I was paid in the pages of this fine publication, because I and the editors of the marvelous publication shared a dirty little secret.

I was the author of the article.

Do not go too hard on me, dear reader, for making this admission, for it was desperation rather than the paralyzing desire for overt homage that drove me to sink so low that I would ghostwrite a rave review of my own movie. (Also, I had recently read that Balzac used to do this kind of thing all the time.) By the time I got around to premiering my film at the First Tarrytown International Film Festival, I knew I was in a deep hole, a hole that no number of screenings in Providence, Rhode Island, or Chappaqua, New York, was going to help me climb out of. It was nice to get the publicity on Imus, in the *Washington Post,* through the Associated Press. It was nice to hear the accolades, garner the florid kudos, bask in the glow of the lavish praise. But florid kudos and lavish praise weren't going to pay my bills. What I needed now was some cash.

The cash did not come. Over the next few months, one promising avenue after another would turn into a blind alley. For starters, the Film Forum in New York didn't agree with my friend Andy Aaron's assessment of the film. They thought it sucked. They sent it back almost overnight with a nasty little note reading: "There is some very funny material in here, but the truly awful acting (the cop is passable) detracts from my appreciation of the script. I'm sorry, but it's not for us."

I didn't take this news that badly, because the Film Forum mostly shows movies by hermaphrodite Turks and experimental Huguenot crossdressers, and because Miramax now had a copy of the film, and because I was still confident of hearing from Amblin. But then more bad news swept in. The theatrical producers my friend Andy Aaron introduced me to spent an hour and forty-five minutes telling me how funny they found the movie, how much they laughed when they screened it, how immensely clever they thought I was. Their comments couldn't have been nicer. Their enthusiasm couldn't have been more genuine. Then they said that the film had absolutely no chance of getting a commercial release. *Anywhere.* They explained that the costs of publicizing and advertising a cult film such as *Twelve Steps to Death*—a minimum of $750,000—were simply too great to tempt prospective distributors. They said that I did have a brilliant future as a screenwriter or a script doctor ahead of me if that was the path I chose to follow. But that was not the path that I chose to follow. I had no interest in writing screenplays. I wanted to sell this sucker.

After that, *le déluge.* Amblin never called back. Miramax passed on the film. New Line never responded one way or the other. Connie Chung got axed by CBS, and the producers at *Eye to Eye* couldn't say when, if ever, the segment about the making of *Twelve Steps to Death* would finally run. On a positive note, the Warner Library in Tarrytown did offer to host a second screening of the film in an upstairs conference room that could seat 120 comfortably, provided I supplied the 16mm projector. I passed.

The famous philosopher, Rogers de Vegas, once declared: "There's a time to hold 'em, and a time to fold 'em." I realized it was time to fold 'em while I was standing in Dealey Plaza in downtown Dallas on April 24, 1995, the night my film was screened at the 25th Annual USA Film Festival. I'd flown down to Dallas four days earlier to be a judge on the Short Films Jury and had spent three entire days locked in a hotel room watching films about lesbians who were afraid to tell their parents they were lesbians; gay teenagers from Cicero, Illinois, who joined the wrestling team so they could get closer to other guys; lesbians who wanted their straight male friends to donate some sperm so one of them could have a baby; gay farmers from Alkali, Iowa, who were finding that gay farming in Alkali, Iowa, was no picnic; and unhappy people with Tourette's syndrome. Then at night, I would go over to the world's largest honky-tonk in Fort Worth and watch a bunch of bogus shitkickers sing sad, sad songs about good love gone bad.

When I'd arrived in Dallas, I'd expected the film festival to be held in some kind of ancient movie house where the red upholstered seats had been rubbed all shiny and threadbare by three generations of wriggling Satyajit Ray aficionados. But Dallas doesn't have any theaters like that. Dallas doesn't have any buildings that are more than twenty minutes old. So the film festival wasn't held in an artsy environment at all. It was held in the AMC Glen Lakes Multiplex. The AMC Glen Lakes Multiplex has eight screens.

Every night, luminaries as varied as Dennis Hopper, Dana Delany, Paul Schrader, and Marvin Hamlisch would come trooping in, say a few words, sit through a screening of some deeply troubled Hollywood film, say a few more words, and then leave. Then everyone else would go out to a party and get wasted. Frequently, actor/director Robert Wuhl, costar of *Batman, Cobb,* and *Bull Durham,* could be spotted at the periphery of the crowd, desperately seeking a distributor for his quirky comedy *Open Season,* which deals with a malfunction in TV ratings boxes that causes network executives to believe that public television has the highest ratings in the country. He may still be there.

Well, it was quite a festival and a terrific honor to be present at a party featuring *both* Dana Delany and Jimmy Smits, but hobnobbing with microcelebrities wasn't what I'd come to Texas for. I'd come to meet the powers-that-be. But the powers-that-be didn't seem to be there. They were being powerful elsewhere. The weekend dragged on, with many more trips to local rib houses and honkytonks. Finally, on Monday night at 7:00 P.M., it was time for the public debut of *Twelve Steps to Death.* Sure, I'd held my own film festival in Tarrytown, and yes, six hundred people had turned up for the event. But that was a full-tilt rig job. Tonight was the first time that anyone would actually *pay* to see my movie.

What a rush I got as I alighted from the car that evening. Outside the cinema stood Marvin Hamlisch, here to plug the Robert Wuhl movie he'd just written the music for. He didn't look happy. I immediately strolled up to him, introduced myself, and told him a nice little story. Two years earlier, while on a book tour in Los Angeles, I'd been shepherded around town by a very likable woman from a literary escort service. When I'd first heard about literary escort services, I naturally assumed they were discreet companies that provided visiting authors with nubile female companions who would read excerpts from *The Mill on the Floss* while administering exquisite blow jobs. I was sadly mistaken. Literary escort services were private livery services that provided writers with media-savvy chaperones who would ferry them all around the metropolitan area and fill them in on all the relevant information about the people who were going to interview them that day, i.e., this one is a fascist, this one has a fake English accent, this one hasn't read your book, and so forth.

Anyway, my driver, a charming, perky middle-aged woman, spent most of our three days together talking about how awful most writers were. This one was a wuss. This one was a lecher. This one was a whiner. This one sat in the backseat of the car and wouldn't talk to me for three days. Finally, I asked if she had ever driven—that is, *escorted*—anyone who wasn't a complete prick.

"Marvin Hamlisch," she said, without a word of hesitation. "He's the nicest man in the business."

I told this story to Marvin Hamlisch, and he seemed really impressed. He shook my hand and thanked me for being so friendly. I think it was the first nice thing that had happened to him in Dallas.

I strolled into the theater, prepared to introduce my film. As soon as I entered the building, my heart stopped. There, on the tiny marquee poised above the first theater, was the word *Outbreak*. Next to it, in theater 3, were the words *Bad Boys*. There was also a room with a sign advertising *Don Juan de Marco* and another advertising *Richie Rich*. And there, in theater 2, lit up for all to see, were the words *Twelve Steps to Death*. My own film. In my very own theater. Not a screening room, but a theater. Filled with people who had paid $6.50 to see the film.

Well, not exactly *filled*. The room, which was a bit on the vast side, could probably hold around 600 patrons. When I arrived, there were twelve paying customers. Gradually, the crowd swelled to twenty-five. Thirty. Forty. By the time the festival director was ready to introduce me, there were probably fifty people in the room. Not quite the opening of *Jurassic Park*, but certainly no abject disgrace. Better than most Lara Flynn Boyle movies.

Festival Director Alonso Duralde introduced me; I got a bit of applause; I cracked a few jokes; we showed the film. People giggled. People laughed. They liked the O.J. joke. They liked the cunnilingus joke. Folks seemed to have a genuinely good time. Afterwards, I strolled back up to the podium and handled questions and answers for twenty minutes. More chuckles. More gags. Then it was over. After the wrap-up session, a critic from *The Hollywood Reporter* asked me a couple of questions, as did a writer from *Film Threat*. They seemed harmless enough. As I left the theater, I noticed that the sign reading *Twelve Steps to Death* had now been replaced by one reading *Mishima* or something. The festival was screening all of Paul Schrader's films and presenting him with some kind of career achievement award for being such a maverick, cutting-edge, indy-prod type guy whose movies never made any money. Personally, I'd always felt that Schrader's scripts were terrific, but that his films sucked. So I got out of there in a hurry.

With the presentation of *Twelve Steps to Death* at a legitimate venue, I felt that a tremendous weight had been lifted from my shoulders. The film had now played to a paying audience. The crowd seemed to enjoy it. Nobody booed or threw rotting vegetables or walked out. Mine was an admittedly small triumph. But it was a triumph all the same.

To celebrate the commercial debut of my film, I drove to Dealey Plaza with a friend. Dealey Plaza, the site of John F. Kennedy's assassination in 1963, was admittedly an odd place to go to celebrate. But there is literally nothing else to do in Dallas. So off to Dealey Plaza I went.

As soon as I arrived at the Book Depository building, I knew that I had made a huge mistake. When I turned the corner and spotted the famous grassy knoll, I sensed at some primal, intuitive level that something horrible was going to happen to me before I left Dallas. Suddenly, in an emotional thunderbolt, the eerie parallels between JFK's life and my own hit me. JFK was in his mid-forties when he died. I was in my mid-forties. My birthday fell in November. JFK died in November. JFK had two children: an older daughter and a younger son. I had two children: an older daughter and a younger son. JFK was a charismatic, good-looking Irish-American from a venerable East Coast city whose mere presence caused women to swoon. I was a charismatic, good-looking Irish-American from a venerable East Coast city whose mere presence caused women to swoon. JFK's final moments as president were captured on a controversial, low-quality home movie—the Zapruder film—that would forever be linked with Dallas. Was it possible that my final moments as a director, producer, screenwriter, and film star were also to be captured on a controversial, low-quality home movie—*Twelve Steps to Death*—that would forever be linked with Dallas?

I cannot begin to express the sense of foreboding I felt that evening as I ambled into Dealey Plaza. Somewhere in that infamous public square, I was certain, my destiny lay waiting. Somehow, tonight, I knew that my career as a filmmaker would end in that plaza. A speeding bullet? A drive-by shooting? An out-of-control Trans-Am? No, the murder weapon was of an infinitely more subtle variety.

The *Dallas Observer.*

Looking back on the events of that evening, I can only recall with infinite regret how close I came to dodging the bullet that would end my career as a filmmaker. Just as JFK could have escaped an assassin's bullet if his limousine had only accelerated a bit faster, I could have escaped a journalistic bullet if I had only climbed back into my friend's car and sped out of the plaza. But for some reason, I felt irresistibly drawn to a tiny orange kiosk on a street corner in the shadow of the Book Depository. The kiosk was operated by the *Dallas Observer,* the local giveaway alternative newspaper (Dallas has three gays, a bisexual, one hermaphrodite, and four people who know who Kurt Cobain was; the paper has an estimated circulation of nine). The cover of the April 20–26 issue was emblazoned with a headline reading: HOW THE FEST WAS WON STARS! SEX! FUNKY FLICKS! THE USA FILM FESTIVAL DELIVERS THE BEST LINEUP IN YEARS.

Trembling with anticipation, yet quivering with dread, I tore open the newspaper. An astounding twenty pages of the issue were devoted to the festival. And oh, how they raved!

"Virtually every detail of the Silver Anniversary Schedule, from programming choices to celebrity guests, is dead-on perfect," the editors gushed. "This year's festival is simply terrific—about as close to representing all things to all moviegoers as anyone could have wished."

I tore through the special supplement, breathing a sigh of relief. Perhaps my premonitions of doom had been ill-founded. Maybe I'd gone just a little bit over the top with all those weird JFK parallels. Maybe the wonderful, caring, sophisticated, megahip citizens of Dallas, having murdered my beloved president thirty-two years earlier—an event from which neither I nor my parents nor the Democratic Party nor the country itself ever really recovered—would now make it up to me by giving my film a rave review.

Breathlessly, I raced through the supplement. (The editors of the newspaper had seen all the films on video before the festival even started, and had written something about every single one.) My hopes rose to the sky as the editors delivered their verdicts on a number of cutting-edge/low budget/indy-prod/intrepid-maverick releases. They loved the "verbal roughhousing and poignant moments of compromise" in *The Sum of Us*, Kevin Dowling's touching film about an Australian homosexual and his understanding heterosexual father. They said *Pom Poko*, a full-length cartoon about a supernatural raccoon, was "a must-see for Japanimation fans who crave that unique blend of science fiction, mysticism, mythology, and social commentary in which Japanese animators specialize." They went nuts over a "cannibalacious horror comedy" called *Spider Baby*. They positively adored films with names as unprepossessing as *Organized Crime and Triad Bureau*, *Cyberstalker*, *My Old Fiddle*, *Plutonium Circus*, *Wigstock*, and *Joe's Rotten World*. Then, under the heading "Short Film and Video Winners," the editors noted, "All the judges will be present to discuss the future of cinema after the screening. A pretty tall order, but they can probably fill it—especially when you consider the presence of *the indomitable Queenan, who can write 11-page articles about actors with bad hair and never bore his readers . . .*"

"Now, you're talking!" I said to myself.

Then I turned to page 27, and my eyes tumbled onto a review of *Twelve Steps to Death*. It hit me with the impact of three direct blasts from a vintage Mannlicher-Carcano rifle in the hands of a commie lunatic with right-wing connections to the CIA, the KGB, the Mafia, and assorted Miami-based cadres of deranged Cuban exiles hell-bent on deposing Fidel Castro. It read:.

> Joe Queenan is a humorist best-known for his extravagant, archly observant essays on film trends in *Movieline*, so fans will be eager to see Queenan's first foray into low-budget filmmaking. Sadly, his debut as producer-writer-director, *Twelve Steps to Death*, displays the cardinal sin of satirical cinema—an unfunny script that lurches on its course like a flatulent snuff-alufagus, pausing before each target and expelling noxious gas that lingers unpleasantly in the air but never quite achieves the necessary rudeness.
>
> Indeed, Queenan bludgeons the culture of codependency, recovery, and the Catholic Church with such monomaniacal clumsiness that the only sound you hear is an axe being ground till it's blunt. Stick to the word processor, Joe.

I staggered out of the plaza, mortally wounded. Like the valiant John F. Kennedy so many years ago, I would hang on desperately for a few more minutes, but by the time I got back to my hotel room that evening, I knew that the wound was fatal. Back in New York the next day, my loyal, faithful wife would try to console me with the thought that I had merely been dissed by a dork from Dallas. But I knew better. I knew that *Twelve Steps to Death* was a goner. In the weeks and months to come, there would be many more overtures, come-ons, proposals, and meetings, but in my heart of hearts I knew that the Quest for the Grail was over. New Line would never respond to Don Imus's overtures. Amblin would never call back. Cash-laden overseas distributors with a ravenous appetite for American *film noir* would not beat a path to my door. Not for a film that lurched on its course like a flatulent snuffalufagus, pausing before each target and expelling noxious gas that lingered unpleasantly in the air but never quite achieved the necessary rudeness. *Twelve Steps to Death* would never, ever, get a commercial release.

The *Dallas Observer* was not the only publication that would heap derision on my film debut. As the days passed, a tidal wave of abuse poured
in. And this came from much more credible media outlets. The *Dallas
Morning News* hated it. *The Hollywood Reporter* said my script was funny,
but as a director I was a flop. *Film Threat* didn't even bother to review
the film. *Daily Variety* said it was "Slight, undernourished, and only in-
termittently funny," noting: "Theatrical prospects for this amateurish, no-
budget exercise are slim." To make matters worse, the reviewer—Emanuel
Levy—had been one of my fellow judges at the U.S.A. Film Festival.

WHERE WAS BERNIE WEINRAUB of *The New York Times* when I needed
him?

The final nail in the coffin was hammered in on the night of June 23,
1995, when the beleaguered Connie-Chungless *Eye to Eye* would finally
air its segment about the making of the film. Mike Silberman, Margaret
Bailey, and all the others would really go to bat for me that evening, framing the events of the previous August in a humorous, touching, life-
affirming fashion. In a segment that ran a full eight minutes, they would
depict my adventure in low-budget cinema as a noble effort by an irreverent maverick to beat the odds.

My friends and neighbors, gathered around the TV screen in my family room, would laugh heartily as they recalled their fleeting moments of
glory the previous summer before they had to go back to their pathetic
jobs and horrible families. And, yes, their hearts would miss a beat or two
when the segment drew to its conclusion and the phone in the hallway
began to ring off the hook. But the person on the other end of the line
was not Samuel Goldwyn, Jr., or Michael Eisner, or Quentin Tarantino,
or Steven Spielberg. The first caller was an unemployed actor from San
Jose. The second caller was a doomed filmmaker from Michigan, trapped
in I-had-to-put-it-on-all-on-my-credit-card-and-still-can't-get-anybody-
interested-in-distributing-it hell. And the third caller—well, who really
cares who the third caller was?

As I staggered up to bed that evening, my wife tried desperately to console me with classic British stiff-upper-lip material. There'll be more calls

in the morning, she assured me. These things take time. Rome wasn't built in a day. Whatever goes around comes around. Keep your sunny side up. It's a long way to Tipperary. Just you wait, Henry Higgins, just you wait. But when I looked in the mirror as I brushed my teeth that night, all I saw staring back at me was one very defeated cutting-edge/low-budget/indy-prod/intrepid-maverick Robert Rodriguez wannabe. Sure, there would be more calls in the morning. Sure, there'd be more faxes. But they'd always be from the wrong people. A failed actor from West Hartford, Connecticut. A low-budget filmmaker from New Brunswick. A guy who wrote music for children's cartoons. But no calls from Miramax. No calls from Amblin.

I had come to the end of the line. A proposal to turn the movie into a TV series would come to nothing. A proposal to show it on cable-TV hit a dead end. Assorted overtures from overseas distributors would lead nowhere. The story would not have a happy ending. I was not going to be the next Orson Welles. I was not even going to be the next Robert Rodriguez. I was going to be the last Ed Wood.

At long last, it was time to get out the pocket calculator and tote up the carnage. The final figure for making the movie was $49,960.39. But if you tossed in the $4,000 I paid John Domesick as a "consultant," the $2,558.73 I had to shell out to make the videotapes, the $1,969.72 it cost to hold the First Tarrytown International Film Festival, the $565.07 I spent on T-shirts and caps, the $5,000 I forked over for publicity, and a bunch of other niggling expenses, the grand total came to $65,193.67. When you factored in the many months of lost income incurred while making the film, the total devastation easily surpassed the $100,000 mark. My finances lay in ruins. My dreams of glory had been shattered. My clock had been thoroughly cleaned.

What then did I learn from my experiences? First off, don't believe everything you read in the newspapers. Especially if that knucklehead Bernie Weinraub is the guy throwing around the figures. If I'd had any inkling when I read that *New York Times* article back in January 1993 that the $7,000 movie Robert Rodriguez originally shot bore no relationship to the *El Mariachi* that was finally released, I probably would have never gotten involved in this doomed undertaking. And imagine how I felt when a friend sent me a November 27, 1994, story from *The Los Angeles Times* reporting that *El Mariachi*, despite all the hype and hoopla, never actually made any money for the studio that released it. Alas, we get too fast old, and too late smart.

Today, I am a penniless, dreamless, broken-down, independent filmmaker condemned to spending the rest of my life trying to rebuild my family's ravaged financial infrastructure. Yes, when all is said and done, I did go out and do what I'd set out to do. But so did Christopher Columbus, and look where it got him. And at least Christopher Columbus did it with other people's money.

Has anything positive come out of this experience? Yes. Before I started making movies, a lot of people dismissed my writing as the addled ramblings of a talentless, mean-spirited jerk. But as my treatment at the hands of the Dallas Observer and The Hollywood Reporter make clear, it's a good career move to try doing something you don't know how to do because then all your critics will say that you're a terrible filmmaker, a rotten actor, an abysmal screenwriter, and a horrible human being, but one hell of a journalist. This raises the tantalizing possibility that if I now started writing symphonies, people would say, "He should stick to what he knows best: journalism and filmmaking. He's a crackerjack reporter, a brilliant satirist, and a wonderful director. But his symphonies eat it raw."

Is there any possibility that I will ever make another motion picture? It's a question that numerous colleagues have asked me since the Disaster in Dallas. Knowing what I know now, they wonder, would I dare to step once more into the breach and see if I could get it right? Maybe use real actors this time around? Hire a real director? Shoot a picture where the camera actually moves once in a while?

The answer, sad to say, is a resounding no. Knowing what I know now, I know that I shouldn't have done what I did then. What's more, if I tried to do a better job in the future, things might turn out worse. This time, my wife might kill me. Even if I could get other people to give me the money, there's no way on earth she would agree to go through this emotional hecatomb again. She'd cheerfully put a bullet through my head. And no jury in the land would convict her. Besides, nobody's going to give me the money to make another film.

So, no, there will be no sequel to *Twelve Steps to Death*. I've learned my lesson. I've shot my wad. My flirtation with the silver screen is over. Yes, I have enjoyed the celebrity status I've attained in Tarrytown since the Night of the Living Film Festival. Yes, it was gratifying to present the film to fifty paying customers in a multiplex cinema two thousand miles from my home. And, yes, I will cherish forever the memories of the night I summoned my neighbors and friends to the ramparts of Axe Castle to spread a bit of fairydust among them. But $65,193.67 is a shitload of fairydust. Sixty-five thousand one hundred ninety-three dollars and sixty-seven cents is an awful lot of money to shell out just to be the most respected independent filmmaker in Tarrytown, New York.

So when people around here say, "Wouldn't it be great to make a sequel?" I turn a deaf ear. And when Ted and Kenna call and say, "There's this independent producer we'd like you to meet," I beg off. And when Gordon promises that the next time he won't quit halfway through the filming of the movie, that the next time he'll be on his best behavior, I gruffly remind him that I have no money, no backers, and no energy to go through this ordeal ever again. Besides, even if I did want to make another low-budget movie, what would be the story line? What would be the plot? After all, the only other really good idea for a movie that I ever came up with was the one about the dying stand-up comic who goes to Antarctica so he can be the funniest person on an entire continent.

But shooting a movie like that would be prohibitively expensive. For starters, I'd have to go all the way to the South Pole. There'd be no two ways about *that*. Unless I used stock footage of Antarctica. And filmed all the shots at incredibly tight angles on a bed of ice in the middle of the winter in Harriman State Park. And talked the crew into working for nothing. And got a really good break on film, and persuaded Sound One to let me edit the footage in the middle of the night, and got my friend Andy Aaron, who had worked on *Ishtar,* to lend me his recording equipment, and . . .